MRS. JACK DETWILER
(YONG LING ING)

III.

For further testimony of the poets to their own practice first take this from Gray, which appears in one of his letters to Mason: "Extreme conciseness of expression, yet pure, perspicuous and musical is one of the grand beauties of lyric poetry. This I have always aimed at, and never could attain. The necessity of rhyming is one great obstacle to it: another and perhaps a stronger, is that way you have chosen, of casting down your first thoughts carelessly and at large, and then clipping them here and there at leisure. This method, after all possible pains, will leave behind it a laxity, a diffuseness." The passage is worth note, if only for the memorable *Triad*—"pure, perspicuous, and musical," which may be set beside Milton's "simple, sensuous, passionate," spoken of poetic style in general. Elsewhere, in another letter to Mason, Gray has a passage which is very consoling to those who believe in the lyric function, and its equal rights with epic and dramatic verse: "The true lyric style," he says, "with all its flights of fancy, ornaments, and heightening of expression and harmony of sound, is in its nature superior to every other style." There is a touch of enthusiasm in this, a fine excess, less unusual with Gray than is commonly supposed; and, subtleties apart, we may all agree that the lyric imagination at its highest, like the dramatic imagination at its broadest, can reach the essence, as well as touch the accidents, of all human experience.

The direct opposite to Gray in his method is his immediate successor—Burns. Burns has been quoted already as a capital instance of the virtue that lies in the musical tradition of poetry. In one of his earlier letters, after speaking of the "wild enthusiasm of passion" aroused in him by the "old Scottish airs," to which his songs were almost always composed, he goes on to say: "When one would compose to them, 'to sowth the tune,' as our Scotch phrase is, over and over, is the readiest way to catch the inspiration and raise the bard into that glorious enthusiasm so strongly characteristic of our old Scotch poetry."

old Scotch air!" says Burns in a letter to Margaret Chalmers of October 26, 1787; and the names of old tunes at the head of most of his songs show us how musically guided his inspiration was.

But to return to Wordsworth, and the more complex forms. In the same preface of 1815, he attempts a classification of poetry, in which the third of his six divisions is the Lyrical. Under this head he includes "the Hymn, the Ode, the Elegy, the Song, and the Ballad," in all which, he adds, "for the production of their full effect, an accompaniment of music is indispensable." Even this shuts out many kinds of poems which latterly we have come to admit as lyrical to all intents and purposes, but which Wordsworth ranks under his next head of idyllic poetry such as the Sonnet and poems like Milton's *L'Allegro*.

Coleridge too insisted, not only in the pages of his *Biographia*, on the imagination and its inborn musical faculty: "'The man that hath not music in his soul' can never be a genuine poet. The sense of musical delight, with the power of producing it, is a gift of imagination; and this, together with the power of reducing multitude into unity of effect, and modifying a series of thoughts by some one predominant thought or feeling, may be cultivated and improved, but can never be learned." Compare this with Blake's words: "One power alone makes a poet. Imagination, the Divine Vision." Again, attacking Wordsworth's faith in the influence of Nature and natural objects upon the poet, Blake wrote: "Natural objects always weaken, deaden and obliterate imagination in me." Against Blake, set William Morris's blunt disclaimer, which occurs in a letter quoted by Mr. Mackail: "That talk of inspiration is sheer nonsense. I may tell you that flat: . . . there is no such thing; it is a mere matter of craftsmanship." At another time, he said: "If a chap can't compose an epic poem while he's weaving tapestry, he had better shut up. . . ."

which transcends our human doctrine: "It riseth higher, as by a divine instinct, when it contemns common and known conceptions. . . . Then it gets aloft and flies away with his rider, whither before it was doubtful to ascend." This the poets understood by their *Helicon, Pegasus,* or *Parnassus;* and this made Ovid to boast

> Est deus in nobis, agitante calescimus illo:
> Sedibus æthereis spiritus ille venit.

Wordsworth in a later preface—the preface to his volume of 1815—leads us back to the musical, as related to the poetic idea.

"All poets," he writes, "except the dramatic, have been in the practice of feigning that their works were composed to the music of the harp or the lyre: with what degree of affectation this has been done in modern times, I leave to the judicious to determine. For my own part, I have not been disposed to violate probability so far, or to make such a large demand upon the Reader's charity. Some of these pieces are essentially lyrical; and, therefore, cannot have their due force without a supposed musical accompaniment; but, in much the greatest part, as a substitute for the classic lyre of romantic harp, I require nothing more than an animated or impassioned recitation, adapted to the subject. . . ."

Since Wordsworth, clearly, we have moved a step, for much that claims to be lyric poetry to-day is pictorial, rather than lyrical, in its conception; written for the eye, and not for the ear. No doubt, as in Wordsworth's own case, some of the best lyric poetry which we possess has been written by poets who have had no ear for music itself. There is a second harmony of words, which may be enough for verse essentially literary. But the true lyric is still first of all a song, and the further away we get from music as the companion of poetry, the further we shall be from "the wellspring of the elder muse." This is one reason why the Elizabethans, and Burns, and a few Scotch song-writers, wrote songs so much more musical and singable than the too literary poets of another day. "If I could hit on some glorious right mind, so the lyric poets are not in their right mind when they are composing their beautiful strains; but when falling under the power of music and metre they are inspired and possessed; like Bacchic maidens who draw milk and honey from the rivers when they are under the influence of Dionysus, but not when they are in their right mind. And the soul of the lyric poet does the same, as they themselves say; for they tell us that they bring songs from the honeyed fountains, calling them out of the gardens and dells of the Muses; they, like the bees, winging their way from flower to flower. And this is true, for the poet is a light and winged and holy thing, and there is no invention in him until he has been inspired and is out of his senses, and the mind is no longer in him."

This passage leads on naturally to Shelley's *Defence;* but before he wrote, Lodge and Sidney, Coleridge and Blake, had written making the same high claim. Lodge wrote, "Whereas the poets were said to call for the Muses' help, their meaning was no other . . . but to call for heavenly inspiration from above to direct their endeavours. . . . Sibylla in her answers to Æneas against her will, as the poet telleth us, was possessed with this fury; yea, weigh considerately but of the writing of poets, and you shall see that when their matter is most heavenly their style is most lofty, a strange token of the wonderful efficacy of the same." Join to it Shakespeare's paraphrase of Plato:

> Lovers and madmen have such seething brains,
> Such shaping fantasies, that apprehend
> More than cool reason ever comprehends.
> The lunatic, the lover, and the poet
> Are of imagination all compact:
> One sees more devils than vast hell can hold,
> That is, the madman; the lover, all as frantic,
> Sees Helen's beauty in a brow of Egypt;
> The poet's eye, in a fine frenzy rolling,
> Doth glance from heaven to earth, from earth to heaven;
> And, as imagination bodies forth
> The forms of things unknown, the poet's pen
> Turns them to shapes, and gives to airy nothing
> A local habitation and a name.

Add Ben Jonson's comment on that poetic rapture

In this defence of the poet's art there are some tems that are inevitable and carry their justification on the face of them. The *Apologie* of Sidney, the *Defence* of Shelley, the passages from Milton, one essay at least of Dryden, Wordsworth's preface to his *Lyrical Ballads*, and Coleridge's complementary chapter: these must have a place. But when we turn to some other poets, the ground is not so clear. The book may serve, as it is, its function of pocket-guide to Parnassus, which discourses easily, if often argumentatively, on the regions, the laws and liberties, the great language, and the associations of the way. It learns what the old Welsh bards would call a *Triad*—a definition in three terms, from Milton, and another from Gray. It knits up the fine threads of these poets, and shows their succession in fame and time. Especially, it shows whatever continuity there is in what we may call the lyric line in English poetry, which follows the most simple form of the art, the natural antithesis to prose. Prose is written speech; lyric poetry is written song: that is the beginning of the whole matter, the radical definition which we may elaborate but can hardly make clearer.

II.

We talk more to-day about the art of poetry and less about its inspiration, and indeed the last is a matter about which the poets themselves are not agreed. For that reason, since Plato is so often referred to in the following essays, the passage in *Ion*, where Socrates declares that poetry is an inspiration and not an art, may be recalled. He says it, no doubt, half with the idea of showing that the poet are an irresponsible race, only noble when they are inspired by the gods. But the passage is one to be remembered now that the primitive inspiration of poetry has become for most of us a mere convention.

"All good poets," says Socrates, "epic as well as lyric, compose their beautiful poems not by art, but because they are inspired and possessed. And as the Corybantian revellers when they dance are not in their

INTRODUCTION

I.

FROM the English poets, from Sidney and Milton, from Coleridge, Wordsworth, Shelley and their successors, we have brought together here some of the arguments they have stated on behalf of their infinite art. It is the natural opening to their poetry, the one confession of their faith which may claim to be inspired, and if it does not give us the whole philosophy of the subject, it affords as much theory as is likely to be listened to profitably within hearing of the muse herself.

The Prelude to Poetry originally opened a series of Lyric Poets, whose volumes were too small to give their authors much space. But it was intended one day to reissue the book in a more complete form, printing at length some of the essays on poetry there represented only in brief, such as Campion's *Observations* and Daniel's vigorous counterblast in his *Defence of Ryme*. Both these famous disputations are now given in full. Among the later additions to the book are Dryden's essay on "Poetic License and the Heroic in Poetry," Gray's essay on Metre, the salient passages from Byron's reply to Bowles' strictures on Pope, and some notes by Burns from his rough commonplace-book on Scottish songs. In the nineteenth century we have Scott's essay on Ballad Poetry, three brief contributions by Keats from his letters and his preface to *Endymion*, and Browning's tribute to the genius of Shelley. Then follow some passages from Matthew Arnold's volume, *On Translating Homer*: and last of all an extract from Dr. Robert Bridges' too little known Tredegar address on *The Function of Poetry*.[1]

---

[1] Originally delivered as an address to an audience of Welsh working men at Tredegar, reprinted here by the courtesy and with the consent of the author and the Oxford University Press.

THE PRELUDE TO POETRY

THE ENGLISH POETS IN DEFENCE AND
PRAISE OF THEIR OWN ART

EDITED BY ERNEST RHYS

LONDON: J. M. DENT & SONS LTD
NEW YORK: E. P. DUTTON & CO. INC.

All rights reserved
Made in Great Britain
Printed by The Northumberland Press Gateshead-on-Tyne
and bound at The Temple Press Letchworth Herts
for
J. M. Dent & Sons Ltd.
Aldine House Bedford St. London
First published in this edition 1927
Last reprinted 1951

Everyman, I will go with thee, and be thy guide,
In thy most need to go by thy side.

EVERYMAN'S LIBRARY

No. 789

ESSAYS & BELLES-LETTRES

THE PRELUDE TO POETRY
Essays and Comments by English
Poets on their own Art

sionate is eternally interesting; and interesting solely in proportion to its greatness and to its passion."

This may be contrasted with Wordsworth's theory, stated in his preface, and with the bolder contemporary claims made by Walt Whitman. Arnold's much contested other statement that poetry is "a criticism of life" has been too often quoted without its qualifying clause; for he said explicitly it was to be a criticism of life "under the conditions fixed by the laws of poetic truth and poetic beauty." Which makes all the difference.

Arnold's own practice of verse, with his attention to classic form, is the more significant to us now because he arrived in *The Strayed Reveller* and other poems, at a very effective use of unrhymed verse, and gave us, paradoxically enough, *vers libre* by a classic revoke.

Another familiar phrase bearing on the art of verse is due to Swinburne, who wrote, "Art for art's sake first of all. . . ." "The one fact for art," he added, "worth taking account of, is simply mere excellence of verse or colour, which involves all manner of truth and loyalty necessary to her well-being. That is the important thing; to have her work supremely well done. . . ." And, writing of William Blake, he quoted the three lines:

> Silent, silent night,
> Quench the holy light
> Of thy torches bright,

with the comment that verse more nearly faultless was never written. . . . "The sweet facility" of the great lyrical poets was always, he said, "varying the art-for-art formula, an especial quality of Blake's. To go the right way and do the right thing, was in the nature of his metrical gift—a faculty mixed into the very flesh and blood of his verse."

From another Blake lover, Dante Gabriel Rossetti, we may take a word about imaginative atmosphere with which Blake would have agreed: "I must confess to a need, in narrative dramatic poetry (unless so simple in structure as *Auld Robin Gray*, for instance), of something rather exciting and indeed I believe something of the romantic element, to rouse my mind to anything like the moods produced by personal emotion in my own life. . . . Keats' narrative works are of the kind I mean. . . ."

The further clues to the poets' testament must be picked up in the following text. Even there we must not expect to find the whole philosophy of the subject, which will never be fully exploited until we have the impossible, a perfect poet and a perfect philosopher rolled into one. This, in spite of Coleridge, who said, " No man was ever yet a great poet, without being at the same time a profound philosopher." But the poet adopts the service of philosophy, it would seem, witness Coleridge himself, with some risk to his own proper art; he cannot serve two masters.

What we do find in these contributions by Sir Philip Sidney, Milton, Dryden, Coleridge and their successors, is a set of testimonies not all agreed or conclusive, but such as they are making a much more delightful and natural companion to the poetic anthology than any more formal body of criticism could do. Taken in themselves, severally, they are full of wise and fine things, said in a way not readily to be forgotten. Taken historically, they touch in very telling fashion the periods in English poetry, from Chaucer to Spenser, on through the Elizabethan golden age to the beginning of the century when Wordsworth and Coleridge were still in their heat of youth and Shelley and Keats still potential, and so to our own day.

CONTENTS

	PAGE
INTRODUCTION	vi
GEOFFREY CHAUCER	1
Invocation from *The Hous of Fame*	
EDMUND SPENSER	3
The Perfect Paterne of a Poet	
SIR PHILIP SIDNEY	9
An Apologie for Poetrie	
THOMAS CAMPION	61
Observations on the Art of English Poesie	
SAMUEL DANIEL	86
A Defence of Ryme	
BEN JONSON	112
Poets and Poetry	
JOHN MILTON	118
A School of Poetry	
JOHN DRYDEN	123
Heroic Poetry and Poetic Licence	
ALEXANDER POPE	135
The Lyric Style and a Style of Sound	
THOMAS GRAY	136
Metrum: Observations on English Metre	
ROBERT BURNS	146
Songs and Song Writing	
SIR WALTER SCOTT	153
On Ballad Poetry	
WILLIAM WORDSWORTH	168
Observations and a Passage on Poetic Diction	

CONTENTS

	PAGE
SAMUEL TAYLOR COLERIDGE	199
Wordsworth and the Art of Poetry	
PERCY BYSSHE SHELLEY	207
A Defence of Poetry	
LORD BYRON	242
The Present State of English Poetry	
JOHN KEATS	252
The Genius of Poetry, and his Own Art	
WALTER SAVAGE LANDOR	255
Poetry without Body	
ROBERT BROWNING	256
Shelley and the Art of Poetry	
MATTHEW ARNOLD	275
On Translating Homer	
ROBERT BRIDGES	285
Poetry and Poetic Diction	

THE PRELUDE TO POETRY

GEOFFREY CHAUCER

(1340–1400)

INVOCATION AND LINES UPON THE MUSE
From " The Hous of Fame," 1383–4.

O GOD of science and of light,
Apollo, through thy grete might,
This litel laste book thou gye!
Nat that I wilne, for maistrye,
Here Art Poetical be shewed;
But, for the rym is light and lewed,
Yit make hit sumwhat agreable,
Though som vers faile in a sillable;
And that I do no diligence,
To shewe crafte, but o sentence.
And if divyne vertu, thou
Wilt helpe me to shewe now
That in myn hede y-marked is,—
Lo, that is for to menen this,
The Hous of Fame to descryve,—
Thou shalt see me go, as blyve,
Unto the nexte laure I see,
And kisse hit, for hit is thy tree.

*　　*　　*　　*

But in this riche lusty place,
That Fames halle called was,
Ful moche prees of folk ther nas,
Ne crouding, for to mochil prees,
But al on hye, above a dees,
Sitte in a see imperial,
That maad was of a rubee al,
Which that a carbuncle is y-called,
I saugh, perpetually y-stalled,
A feminyne creature;

That never formed by nature
Nas swich another thing y-seye.
For altherfirst, soth for to seye,
Me thoughte that she was so lyte,
That the lengthe of a cubyte
Was lenger than she seemed be;
But thus sone, in a whyle, she
Hir tho so wonderliche streighte,
That with hir feete she therthe reighte,
And with hir heed she touched hevene,
Ther as shynen sterres sevene.

* * * *

But, lord! the perrie and the richesse
I saugh sitting on this goddesse!
And, lord! the hevenish melodye
Of songes, ful of armonye,
I herde aboute her trone y-songe,
That al the paleys-walles ronge!
So song the mighty Muse, she
That cleped is Caliopee.
And hir eighte sustren eke,
That in hir face semen meke;
And evermo, eternally,
They songe of Fame, as tho herde I:—
"Heried be thou and thy name,
Goddesse of renoun and of fame!"

EDMUND SPENSER

(1552-1599)

THE PERFECTE PATERNE OF A POETE

From " The Shepheards Calender," 1579
[With Notes on Poetry, and on Music].

This Poem forms the October Eclogue of the Calendar. The Prose Argument and Notes were part of the Commentary supposed to be written by E. K. E. K. was Spenser's friend, Edward Kirke, possibly on occasion his mouthpiece.

ARGUMENT.

In Cuddie is set out the perfecte paterne of a Poete, whiche, finding no maintenaunce of his state and studies, complayneth of the contempte of Poetrie, and the causes thereof: Specially having bene in all ages, and even amongst the most barbarous, always of singular accoumpt and honor, and being indede so worthy and commendable an arte ; or rather no arte, but a divine gift and heavenly instinct not to bee gotten by laboure and learning, but adorned with both ; and poured into the witte by a certain Ἐνθουσιασμὸς and celestiall inspiration, as the Author hereof els where at large discourseth in his booke called "The English Poete," which booke being lately come to my hands, I mynde also by Gods grace, upon further advisement to publish.

PIERS.

CUDDIE, for shame! hold up thy heavye head,
And let us cast with what delight to chace,
And weary thys long lingring Phœbus race.
Whilome thou wont the shepheards laddes to leade
In rymes, in ridles, and in bydding base ;
Now they in thee, and thou in sleepe art dead.

CUDDIE.

Piers, I have pyped erst so long with payne,
That all mine Oten reedes bene rent and wore,
And my poore Muse hath spent her spared store

Yet little good hath got, and much lesse gayne.
Such pleasaunce makes the Grashopper so poore,
And ligge so layd, when Winter doth her straine.

The dapper ditties, that I wont devise
To feede youthes fancie, and the flocking fry,
Delighten much; what I the bett for-thy?
They han the pleasure, I a sclender prise;
I beate the bush, the byrds to them doe flye:
What good thereof to Cuddie can arise?

PIERS.

Cuddie, the prayse is better then the price,
The glory eke much greater then the gayne:
O! what an honor is it, to restraine
The lust of lawlesse youth with good advice,
Or pricke them forth with pleasaunce of thy vaine,
Whereto thou list their trayned willes entice.

Soone as thou gynst to sette thy notes in frame,
O, how the rurall routes to thee doe cleave!
Seemeth thou dost their soule of sence bereave;
All as the shepheard that did fetch his dame
From Plutoes balefull bowre withouten leave,
His musicks might the hellish hound did tame.

CUDDIE.

So praysen babes the Peacoks spotted traine,
And wondren at bright Argus blazing eye;
But who rewards him ere the more for-thy,
Or feedes him once the fuller by a graine?
Sike prayse is smoke, that sheddeth in the skye;
Sike words bene wynd, and wasten soone in vayne.

PIERS.

Abandon, then, the base and viler clowne;
Lyft up thy selfe out of the lowly dust,
And sing of bloody Mars, of wars, of giusts;
Turne thee to those that weld the awful crowne,
To doubted Knights, whose woundlesse armour rusts,
And helmes unbruzed wexen dayly browne.

There may thy Muse display her fluttryng wing,
And stretch her selfe at large from East to West
Whither thou list in fayre Elisa rest,
Or, if thee please in bigger notes to sing,
Advaunce the worthy whome shee loveth best,
That first the white beare to the stake did bring.

And, when the stubborne stroke of stronger stoundes
Has somewhat slackt the tenor of thy string,
Of love and lustihead tho mayst thou sing,
And carroll lowde, and leade the Myllers rownde,
All were Elisa one of thilke same ring ;
So mought our Cuddies name to heaven sownde.

CUDDIE.

Indeede the Romish Tityrus, I heare,
Through his Mecænas left his Oaten reede,
Whereon he earst had taught his flocks to feede,
And laboured lands to yield the timely eare,
And eft did sing of warres and deadly drede,
So as the Heavens did quake his verse to here.

But ah ! Mecænas is yclad in claye,
And great Augustus long ygoe is dead,
And all the worthies liggen wrapt in leade,
That matter made for Poets on to play :
For ever, who in derring-doe were dreade,
The loftie verse of hem was loved aye.

But after vertue gan for age to stoope,
And mightie manhode brought a bedde of ease,
The vaunting Poets found nought worth a pease
To put in preace emong the learned troupe :
Tho gan the streames of flowing wittes to cease,
And sonne-bright honour pend in shamefull coupe.

And if that any buddes of Poesie,
Yet of the old stocke, gan to shoote agayne,
Or it mens follies mote be forst to fayne,
And rolle with rest in rymes of rybaudrye ;
Or, as it sprong, it wither must agayne :
Tom Piper makes us better melodie.

PIERS.

O pierlesse Poesye! where is then thy place?
If nor in Princes pallace thou doe sitt,
(And yet is Princes pallace the most fitt,)
Ne brest of baser birth doth thee embrace,
Then make thee winges of thine aspyring wit,
And, whence thou camst, flye backe to heaven apace.

CUDDIE.

Ah, Percy! it is all to weake and wanne,
So high to sore and make so large a flight;
Her peeced pyneons bene not so in plight:
For Colin fittes such famous flight to scanne;
He, were he not with love so ill bedight,
Would mount as high, and sing as soote as Swanne.

PIERS.

Ah, fon! for love does teach him climbe so hie,
And lyftes him up out of the loathsome myre:
Such immortal mirrhor, as he doth admire,
Would rayse ones mynd above the starry skie,
And cause a caytive corage to aspire;
For lofty love doth loath a lowly eye.

CUDDIE.

All otherwise the state of Poet stands;
For lordly love is such a Tyranne fell,
That where he rules all power he doth expell;
The vaunted verse a vacant head demaundes,
Ne wont with crabbed care the Muses dwell:
Unwisely weaves, that takes two webbes in hand.

Who ever casts to compasse weightye prise,
And thinkes to throwe out thondring words of threate,
Let powre in lavish cups and thriftie bitts of meate,
For Bacchus fruite is frend to Phœbus wise;
And, when with Wine the braine begins to sweate,
The nombers flowe as fast as spring doth ryse.

Thou kenst not, Percie, howe the ryme should rage,
O! if my temples were distain'd with wine,
And girt in girlonds of wild Yvie twine,
How I could reare the Muse on stately stage,
And teache her tread aloft in buskin fine,
With queint Bellona in her equipage!

But ah! my corage cooles ere it be warme:
For-thy content us in thys humble shade,
Where no such troublous tydes han us assayde;
Here we our slender pypes may safely charme.

* * * *

NOTES.

ON THE ABOVE POEM.

This Æglogue is made in imitation of Theocritus his **xvi.** Idilion, wherein he reproved the Tyranne Hiero of Syracuse for his nigardise towarde Poetes, in whome is the power to make men immortall for theyr good dedes, or shameful for their naughty lyfe. And the lyke also is in Mantuane. The style hereof, as also that in Theocritus, is more loftye then the rest, and applyed to the heighte of Poeticall witte.

"THE FIRST INVENTION OF POETRY."

[*See Stanza IV.*]

This place seemeth to conspyre with Plato, who in his first booke de Legibus sayth, that the first invention of Poetry was of very vertuous intent. For at what time an infinite number of youth usually came to theyr great solemne feastes called Panegyrica, which they used every five yeere to hold, some learned man, being more hable then the rest for speciall gyftes of wytte and Musicke, would take upon him to sing fine verses to the people, in prayse eyther of vertue or of victory, or of immortality, or such like. At whose wonderfull gyft al men being astonied, and as it were ravished with delight, thinking (as it was indeed) that he was inspired from above, called him vatem: which kinde of men afterward framing their verses to lighter musick (as of musick be many kinds, some sadder, some lighter, some martiall, some heroicall, and so diversely eke affect the mynds of men,) found out lighter matter of Poesie also, some playing wyth love, some scorning at mens fashions, some powred out in pleasures: and so were called Poetes or makers.

"THE SECRETE WORKING OF MUSICK."
[See Stanza V.]

What the secrete working of Musick is in the myndes of men, as well appeareth hereby, that some of the auncient Philosophers, and those the moste wise, as Plato and Pythagoras, held for opinion, that the mynd was made of a certaine harmonie and musicall nombers, for the great compassion, and likenes of affection in thone and in the other, as also by that memorable history of Alexander: to whom when as Timotheus the great Musitian playd the Phrygian melody, it is said, that he was distraught with such unwonted fury, that, streightway rysing from the table in great rage, he caused himselfe to be armed, as ready to goe to warre, (for that musick is very warlike.) And immediately when as the Musitian chaunged his stroke into the Lydian and Ionique harmony, he was so furr from warring, that he sat as styl, as if he had bene in matters of counsell. Such might is in musick: wherefore Plato and Aristotle forbid the Arcadian Melodie from children and youth. For that being altogither on the fyft and vii tone, it is of great force to molifie and quench the kindly courage, which useth to burne in yong brests. So that it is not incredible which the Poete here sayth, that Musick can bereave the soule of sence.

SIR PHILIP SIDNEY

(1554–1586)

AN APOLOGIE FOR POETRIE.

The "Apologie" was written about 1581,—the date is not absolutely certain. The first edition is the quarto of 1595, whose text we take, following the reprint of Professor Arber.

WHEN the right vertuous *Edward Wotton*, and I, were at the Emperors Court together, wee gave our selves to learne horsemanship of *John Pietro Pugliano*: one that with great commendation had the place of an Esquire in his stable. And hee, according to the fertilnes of the Italian wit, did not onely afoord us the demonstration of his practise, but sought to enrich our mindes with the contemplations therein, which hee thought most precious. But with none I remember mine eares were at any time more loden, then when (either angred with slowe paiment, or mooved with our learner-like admiration,) he exercised his speech in the prayse of his facultie. Hee sayd, Souldiours were the noblest estate of mankinde, and horsemen, the noblest of Souldiours. Hee sayde, they were the Maisters of warre, and ornaments of peace: speedy goers, and strong abiders, triumphers both in Camps and Courts. Nay, to so unbeleeved a poynt hee proceeded, as that no earthly thing bred such wonder to a Prince, as to be a good horseman. Skill of government, was but a Pedanteria in comparison: then would hee adde certaine prayses, by telling what a peerlesse beast a horse was. The onely serviceable Courtier without flattery, the beast of most beutie, faithfulnes, courage, and such more, that if I had not beene a peece of a Logician before I came to him, I think he would have perswaded mee to have wished my selfe a horse. But thus much at least with his no fewe words hee drave into me, that selfe-love is better then any guilding to make that seeme gorgious, wherein our selves are parties. Wherein, if *Pugliano* his strong affection and weake arguments will not satisfie you, I wil give you a neerer example of my selfe, who (I knowe not by what mischance) in these my not old yeres and idelest times, having slipt into the title of a Poet, am provoked to say somthing unto you in the defence of that my unelected vocation, which if I handle with more good will then good reasons, beare with me, sith the scholler is to be pardoned that foloweth the steppes of his Maister. And yet I must say, that as I have just cause to make a pittiful defence of poore Poetry, which from almost the highest estimation of learning, is fallen to be the laughingstocke of children. So have I need to bring some more availeable proofes: sith the former is by no man barred of his deserved credite, the silly latter hath had even the names of Philosophers used to the defacing of it, with great danger of civill war among the Muses. And first, truly to al them that professing learning inveigh against Poetry, may justly be objected, that they goe very neer to ungratfulnes, to seek to deface that, which in the noblest nations and languages that are knowne, hath been the first light-giver to ignorance, and first Nurse, whose milk by little and little enabled them to feed afterwards of tougher knowledges: and will they now play the Hedghog, that being received into the den, drave out his host? or rather the Vipers, that with theyr birth kill their Parents? Let learned Greece in any of her manifold Sciences, be able to shew me one booke, before *Musæus*, *Homer*, and *Hesiodus*, all three nothing els but Poets. Nay, let any historie be brought, that can say any Writers were there before them, if they were not men of the same skil, as *Orpheus*, *Linus*, and some other are named: who having beene the first of that Country, that made pens deliverers of their knowledge to their posterity, may justly challenge to bee called their Fathers in learning: for not only in time they had this priority (although in it self antiquity be venerable) but went before them, as causes to drawe with their charming sweetnes, the wild untamed wits

AN APOLOGIE FOR POETRIE

to an admiration of knowledge. So as *Amphion* was sayde to move stones with his Poetrie, to build Thebes. And *Orpheus* to be listened to by beastes, indeed, stony and beastly people. So among the Romans were *Livius*, *Andronicus*, and *Ennius*. So in the Italian language, the first that made it aspire to be a Treasurehouse of Science, where the Poets *Dante*, *Boccace*, and *Petrarch*. So in our English were *Gower* and *Chawcer*.

After whom, encouraged and delighted with theyr excellent fore-going, others have followed, to beautifie our mother tongue, as wel in the same kinde as in other Arts. This did so notably shewe it selfe, that the Phylosophers of Greece, durst not a long time appeare to the worlde but under the masks of Poets. So *Thales*, *Empedocles*, and *Parmenides*, sange their naturall Phylosophie in verses: so did *Pythagoras* and *Phocilides* their morrall counsells: so did *Tirteus* in war matters, and *Solon* in matters of policie: or rather, they beeing Poets, dyd exercise their delightful vaine in those points of highest knowledge, which before them lay hid to the world. For that wise *Solon* was directly a Poet, it is manifest, having written in verse, the notable fable of the Atlantick Iland, which was continued by *Plato*.

And truely, even *Plato*, whosoever well considereth, shall find, that in the body of his work, though the inside and strength were Philosophy, the skinne as it were and beautie, depended most of Poetrie: for all standeth upon Dialogues, wherein he faineth many honest Burgesses of Athens to speake of such matters, that if they had been sette on the racke, they would never have confessed them. Besides, his poetical describing the circumstances of their meetings, as the well ordering of a banquet, the delicacie of a walke, with enterlacing meere tales, as *Giges* Ring, and others, which who knoweth not to be flowers of Poetrie, did never walke into *Appolos* Garden.

And even Historiographers (although theyr lippes sounde of things doone, and veritie be written in theyr fore-heads,) have been glad to borrow both fashion, and perchance weight of Poets. So *Herodotus* entituled his Historie, by the name of the nine Muses: and both he and all the rest that followed him, either stole or usurped of Poetrie, their passionate describing of passions, the many particularities of battailes, which no man could affirme : or if that be denied me, long Orations put in the mouthes of great Kings and Captaines, which it is certaine they never pronounced. So that truely, neyther Phylosopher nor Historiographer, coulde at the first have entred into the gates of populer judgements, if they had not taken a great pasport of Poetry, which in all Nations at this day wher learning florisheth not, is plaine to be seene : in all which they have some feeling of Poetry. In Turky, besides their lawe-giving Divines, they have no other Writers but Poets. In our neighbour Countrey Ireland, where truelie learning goeth very bare, yet are theyr Poets held in a devoute reverence. Even among the most barbarous and simple Indians where no writing is, yet have they their Poets, who make and sing songs which they call *Areytos*, both of theyr Auncestors deedes, and praises of theyr Gods. A sufficient probabilitie, that if ever learning come among them, it must be by having theyr hard dull wits softened and sharpened with the sweete delights of Poetrie. For untill they find a pleasure in the exercises of the minde, great promises of much knowledge, will little perswade them, that knowe not the fruites of knowledge. In Wales, the true remnant of the auncient Brittons, as there are good authorities to shewe the long time they had Poets, which they called *Bardes* : so thorough all the conquests of Romaines, Saxons, Danes, and Normans, some of whom did seeke to ruine all memory of learning from among them, yet doo their Poets even to this day, last ; so as it is not more notable in soone beginning then in long continuing. But since the Authors of most of our Sciences were the Romans, and before them the Greekes, let us a little stand uppon their authorities, but even so farre as to see, what names they have given unto this now scorned skill.

Among the Romans a Poet was called *Vates*, which is as much as a Diviner, Fore-seer, or Prophet, as by his conjoyned wordes *Vaticinium* and *Vaticinari*, is manifest : so heavenly a title did that excellent people bestow upon his hart-ravishing knowledge. And so farre were they carried into the admiration thereof, that they thought in the chaunceable hitting uppon any such verses great fore-tokens of their following fortunes were placed. Whereupon grew the worde of *Sortes Virgilianæ*, when by suddaine opening *Virgils* booke, they lighted upon any verse of hys making, whereof the histories of the Emperors lives are full, as of *Albinus* the Governour of our Iland, who in his childehoode mette with this verse

> Arma amens capio nec sat rationis in armis.

And in his age performed it, which although it were a very vaine, and godles superstition, as also it was to think that spirits were commaunded by such verses, whereupon this word charmes, derived of *Carmina* commeth, so yet serveth it to shew the great reverence those wits were helde in. And altogether not without ground, since both the Oracles of *Delphos* and *Sibillas* prophecies, where wholy delivered in verses. For that same exquisite observing of number and measure in words, and that high flying liberty of conceit proper to the Poet, did seeme to have some dyvine force in it.

And may not I presume a little further, to shew the reasonablenes of this worde *Vates*? And say that the holy *Davids* Psalmes are a divine Poem? If I doo, I shall not do it without the testimonie of great learned men, both aunctent and moderne : but even the name Psalmes will speake for mee, which being interpreted, is nothing but songes Then that it is fully written in meeter, as all learned Hebricians agree, although the rules be not yet fully found. Lastly and principally, his handeling his prophecy, which is meerely poetical. For what els is the awaking his musicall instruments? The often and free changing of persons? His notable *Prosopopeias*, when he maketh you as it were, see God comming in his Majestie. His telling of the Beastes joyfulnes and hills leaping, but a heavenlie poesie: wherein almost hee sheweth himselfe a passionate lover, of that unspeakable and everlasting beautie to be seene by the eyes of the minde, onely cleered by fayth. But truely nowe having named him, I feare mee I seeme to prophane that holy name, applying it to Poetrie, which is among us throwne downe to so ridiculous an estimation: but they that with quiet judgements will looke a little deeper into it, shall finde the end and working of it such, as beeing rightly applyed, deserveth not to bee scourged out of the Church of God.

But now, let us see how the Greekes named it, and howe they deemed of it. The Greekes called him a Poet, which name, hath as the most excellent, gone thorough other Languages. It commeth of this word *Poiein*, which is, to make: wherein I know not whether by lucke or wisedome, wee Englishmen have mette with the Greekes, in calling him a maker: which name, how high and incomparable a title it is, I had rather were knowne by marking the scope of other Sciences, then by my partiall allegation.

There is no Arte delivered to mankinde, that hath not the workes of Nature for his principall object, without which they could not consist, and on which they so depend, as they become Actors and Players as it were, of what Nature will have set foorth. So doth the Astronomer looke upon the starres, and by that he seeth, setteth downe what order Nature hath taken therein. So doe the Geometrician, and Arithmetician, in their diverse sorts of quantities. So doth the Musitian in times, tel you which by nature agree, which not. The naturall Philosopher thereon hath his name, and the Morrall Philosopher standeth upon the naturall vertues, vices, and passions of man; and followe Nature (saith hee) therein, and thou shalt not erre. The Lawyer sayth what men have determined. The Historian what men have done. The Grammarian speaketh onely of the rules of speech, and the Rethorician, and Logitian, considering what in Nature will soonest prove and perswade, thereon give artificial rules, which still are compassed within the circle of a question, according to the proposed matter. The Phisition waigheth the nature of a mans bodie, and the nature of things helpeful, or hurtefull unto it. And the Metaphisick, though it be in the seconde and abstract notions, and therefore be counted supernaturall: yet doth hee indeede builde upon the depth of Nature: onely the Poet, disdayning to be tied to any such subjection, lifted up with the vigor of his owne invention, dooth growe in effect, another nature, in making things either better then Nature bringeth forth, or quite a newe formes such as never were in Nature, as the *Heroes, Demigods, Cyclops, Chimeras, Furies,* and such like: so as hee goeth hand in hand with Nature, not inclosed within the narrow warrant of her guifts, but freely ranging onely within the Zodiack of his owne wit.

Nature never set forth the earth in so rich tapistry, as divers Poets have done, neither with plesant rivers, fruitful trees, sweet smelling flowers: nor whatsoever els may make the too much loved earth more lovely. Her world is brasen, the Poets only deliver a golden: but let those things alone and goe to man, for whom as the other things are, so it seemeth in him her uttermost cunning is imployed, and knowe whether shee have brought foorth so true a lover as *Theagines,* so constant a friende as *Pilades,* so valiant a man as *Orlando,* so right a Prince as *Xenophons Cyrus:* so excellent a man every way, as *Virgils Aeneas:* neither let this be jestingly conceived, because the works of the one be essentiall: the other, in imitation or fiction, for any understanding knoweth the skil of the Artificer: standeth in that *Idea* or fore-conceite of the work, and not in the work it selfe. And that the Poet hath that *Idea,* is manifest, by delivering them forth in such excellencie as hee hath imagined them. Which delivering forth also, is not wholie imaginative, as we are wont to say by them that build Castles in the ayre: but so farre substantially it worketh, not onely to make a *Cyrus,* which had been but a particuler excellencie, as Nature might have done, but to bestow a *Cyrus* upon the worlde, to make many *Cyrus's,* if they wil learne aright, why, and how that Maker made him.

Neyther let it be deemed too sawcie a comparison to ballance the highest poynt of mans wit with the efficacie of Nature: but rather give right honor to the heavenly Maker of that maker: who having made man to his owne likenes, set him beyond and over all the workes of that second nature, which in nothing hee sheweth so much as in Poetrie: when with the force of a divine breath, he bringeth things forth far surpassing her dooings, with no small argument to the incredulous of that first accursed fall of *Adam:* sith our erected wit, maketh us know what perfection is, and yet our infected will, keepeth us from reaching unto it. But these arguments wil by fewe be understood, and by fewer granted. Thus much (I hope) will be given me, that the Greekes with some probabilitie of reason, gave him the name above all names of learning. Now let us goe to a more ordinary opening of him, that the trueth may be more palpable: and so I hope, though we get not so unmatched a praise as the Etimologie of his names wil grant, yet his very description, which no man will denie, shall not justly be barred from a principall commendation.

Poesie therefore is an arte of imitation, for so *Aristotle* termeth it in his word *Mimesis,* that is to say, a representing, counterfetting, or figuring foorth: to speake metaphorically, a speaking picture: with this end, to teach and delight; of this have beene three severall kindes. The chiefe both in antiquitie and excellencie, were they that did imitate the inconceivable excellencies of GOD. Such were, *David* in his Psalmes, *Salomon* in his song of Songs, in his Ecclesiastes, and Proverbs: *Moses* and *Debora* in theyr Hymnes, and the writer of *Job;* which beside other, the learned *Emanuell Tremilius* and *Franciscus Junius,* doe entitle the poeticall part of the Scripture. Against these none will speake that hath the holie Ghost in due holy reverence.

In this kinde, though in a full wrong divinitie, were *Orpheus, Amphion, Homer* in his hymes, and many other, both Greekes and Romaines: and this Poesie must be used, by whosoever will follow *S. James* his counsell, in singing Psalmes when they are merry: and I knowe is used with the fruite of comfort by some, when in sorrowfull pangs of their death-bringing sinnes, they find the consolation of the never-leaving goodnesse.

The second kinde, is of them that deale with matters

Philosophicall; eyther morrall, as *Tirteus, Phocilides* and *Cato*, or naturall, as *Lucretius* and *Virgils Georgicks*: or Astronomicall, as *Manilius*, and *Pontanus*: or historical, as *Lucan*: which who mislike, the faulte is in their judgements quite out of taste, and not in the sweet foode of sweetly uttered knowledge. But because thys second sorte is wrapped within the folde of the proposed subject, and takes not the course of his owne invention, whether they properly be Poets or no, let Gramarians dispute: and goe to the thyrd, indeed right Poets, of whom chiefly this question ariseth; betwixt whom, and these second is such a kinde of difference, as betwixt the meaner sort of Painters, (who counterfet onely such faces as are sette before them) and the more excellent: who having no law but wit, bestow that in cullours upon you which is fittest for the eye to see: as the constant, though lamenting looke of *Lucrecia*, when she punished in her selfe an others fault.

Wherein he painteth not *Lucrecia* whom he never sawe, but painteth the outwarde beauty of such a vertue: for these third be they which most properly do imitate to teach and delight, and to imitate, borrow nothing of what is, hath been, or shall be: but range onely rayned with learned discretion, into the divine consideration of what may be, and should be. These bee they, that as the first and most noble sorte, may justly bee termed *Vates*, so these are waited on in the excellen[te]st languages and best understandings, with the fore described name of Poets: for these indeede doo meerely make to imitate: and imitate both to delight and teach: and delight to move men to take that goodnes in hande, which without delight they would flye as from a stranger. And teach, to make them know that goodnes whereunto they are mooved, which being the noblest scope to which ever any learning was directed, yet want there not idle tongues to barke at them. These be subdivided into sundry more speciall denominations. The most notable bee the *Heroick, Lirick, Tragick, Comick, Satirick, Iambick, Elegiack, Pastorall*, and certaine others. Some of these being termed according to the matter they deale with, some by the sorts of verses they liked best to write in, for indeede the greatest part of Poets have apparelled their poeticall inventions in that numbrous kinde of writing which is called verse: indeed but apparelled, verse being but an ornament and no cause to Poetry: sith there have beene many most excellent Poets, that never versified, and now swarme many versifiers that neede never aunswere to the name of Poets. For *Xenophon*, who did imitate so excellently, as to give us *effigiem justi imperij*, the portraiture of a just Empire under the name of *Cyrus*, (as *Cicero* sayth of him) made therein an absolute heroicall Poem.

So did *Heliodorus* in his sugred invention of that picture of love in *Theagines* and *Cariclea*, and yet both these writ in Prose: which I speak to shew, that it is not riming and versing that maketh a Poet, no more then a long gowne maketh an Advocate: who though he pleaded in armor should be an Advocate and no Souldier. But it is that fayning notable images of vertues, vices, or what els, with that delightfull teaching which must be the right describing note to know a Poet by: although indeed the Senate of Poets hath chosen verse as their fittest rayment, meaning, as in matter they passed all in all, so in maner to goe beyond them: not speaking (table talke fashion or like men in a dreame,) words as they chanceably fall from the mouth, but peyzing each sillable of each worde by just proportion according to the dignitie of the subject.

Nowe therefore it shall not bee amisse first to waigh this latter sort of Poetrie by his works, and then by his partes; and if in neyther of these Anatomies hee be condemnable, I hope wee shall obtaine a more favourable sentence. This purifing of wit, this enritching of memory, enabling of judgment, and enlarging of conceyt, which commonly we call learning, under what name soever it com forth, or to what immediat end soever it be directed, the final end is, to lead and draw us to as high a perfection, as our degenerate soules made worse by theyr clayey lodgings, can be capable of. This according to the inclination of the man, bred many formed impressions, for some that thought this

AN APOLOGIE FOR POETRIE

felicity principally to be gotten by knowledge, and no knowledge to be so high and heavenly, as acquaintance with the starres, gave themselves to Astronomie; others, perswading themselves to be *Demigods* if they knewe the causes of things, became naturall and supernaturall Philosophers, some an admirable delight drew to Musicke: and some, the certainty of demonstration, to the Mathematickes. But all, one, and other, having this scope to knowe, and by knowledge to lift up the mind from the dungeon of the body, to the enjoying his owne divine essence. But when by the ballance of experience it was found, that the Astronomer looking to the starres might fall into a ditch, that the enquiring Philosopher might be blinde in himselfe, and the Mathematician might draw foorth a straight line with a crooked hart: then loe, did proofe the over ruler of opinions, make manifest, that all these are but serving Sciences, which as they have each a private end in themselves, so yet are they all directed to the highest end of the mistres Knowledge, by the Greekes called *Arkitecktonike*, which stands, (as I thinke) in the knowledge of a mans selfe, in the Ethicke and politick consideration, with the end of well dooing and not of well knowing onely; even as the Sadlers next end is to make a good saddle: but his farther end, to serve a nobler facultie, which is horsemanship, so the horsemans to souldiery, and the Souldier not onely to have the skill, but to performe the practise of a Souldier: so that the ending end of all earthly learning, being vertuous action, those skilles that most serve to bring forth that, have a most just title to bee Princes over all the rest: wherein if wee can shewe the Poets noblenes, by setting him before his other Competitors, among whom as principall challengers step forth the morrall Philosophers, whom me thinketh, I see comming towards me with a sullen gravity, as though they could not abide vice by day light, rudely clothed for to witnes outwardly their contempt of outward things, with bookes in their hands agaynst glory, whereto they sette theyr names, sophistically speaking against subtility, and angry with any man in whom they see the foule fault

of anger: these men casting larges as they goe, of
Definitions, Divisions, and Distinctions, with a scornefull
interogative, doe soberly aske, whether it bee possible to
finde any path, so ready to leade a man to vertue, as
that which teacheth what vertue is ? and teacheth it
not onely by delivering forth his very being, his causes,
and effects: but also, by making known his enemie
vice, which must be destroyed, and his combersome
servant Passion, which must be maistered, by shewing
the generalities that contayneth it, and the specialities
that are derived from it. Lastly, by playne setting
downe, how it extendeth it selfe out of the limits of a
mans own little world, to the government of families,
and maintayning of publique societies.

The Historian, scarcely giveth leysure to the Moralist,
to say so much, but that he loden with old Mouse-eaten
records, authorising himselfe (for the most part) upon
other histories, whose greatest authorities, are built
upon the notable foundation of Heare-say, having much
a-doe to accord differing Writers, and to pick trueth
out of partiality, better acquainted with a thousande
yeeres a goe, then with the present age: and yet better
knowing how this world goeth, then how his owne wit
runneth: curious for antiquities, and inquisitive of
novelties, a wonder to young folkes, and a tyrant in
table talke, denieth in a great chafe, that any man for
teaching of vertue, and vertuous actions, is comparable
to him. I am *Lux vitæ, Temporum Magistra, Vita
memoriæ, Nuncia vetustatis, &c.*

The Phylosopher (sayth hee) teacheth a disputative
vertue, but I doe an active: his vertue is excellent
in the dangerlesse Academie of *Plato*, but mine sheweth
foorth her honorable face, in the battailes of *Marathon,
Pharsalia, Poitiers,* and *Agincourt.* Hee teacheth vertue
by certaine abstract considerations, but I onely bid
you follow the footing of them that have gone before
you. Olde-aged experience, goeth beyond the fine-
witted Phylosopher, but I give the experience of many
ages. Lastly, if he make the Song-booke, I put the
learners hande to the Lute: and if hee be the guide, I
am the light.

Then woulde hee alledge you innumerable examples, conferring storie by storie, how much the wisest Senatours and Princes, have beene directed by the credite of history, as *Brutus*, *Alphonsus* of *Aragon*, and who not, if need bee? At length, the long lyne of theyr disputation maketh a poynt in thys, that the one giveth the precept, and the other the example.

Nowe, whom shall wee finde (sith the question standeth for the highest forme in the Schoole of learning) to bee Moderator? Trulie, as me seemeth, the Poet; and if not a Moderator, even the man that ought to carrie the title from them both, and much more from all other serving Sciences. Therefore compare we the Poet with the Historian, and with the Morrall Phylosopher, and, if hee goe beyond them both, no other humaine skill can match him. For as for the Divine, with all reverence it is ever to be excepted, not only for having his scope as far beyonde any of these, as eternitie exceedeth a moment, but even for passing each of these in themselves.

And for the Lawyer, though *Jus* bee the Daughter of Justice, and Justice the chiefe of Vertues, yet because hee seeketh to make men good, rather *Formidine pænæ*, then *Virtutis amore*, or to say righter, dooth not indevour to make men good, but that their evill hurt not others: having no care so hee be a good Cittizen; how bad a man he be. Therefore, as our wickedness maketh him necessarie, and necessitie maketh him honorable, so is hee not in the deepest trueth to stande in rancke with these; who all indevour to take naughtines away, and plant goodnesse even in the secretest cabinet of our soules. And these foure are all, that any way deale in that consideration of mens manners, which being the supreme knowledge, they that best breed it, deserve the best commendation.

The Philosopher therfore and the Historian, are they which would win the gole: the one by precept, the other by example. But both not having both, doe both halte. For the Philosopher, setting downe with thorny argument the bare rule, is so hard of utterance, and so mistie to bee conceived, that one that hath no other guide but him, shall wade in him till hee be olde, before he shall finde sufficient cause to bee honest: for his knowledge standeth so upon the abstract and generall, that happie is that man who may understande him, and more happie, that can applye what hee dooth understand.

On the other side, the Historian wanting the precept, is so tyed, not to what shoulde bee, but to what is, to the particuler truth of things, and not to the general reason of things, that hys example draweth no necessary consequence and therefore a lesse fruitfull doctrine.

Nowe dooth the peerelesse Poet performe both: for whatsoever the Philosopher sayth shoulde be doone, hee giveth a perfect picture of it in some one, by whom hee presupposeth it was done. So as hee coupleth the generall notion with the particuler example. A perfect picture I say, for hee yeeldeth to the powers of the minde, an image of that whereof the Philosopher bestoweth but a woordish description: which dooth neyther strike, pierce, nor possesse the sight of the soule, so much as that other dooth.

For as in outward things, to a man that had never seene an Elephant or a Rinoceros, who should tell him most exquisitely all theyr shapes, cullour, bignesse, and particuler markes: or of a gorgeous Pallace, the Architecture, with declaring the full beauties, might well make the hearer able to repeate as it were by rote, all hee had heard, yet should never satisfie his inward conceits, with being witnes to it selfe of a true lively knowledge: but the same man, as soone as hee might see those beasts well painted, or the house wel in moddel, should straightwaies grow without need of any description, to a judicial comprehending of them, so no doubt the Philosopher with his learned definition, bee it of vertue, vices, matters of publick policie, or privat government, replenisheth the memory with many infallible grounds of wisdom: which notwithstanding, lye darke before the imaginative and judging powre, if they bee not illuminated or figured foorth by the speaking picture of Poesie.

Tullie taketh much paynes and many times not without poeticall helpes, to make us knowe the force love of our Countrey hath in us. Let us but heare old *Anchises* speaking in the middest of Troyes flames, or see *Ulisses* in the fulnes of all *Calipso's* delights, bewayle his absence from barraine and beggerly *Ithaca*. Anger the *Stoicks* say, was a short maddnes, let but *Sophocles* bring you *Ajax* on a stage, killing and whipping Sheepe and Oxen, thinking them the Army of Greeks, with theyr Chiefetaines *Agamemnon* and *Menelaus*, and tell mee if you have not a more familiar insight into anger, then finding in the Schoolemen his *Genus* and difference. See whether wisdome and temperance in *Ulisses* and *Diomedes*, valure in *Achilles*, friendship in *Nisus* and *Eurialus*, even to an ignoraunt man, carry not an apparent shyning: and contrarily, the remorse of conscience in *Oedipus*, the soone repenting pride of *Agamemnon*, the selfe-devouring crueltie in his Father *Atreus*, the violence of ambition in the two *Theban* brothers, the sowre-sweetnes of revenge in *Medæa*, and to fall lower, the *Terentian Gnato*, and our *Chaucers* Pandar, so exprest, that we nowe use their names to signifie their trades. And finally, all vertues, vices, and passions, so in their own naturall seates layd to the viewe, that wee seeme not to heare of them, but cleerely to see through them. But even in the most excellent determination of goodnes, what Philosophers counsell can so redily direct a Prince, as the fayned *Cyrus* in *Xenophon*? or a vertuous man in all fortunes, as *Aeneas* in *Virgill*? or a whole Common-wealth, as the way of Sir *Thomas Moores Eutopia*? I say the way, because where Sir *Thomas Moore* erred, it was the fault of the man and not of the Poet, for that way of patterning a Common-wealth was most absolute, though hee perchaunce hath not so absolutely perfourmed it: for the question is, whether the fayned image of Poesie, or the regular instruction of Philosophy, hath the more force in teaching: wherein if the Philosophers have more rightly shewed themselves Philosophers, then the Poets have obtained to the high top of their profession, as in truth,

———Mediocribus esse poetis,
Non Dij, non homines, non concessere Columnæ:

It is I say againe, not the fault of the Art, but that by fewe men that Arte can bee accomplished.

Certainly, even our Saviour Christ could as well have given, the morrall common places of uncharitablenes and humblenes, as the divine narration of *Dives* and *Lazarus*: or of disobedience and mercy, as that heavenly discourse of the lost Child and the gratious Father; but that hys through-searching wisdom, knewe the estate of *Dives* burning in hell, and of *Lazarus* being in *Abrahams* bosome, would more constantly (as it were) inhabit both the memory and judgment. Truly, for my selfe, mee seemes I see before my eyes the lost Childes disdainefull prodigality, turned to envie a Swines dinner: which by the learned Divines, are thought not historicall acts, but instructing Parables. For conclusion, I say the Philosopher teacheth, but he teacheth obscurely, so as the learned onely can understande him: that is to say, he teacheth them that are already taught, but the Poet is the foode for the tenderest stomacks, the Poet is indeed the right Popular Philosopher, whereof *Esops* tales give good proofe: whose pretty Allegories, stealing under the formall tales of Beastes, make many, more beastly then Beasts, begin to heare the sound of vertue from these dumbe speakers.

But now may it be alledged, that if this imagining of matters be so fitte for the imagination, then must the Historian needs surpasse, who bringeth you images of true matters, such as indeede were doone, and not such as fantastically or falsely may be suggested to have been doone. Truely *Aristotle* himselfe in his discourse of Poesie, plainely determineth this question, saying, that Poetry is *Philosophoteron* and *Spoudaioteron*, that is to say, it is more Philosophicall, and more studiously serious, then history. His reason is, because Poesie dealeth with *Katholon*, that is to say, with the universall consideration; and the history with *Kathekaston*, the perticuler; nowe sayth he, the universall wayes what is fit to bee sayd or done, eyther in likelihood or necessity, (which the Poesie considereth in his imposed names,) and the perticuler, onely mark's, whether *Alcibiades* did, or suffered, this or that. Thus farre *Aristotle:* which reason of his, (as all his) is most full of reason. For indeed, if the question were whether it were better to have a perticuler acte truly or falsly set down: there is no doubt which is to be chosen, no more then whether you had rather have *Vespasians* picture right as hee was, or at the Painters pleasure nothing resembling. But if the question be for your owne use and learning, whether it be better to have it set downe as it should be, or as it was: then certainely is more doctrinable the fained *Cirus* of *Xenophon* then the true *Cyrus* in *Justine:* and the fayned *Aeneas* in *Virgil*, then the right *Aeneas* in *Dares Phrigius*.

As to a Lady that desired to fashion her countenance to the best grace, a Painter should more benefite her to portraite a most sweet face, wryting *Canidia* upon it, then to paynt *Canidia* as she was, who *Horace* sweareth, was foule and ill favoured.

If the Poet doe his part a-right, he will shew you in *Tantalus, Atreus*, and such like, nothing that is not to be shunned. In *Cyrus, Aeneas, Ulisses*, each thing to be followed; where the Historian, bound to tell things as things were, cannot be liberall (without hee will be poeticall) of a perfect patterne: but as in *Alexander* or *Scipio* himselfe, shew dooings, some to be liked, some to be misliked. And then how will you discerne what to followe but by your owne discretion, which you had without reading *Quintus Curtius?* And whereas a man may say, though in universall consideration of doctrine the Poet prevaileth; yet that the historie, in his saying such a thing was doone, doth warrant a man more in that hee shall follow.

The aunswere is manifest, that if hee stande upon that was; as if hee should argue, because it rayned yesterday, therefore it shoulde rayne to day, then indeede it hath some advantage to a grose conceite: but if he know an example onlie, informes a conjectured likelihood, and so goe by reason, the Poet dooth so farre exceede him, as hee is to frame his example to that which is most reasonable: be it in warlike, politick, or private matters; where the Historian in his bare *Was*, hath many times that which wee call fortune, to over-rule the best wisdome. Manie times, he must tell events, whereof he can yeelde no cause: or if hee doe, it must be poeticall; for that a fayned example, hath as much force to teach, as a true example: (for as for to moove, it is cleere, sith the fayned may bee tuned to the highest key of passion) let us take one example, wherein a Poet and a Historian doe concur.

Herodotus and *Justine* do both testifie, that *Zopirus*, King *Darius* faithful servaunt, seeing his Maister long resisted by the rebellious *Babilonians*, fayned himselfe in extreame disgrace of his King: for verifying of which, he caused his owne nose and eares to be cut off: and so flying to the *Babylonians*, was received: and for his knowne valour, so far credited, that hee did finde meanes to deliver them over to *Darius*. Much like matter doth *Livie* record of *Tarquinius* and his sonne. *Xenophon* excellently faineth such another stratageme, performed by *Abradates* in *Cyrus* behalfe. Now would I fayne know, if occasion bee presented unto you, to serve your Prince by such an honest dissimulation, why you doe not as well learne it of *Xenophons* fiction, as of the others verity: and truely so much the better, as you shall save your nose by the bargaine: for *Abradates* did not counterfet so far. So then the best of the Historian, is subject to the Poet; for whatsoever action, or faction, whatsoever counsell, pollicy, or warre stratagem, the Historian is bound to recite, that may the Poet (if he list) with his imitation make his own; beautifying it both for further teaching, and more delighting, as it pleaseth him: having all, from *Dante* his heaven, to hys hell, under the authoritie of his penne. Which if I be asked what Poets have done so, as I might well name some, yet say I, and say againe, I speak of the Arte, and not of the Artificer.

Nowe, to that which commonly is attributed to the prayse of histories, in respect of the notable learning is gotten by marking the successe, as though therein

AN APOLOGIE FOR POETRIE

a man should see vertue exalted, and vice punished. Truely that commendation is peculiar to Poetrie, and farre of from History. For indeede Poetrie ever setteth vertue so out in her best cullours, making Fortune her wel-wayting hand-mayd, that one must needs be enamored of her. Well may you see *Ulisses* in a storme, and in other hard plights; but they are but exercises of patience and magnanimitie, to make them shine the more in the neere-following prosperitie. And of the contrarie part, if evill men come to the stage, they ever goe out (as the Tragedie Writer answered, to one that misliked the shew of such persons) so manacled, as they little animate folkes to followe them. But the Historian, beeing captived to the trueth of a foolish world, is many times a terror from well dooing, and an incouragement to unbrideled wickednes.

For, see wee not valiant *Milciades* rot in his fetters? The just *Phocion*, and the accomplished *Socrates*, put to death like Traytors? The cruell *Severus* live prosperously? The excellent *Severus* miserably murthered? *Sylla* and *Marius* dying in theyr beddes? *Pompey* and *Cicero* slaine then, when they would have thought exile a happinesse?

See wee not vertuous *Cato* driven to kyll himselfe? and rebell *Cæsar* so advaunced, that his name yet after 1600 yeares, lasteth in the highest honor? And marke but even *Cæsars* own words of the fore-named *Sylla*, (who in that onely did honestly, to put downe his dishonest tyrannie,) *Literas nescivit*, as if want of learning caused him to doe well. Hee meant it not by Poetrie, which not content with earthly plagues, deviseth new punishments in hel for Tyrants: nor yet by Philosophie, which teacheth *Occidendos esse*, but no doubt by skill in Historie: for that indeede can affoord your *Cipselus, Periander, Phalaris, Dionisius*, and I know not how many more of the same kennell, that speede well enough in theyr abhominable unjustice or usurpation. I conclude therefore, that hee excelleth Historie, not onely in furnishing the minde with knowledge, but in setting it forward, to that which deserveth to be called and accounted good : which setting forward, and mooving to well dooing, indeed setteth the Lawrell crowne upon the Poet as victorious, not onely of the Historian, but over the Phylosopher : howsoever in teaching it may bee questionable.

For suppose it be granted, (that which I suppose with great reason may be denied,) that the Philosopher in respect of his methodical proceeding, doth teach more perfectly then the Poet : yet do I thinke, that no man is so much *Philophilosophos*, as to compare the Philosopher in mooving, with the Poet.

And that mooving is of a higher degree then teaching, it may by this appeare : that it is wel nigh the cause and the effect of teaching. For who will be taught, if hee bee not mooved with desire to be taught ? and what so much good doth that teaching bring forth, (I speak still of morrall doctrine) as that it mooveth one to doe that which it dooth teach ? for as *Aristotle* sayth, it is not *Gnosis*, but *Praxis* must be the fruit. And howe *Praxis* cannot be, without being mooved to practise, it is no hard matter to consider.

The Philosopher sheweth you the way, hee informeth you of the particularities, as well of the tediousnes of the way, as of the pleasant lodging you shall have when your journey is ended, as of the many byturnings that may divert you from your way. But this is to no man but to him that will read him, and read him with attentive studious painfulnes. Which constant desire, whosoever hath in him, hath already past halfe the hardnes of the way, and therefore is beholding to the Philosopher but for the other halfe. Nay truely, learned men have learnedly thought, that where once reason hath so much overmastred passion, as that the minde hath a free desire to doe well, the inward light each minde hath in it selfe, is as good as a Philosophers booke ; seeing in nature we know it is wel, to doe well, and what is well, and what is evill, although not in the words of Arte, which Philosophers bestowe upon us. For out of naturall conceit, the Philosophers drew it, but to be moved to doe that which we know, or to be mooved with desire to knowe, *Hoc opus: Hic labor est.*

Nowe therein of all Sciences, (I speake still of humane, and according to the humane conceits) is our Poet the Monarch. For he dooth not only show the way, but giveth so sweete a prospect into the way, as will intice any man to enter into it. Nay, he dooth as if your journey should lye through a fayre Vineyard, at the first give you a cluster of Grapes: that full of that taste, you may long to passe further. He beginneth not with obscure definitions, which must blur the margent with interpretations, and load the memory with doubtfulnesse: but hee commeth to you with words sent in delightfull proportion, either accompanied with, or prepared for the well inchaunting skill of Musicke; and with a tale forsooth he commeth unto you: with a tale which holdeth children from play, and old men from the chimney corner. And pretending no more, doth intende the winning of the mind from wickednesse to vertue: even as the childe is often brought to take most wholsom things, by hiding them in such other as have a pleasant tast: which if one should beginne to tell them, the nature of *Aloes*, or *Rubarb* they shoulde receive, woulde sooner take their Phisicke at their eares, then at their mouth. So is it in men (most of which are childish in the best things, till they bee cradled in their graves,) glad they will be to heare the tales of *Hercules*, *Achilles*, *Cyrus*, and *Aeneas*: and hearing them, must needs heare the right description of wisdom, valure, and justice; which, if they had been barely, that is to say, Philosophically set out, they would sweare they bee brought to schoole againe.

That imitation whereof Poetry is, hath the most conveniency to Nature of all other, in somuch, that as *Aristotle* sayth, those things which in themselves are horrible, as cruell battailes, unnaturall Monsters, are made in poeticall imitation delightfull. Truely I have knowen men, that even with reading *Amadis de Gaule*, (which God knoweth wanteth much of a perfect Poesie) have found their harts mooved to the exercise of courtesie, liberalitie, and especially courage.

Who readeth *Aeneas* carrying olde *Anchises* on his back, that wisheth not it were his fortune to perfourme so excellent an acte? Whom doe not the words of *Turnus* moove? (the tale of *Turnus*, having planted his image in the imagination,)

———————————Fugientem hæc terra videbit,
Usque adeone mori miserum est?———

Where the Philosophers, as they scorne to delight, so must they bee content little to moove: saving wrangling, whether Vertue bee the chiefe, or the onely good: whether the contemplative, or the active life doe excell: which *Plato* and *Boethius* well knew, and therefore made Mistres Philosophy, very often borrow the masking rayment of Poesie. For even those harde harted evill men, who thinke vertue a schoole name, and knowe no other good, but *indulgere genio*, and therefore despise the austere admonitions of the Philosopher, and feele not the inward reason they stand upon; yet will be content to be delighted: which is all the good felow Poet seemeth to promise: and so steale to see the forme of goodnes (which seene they cannot but love) ere themselves be aware, as if they tooke a medicine of Cherries. Infinite proofes of the strange effects of this poeticall invention might be alledged, onely two shall serve, which are so often remembred, as I thinke all men knowe them.

The one of *Menenius Agrippa*, who when the whole people of Rome had resolutely devided themselves from the Senate, with apparant shew of utter ruine: though hee were (for that time) an excellent Oratour, came not among them, upon trust of figurative speeches, or cunning insinuations: and much lesse, with farre set *Maximes* of Phylosophie, which (especially if they were *Platonick*,) they must have learned Geometrie before they could well have conceived: but forsooth he behaves himselfe, like a homely, and familiar Poet. Hee telleth them a tale, that there was a time, when all the parts of the body made a mutinous conspiracie

AN APOLOGIE FOR POETRIE 31

against the belly, which they thought devoured the fruits of each others labour: they concluded they would let so unprofitable a spender starve. In the end, to be short, (for the tale is notorious, and as notorious that it was a tale,) with punishing the belly, they plagued themselves. This applied by him, wrought such effect in the people, as I never read, that ever words brought forth but then, so suddaine and so good an alteration: for upon reasonable conditions, a perfect reconcilement ensued. The other is of *Nathan* the Prophet, who when the holie *David* had so far forsaken God, as to confirme adulterie with murther: when hee was to doe the tenderest office of a friende, in laying his owne shame before his eyes, sent by God to call againe so chosen a servant: how doth he it? but by telling of a man, whose beloved Lambe was ungratefullie taken from his bosome: the applycation most divinely true, but the discourse itselfe, fayned: which made *David*, (I speake of the second and instrumentall cause) as in a glasse, to see his own filthines, as that heavenly Psalme of mercie wel testifieth.

By these therefore examples and reasons, I think it may be manifest, that the Poet with that same hand of delight, doth draw the mind more effectually, then any other Arte dooth, and so a conclusion not unfitlie ensueth: that as vertue is the most excellent resting place for all worldlie learning to make his end of: so Poetrie, beeing the most familiar to teach it, and most princelie to move towards it, in the most excellent work, is the most excellent workman. But I am content, not onely to decipher him by his workes, (although works in commendation or disprayse, must ever holde an high authority,) but more narrowly will examine his parts: so that (as in a man) though altogether may carry a presence ful of majestie and beautie, perchance in some one defectious peece, we may find a blemish: now in his parts, kindes, or *Species*, (as you list to terme them) it is to be noted that some Poesies have coupled together two or three kindes, as Tragicall and Comicall, wher-upon is risen, the Tragi-comicall. Some in the like manner have mingled Prose and

Verse, as *Sanazzar* and *Boetius*. Some have mingled matters Heroicall and Pastorall. But that commeth all to one in this question, for if severed they be good, the conjunction cannot be hurtfull. Therefore perchaunce forgetting some, and leaving some as needlesse to be remembred, it shall not be amisse in a worde to cite the speciall kindes, to see what faults may be found in the right use of them.

Is it then the Pastorall Poem which is misliked? (for perchance, where the hedge is lowest, they will soonest leape over.) Is the poore pype disdained, which sometime out of *Melibeus* mouth, can shewe the miserie of people, under hard Lords, or ravening Souldiours? And again, by *Titirus*, what blessednes is derived to them that lye lowest from the goodnesse of them that sit highest? Sometmes, under the prettie tales of Wolves and Sheepe, can include the whole considerations of wrong dooing and patience. Sometimes shew, that contention for trifles, can get but a trifling victorie. Where perchaunce a man may see, that even *Alexander* and *Darius*, when they strave who should be Cocke of this worlds dunghill, the benefit they got, was, that the after-livers may say,

> Hæc memini et victum frustra contendere Thirsin:
> Ex illo Coridon, Coridon est tempore nobis.

Or is it the lamenting Elegiack, which in a kinde hart would moove rather pitty then blame, who bewailes with the great Philosopher *Heraclitus*, the weakenes of man-kind, and the wretchednes of the world: who surely is to be praysed, either for compassionate accompanying just causes of lamentation, or for rightly paynting out how weake be the passions of wofulnesse. Is it the bitter, but wholsome Iambick, which rubs the galled minde, in making shame the trumpet of villanie, with bolde and open crying out against naughtines; Or the Satirick, who

> Omne vafer vitium, ridenti tangit amico?

Who sportingly never leaveth, until hee make a man laugh at folly, and at length ashamed, to laugh at himselfe: which he cannot avoyd, without avoyding the follie. Who while

<blockquote>Circum præcordia ludit,</blockquote>

giveth us to feele, how many head-aches a passionate life bringeth us to. How when all is done,

<blockquote>Est ulubris animus si nos non deficit æquus?</blockquote>

No perchance it is the Comick, whom naughtie Play-makers and Stage-keepers, have justly made odious. To the argument of abuse, I will answer after. Onely thus much now is to be said, that the Comedy is an imitation of the common errors of our life, which he representeth, in the most ridiculous and scornefull sort that may be. So as it is impossible, that any beholder can be content to be such a one.

Now, as in Geometry, the oblique must be knowne as wel as the right: and in Arithmetick, the odde aswell as the even, so in the actions of our life, who seeth not the filthines of evil, wanteth a great foile to perceive the beauty of vertue. This doth the Comedy handle so in our private and domestical matters, as with hearing it, we get as it were an experience, what is to be looked for of a nigardly *Demea*: of a crafty *Danus*: of a flattering *Gnato*: of a vaine glorious *Thraso*: and not onely to know what effects are to be expected, but to know who be such, by the signifying badge given them by the Comedian. And little reason hath any man to say, that men learne evill by seeing it so set out: sith as I sayd before, there is no man living, but by the force trueth hath in nature, no sooner seeth these men play their parts, but wisheth them in *Pistrinum*: although perchance the sack of his owne faults, lye so behinde his back, that he seeth not himselfe daunce the same measure: whereto, yet nothing can more open his eyes, then to finde his own actions contemptibly set forth. So that the right use of Comedy will (I thinke) by no body be blamed, and much lesse of the high and excellent Tragedy, that openeth the greatest wounds, and sheweth forth the Vlcers, that are covered with Tissue: that maketh

Kinges feare to be Tyrants, and Tyrants manifest their tirannicall humors: that with sturring the affects of admiration and commiseration, teacheth, the uncertainety of this world, and upon how weake foundations guilden roofes are builded. That maketh us knowe,

> Qui sceptra sœvus, duro imperio regit,
> Timet timentes, metus in authorem redit.

But how much it can moove, *Plutarch* yeeldeth a notable testimonie, of the abhominable Tyrant, *Alexander Pherœus;* from whose eyes, a Tragedy wel made, and represented, drewe aboundance of teares: who without all pitty, had murthered infinite nombers, and some of his owne blood. So as he, that was not ashamed to make matters for Tragedies, yet coulde not resist the sweet violence of a Tragedie.

And if it wrought no further good in him, it was, that he in despight of himselfe, withdrewe himselfe from harkening to that, which might mollifie his hardened heart. But it is not the Tragedy they doe mislike: For it were too absurd to cast out so excellent a representation of whatsoever is most worthy to be learned. Is it the Liricke that most displeaseth, who with his tuned Lyre, and wel accorded voyce, giveth praise, the reward of vertue, to vertuous acts? who gives morrall precepts, and naturall Problemes, who sometimes rayseth up his voice to the height of the heavens, in singing the laudes of the immortall God. Certainly I must confesse my own barbarousnes, I never heard the olde song of *Percy* and *Duglas,* that I found not my heart mooved more then with a Trumpet: and yet is it sung but by some blinde Crouder, with no rougher voyce, then rude stile: which being so evill apparrelled in the dust and cob-webbes of that uncivill age, what would it worke trymmed in the gorgeous eloquence of *Pindar?* In *Hungary* I have seene it the manner at all Feasts, and other such meetings, to have songes of their Auncestours valour; which that right Souldier-like Nation thinck the chiefest kindlers of brave courage. The incomparable *Lacedemonians*, did not only carry that kinde of Musicke ever with them to the field, but even at home, as such songs were made, so were they all content to bee the singers of them, when the lusty men were to tell what they dyd, the olde men, what they had done, and the young men what they wold doe. And where a man may say, that *Pindar* many times prayseth highly victories of small moment, matters rather of sport then vertue: as it may be aunswered, it was the fault of the Poet, and not of the Poetry; so indeede, the chiefe fault was in the tyme and custome of the Greekes, who set those toyes at so high a price, that *Phillip* of *Macedon* reckoned a horse-race wonne at *Olimpus*, among hys three fearefull felicities. But as the unimitable *Pindar* often did, so is that kinde most capable and most fit, to awake the thoughts from the sleep of idlenes, to imbrace honorable enterprises.

There rests the Heroicall, whose very name (I thinke) should daunt all back-biters; for by what conceit can a tongue be directed to speak evill of that, which draweth with it, no lesse Champions then *Achilles*, *Cyrus*, *Aeneas*, *Turnus*, *Tideus*, and *Rinaldo?* who doth not onely teach and move to a truth, but teacheth and mooveth to the most high and excellent truth. Who maketh magnanimity and justice shine, throughout all misty fearefulnes and foggy desires. Who, if the saying of *Plato* and *Tullie* bee true, that who could see Vertue, would be wonderfully ravished with the love of her beauty: this man sets her out to make her more lovely in her holyday apparell, to the eye of any that will daine, not to disdaine, untill they understand. But if any thing be already sayd in the defence of sweete Poetry, all concurreth to the maintaining the Heroicall, which is not onely a kinde, but the best, and most accomplished kinde of Poetry. For as the image of each action styrreth and instructeth the mind, so the loftie image of such Worthies, most inflameth the mind with desire to be worthy, and informes with counsel how to be worthy. Only let *Aeneas* be worne in the tablet of your memory, how he governeth himselfe in the ruine of his Country, in the preserving his old Father, and carrying away his religious ceremonies : in obeying the Gods commandement to leave *Dido*, though not onely all passionate kindenes, but even the humane consideration of vertuous gratefulnes, would have craved other of him. How in storms, howe in sports, howe in warre, howe in peace, how a fugitive, how victorious, how besiedged, how besiedging, howe to strangers, howe to allyes, how to enemies, howe to his owne : lastly, how in his inward selfe, and how in his outward government. And I thinke, in a minde not prejudiced with a prejudicating humor, hee will be found in excellencie fruitefull : yea, even as *Horace* sayth

Melius Chrisippo et Crantore.

But truely I imagine, it falleth out with these Poet whyppers, as with some good women, who often are sicke, but in fayth they cannot tel where. So the name of Poetrie is odious to them, but neither his cause, nor effects, neither the sum that containes him, nor the particularities descending from him, give any fast handle to their carping disprayse.

Sith then Poetrie is of all humane learning the most aunciext, and of most fatherly antiquitie, as from whence other learnings have taken theyr beginnings : sith it is so universall, that no learned Nation dooth despise it, nor no barbarous Nation is without it : sith both Roman and Greek gave divine names unto it : the one of prophecying, the other of making. And that indeede, that name of making is fit for him ; considering, that where as other Arts retaine themselves within their subject, and receive as it were, their beeing from it : the Poet onely, bringeth his owne stuffe, and dooth not learne a conceite out of a matter, but maketh matter for a conceite : Sith neither his description, nor his ende, contayneth any evill, the thing described cannot be evill : Sith his effects be so good as to teach goodnes and to delight the learners : Sith therein, (namely in morrall doctrine, the chiefe of all knowledges,) hee dooth not onely farre passe the Historian, but for instructing, is well nigh comparable to the Philosopher: and for moving, leaves him behind him: Sith the holy scripture (wherein there is no uncleannes) hath whole parts in it poeticall. And that even our Saviour Christ, vouchsafed to use the flowers of it: Sith all his kindes are not onlie in their united formes, but in their severed dissections fully commendable, I think, (and think I thinke rightly) the Lawrell crowne appointed for tryumphing Captaines, doth worthilie (of al other learnings) honor the Poets tryumph. But because wee have eares aswell as tongues, and that the lightest reasons that may be, will seeme to weigh greatly, if nothing be put in the counter-balance: let us heare, and aswell as wee can ponder, what objections may bee made against this Arte, which may be worthy, eyther of yeelding, or answering.

First truely I note, not onely in these *Mysomousoi* Poet-haters, but in all that kinde of people, who seek a prayse by dispraysing others, that they doe prodigally spend a great many wandering wordes, in quips, and scoffes; carping and taunting at each thing, which by styrring the Spleene, may stay the braine from a through beholding the worthines of the subject.

Those kinde of objections, as they are full of very idle easines, sith there is nothing of so sacred a majestie, but that an itching tongue may rubbe it selfe upon it: so deserve they no other answer, but in steed of laughing at the jest, to laugh at the jester. Wee know a playing wit, can prayse the discretion of an Asse; the comfortablenes of being in debt, and the jolly commoditie of beeing sick of the plague. So of the contrary side, if we will turne *Ovids* verse,

Ut lateat virtus, proximitate mali,

that good lye hid in neerenesse of the evill: *Agrippa* will be as merry in showing the vanitie of Science, as *Erasmus* was in commending of follie. Neyther shall any man or matter escape some touch of these smyling raylers. But for *Erasmus* and *Agrippa*, they had another foundation then the superficiall part would promise. Mary, these other pleasant Fault-finders, who wil correct the Verbe, before they understande the Noune, and confute others knowledge before they confirme theyr owne : I would have them onely remember, that scoffing commeth not of wisedom. So as the best title in true English they gette with their merriments, is to be called good fooles: for so have our grave Forefathers ever termed that humorous kinde of jesters: but that which gyveth greatest scope to their scorning humors, is ryming and versing. It is already sayde (and as I think, trulie sayde) it is not ryming and versing, that maketh Poesie. One may bee a Poet without versing, and a versifier without Poetry. But yet, presuppose it were inseparable (as indeede it seemeth *Scaliger* judgeth) truelie it were an inseparable commendation. For if *Oratio*, next to *Ratio*, Speech next to Reason, bee the greatest gyft bestowed upon mortalitie : that can not be praiselesse, which dooth most pollish that blessing of speech, which considers each word, not only (as a man may say) by his forcible qualitie, but by his best measured quantitie, carrying even in themselves, a Harmonie : (without (perchaunce) Number, Measure, Order, Proportion, be in our time growne odious.) But lay a side the just prayse it hath, by beeing the onely fit speech for Musick, (Musick I say, the most divine striker of the sences :) thus much is undoubtedly true, that if reading bee foolish, without remembring, memorie being the onely treasurer of knowled[g]e, those words which are fittest for memory, are likewise most convenient for knowledge.

Now, that Verse farre exceedeth Prose in the knitting up of the memory, the reason is manifest. The words, (besides theyr delight which hath a great affinitie to memory,) beeing so set, as one word cannot be lost, but the whole worke failes : which accuseth it selfe, calleth the remembrance backe to it selfe, and so most strongly confirmeth it ; besides, one word so as it were begetting another, as be it in ryme or measured verse, by the former a man shall have a neere gesse to the follower : lastly, even they that have taught the Art of memory, have shewed nothing so apt for it, as a certaine roome devided into many places well and throughly knowne. Now, that hath the verse in effect perfectly; every word having his naturall seate, which seate, must needes make the words remembred. But what needeth more in a thing so knowne to all men? who is it that ever was a scholler, that doth not carry away some verses of *Virgill, Horace,* or *Cato,* which in his youth he learned, and even to his old age serve him for howrely lessons? but the fitnes it hath for memory, is notably proved by all delivery of Arts: wherein for the most part, from Grammer, to Logick, Mathematick, Phisick, and the rest, the rules chiefly necessary to bee borne away, are compiled in verses. So that, verse being in it selfe sweete and orderly, and beeing best for memory, the onely handle of knowledge, it must be in jest that any man can speake against it. Nowe then goe wee to the most important imputations laid to the poore Poets, for ought I can yet learne, they are these, first, that there beeing many other more fruitefull knowledges, a man might better spend his tyme in them, then in this. Secondly, that it is the mother of lyes. Thirdly, that it is the Nurse of abuse, infecting us with many pestilent desires: with a Syrens sweetnes, drawing the mind to the Serpents tayle of sinfull fancy. And heerein especially, Comedies give the largest field to erre, as *Chaucer* sayth: howe both in other Nations and in ours, before Poets did soften us, we were full of courage, given to martiall exercises; the pillers of manlyke liberty, and not lulled a sleepe in shady idlenes with Poets pastimes. And lastly, and chiefely, they cry out with an open mouth, as if they out shot *Robin Hood,* that *Plato* banished them out of hys Common-wealth. Truely, this is much, if there be much truth in it. First to the first: that a man might better spend his time, is a reason indeede: but it doth (as they say) but *Petere principium:* for if it be as I affirme, that no learning is so good, as that which teacheth and mooveth to vertue; and that none can both teach and move thereto so much as Poetry: then is the conclusion manifest, that Incke and Paper cannot be to a more profitable purpose employed. And certainly, though a man should graunt their first assumption, it should

followe (me thinkes) very unwillingly, that good is
not good, because better is better. But I still and
utterly denye, that there is sprong out of earth a more
fruitefull knowledge. To the second therefore, that
they should be the principall lyars; I aunswere paradoxically, but truely, I thinke truely; that of all
Writers under the sunne, the Poet is the least lier;
and though he would, as a Poet can scarcely be a lyer,
the Astronomer, with his cosen the Geometrician, can
hardly escape, when they take upon them to measure
the height of the starres.

How often, thinke you, doe the Phisitians lye, when
they aver things, good for sicknesses, which afterwards
send *Charon* a great number of soules drown[e]d in a
potion before they come to his Ferry. And no lesse
of the rest, which take upon them to affirme. Now, for
the Poet, he nothing affirmes, and therefore never lyeth.
For, as I take it, to lye, is to affirme that to be true which
is false. So as the other Artists, and especially the
Historian, affirming many things, can in the cloudy
knowledge of mankinde, hardly escape from many
lyes. But the Poet (as I sayd before) never affirmeth.
The Poet never maketh any circles about your imagination, to conjure you to beleeve for true what he writes.
Hee citeth not authorities of other Histories, but even
for hys entry, calleth the sweete Muses to inspire into
him a good invention: in troth, not labouring to tell
you what is, or is not, but what should or should not
be: and therefore, though he recount things not true,
yet because hee telleth them not for true, he lyeth not,
without we will say, that *Nathan*, lyed in his speech,
before alledged to *David*. Which as a wicked man durst
scarce say, so think I none so simple would say, that
Esope lyed in the tales of his beasts: for who thinks that
Esope writ it for actually true, were well worthy to have
his name c[h]ronicled among the beastes hee writeth of.

What childe is there, that comming to a Play, and
seeing *Thebes* written in great Letters upon an olde doore,
doth beleeve that it is *Thebes*? If then, a man can arive,
at that childs age, to know that the Poets persons and
dooings, are but pictures what should be, and not

AN APOLOGIE FOR POETRIE 41

stories what have beene, they will never give the lye, to things not affirmatively, but allegorically, and figurativelie written. And therefore, as in Historie, looking for trueth, they goe away full fraught with falsehood: so in Poesie, looking for fiction, they shal use the narration, but as an imaginative groundplot of a profitable invention.

But heereto is replyed, that the Poets gyve names to men they write of, which argueth a conceite of an actuall truth, and so, not being true, prooves a falsehood. And doth the Lawyer lye then, when under the names of *John a stile* and *John a noakes*, hee puts his case? But that is easily answered. Theyr naming of men, is but to make theyr picture the more lively, and not to builde any historie: paynting men, they cannot leave men namelesse. We see we cannot play at Chesse, but that wee must give names to our Chesse-men; and yet mee thinks, hee were a very partiall Champion of truth, that would say we lyed, for giving a peece of wood, the reverend title of a Bishop. The Poet nameth *Cyrus* or *Aeneas*, no other way, then to shewe, what men of theyr fames, fortunes, and estates, should doe.

Their third is, how much it abuseth mens wit, trayning it to wanton sinfulnes, and lustfull love: for indeed that is the principall, if not the onely abuse I can heare alledged. They say, the Comedies rather teach, then reprehend, amorous conceits. They say, the Lirick, is larded with passionate Sonnets. The Elegiack, weepes the want of his mistresse. And that even to the Heroical, *Cupid* hath ambitiously climed. Alas Love, I would, thou couldest as well defende thy selfe, as thou canst offende others. I would those, on whom thou doost attend, could eyther put thee away, or yeelde good reason, why they keepe thee. But grant love of beautie, to be a beastlie fault, (although it be very hard, sith onely man, and no beast, hath that gyft, to discerne beauty.) Grant, that lovely name of Love, to deserve all hatefull reproches: (although even some of my Maisters the Phylosophers, spent a good deale of theyr Lamp-oyle, in setting foorth the excellencie of it.) Grant, I say, what soever they wil have granted; that not onely love, but lust, but vanitie, but, (if they list) scurrilitie, possesseth many leaves of the Poets bookes: yet thinke I, when this is granted, they will finde, theyr sentence may with good manners, put the last words foremost: and not say, that Poetrie abuseth mans wit, but that, mans wit abuseth Poetrie.

For I will not denie, but that mans wit may make Poesie, (which should be *Eikastike*, which some learned have defined, figuring foorth good things,) to be *Phantastike:* which doth contrariwise, infect the fancie with unworthy objects. As the Painter, that shoulde give to the eye, eyther some excellent perspective, or some fine picture, fit for building or fortification: or contayning in it some notable example, as *Abraham*, sacrificing his Sonne *Isaack*, *Judith* killing *Holofernes*, *David* fighting with *Goliah*, may leave those, and please an ill-pleased eye, with wanton shewes of better hidden matters. But what, shall the abuse of a thing, make the right use odious? Nay truely, though I yeeld, that Poesie may not onely be abused, but that beeing abused, by the reason of his sweete charming force, it can doe more hurt than any other Armie of words: yet shall it be so far from concluding, that the abuse, should give reproch to the abused, that contrariwise it is a good reason, that whatsoever being abused, dooth most harme, beeing rightly used: (and upon the right use each thing conceiveth his title) doth most good.

Doe wee not see the skill of Phisick, (the best rampire to our often-assaulted bodies) beeing abused, teach poyson the most violent destroyer? Dooth not knowledge of Law, whose end is, to even and right all things being abused, grow the crooked fosterer of horrible injuries? Doth not (to goe to the highest) Gods word abused, breed heresie? and his Name abused, become blasphemie? Truely, a needle cannot doe much hurt, and as truely, (with leave of Ladies be it spoken) it cannot doe much good. With a sword, thou maist kill thy Father, and with a sword thou maist defende thy Prince and Country. So that, as in their calling Poets the Fathers of lyes, they say nothing: so in this theyr argument of abuse, they proove the commendation.

AN APOLOGIE FOR POETRIE

They alledge heere-with, that before Poets beganne to be in price, our Nation, hath set their harts delight upon action, and not upon imagination: rather doing things worthy to bee written, then writing things fitte to be done. What that before tyme was, I thinke scarcely *Sphinx* can tell: Sith no memory is so auncient, that hath the precedence of Poetrie. And certaine it is, that in our plainest homelines, yet never was the *Albion* Nation without Poetrie. Mary, thys argument, though it bee leaveld against Poetrie, yet is it indeed, a chaine-shot against all learning, or bookishnes, as they commonly tearme it. Of such minde were certaine *Goethes*, of whom it is written, that having in the spoile of a famous Citie, taken a fayre librarie: one hangman (bee like fitte to execute the fruites of their wits) who had murthered a great number of bodies, would have set fire on it: no sayde another, very gravely, take heede what you doe, for whyle they are busie about these toyes, wee shall with more leysure conquer their Countries.

This indeede is the ordinary doctrine of ignorance, and many wordes sometymes I have heard spent in it: but because this reason is generally against all learning, aswell as Poetrie; or rather, all learning but Poetry: because it were too large a digression, to handle, or at least, to superfluous: (sith it is manifest, that all government of action, is to be gotten by knowledg, and knowledge best, by gathering many knowledges, which is, reading,) I onely with *Horace*, to him that is of that opinion,

Iubeo stultum esse libenter;

for as for Poetrie it selfe, it is the freest from thys objection. For Poetrie is the companion of the Campes.

I dare undertake, *Orlando Furioso*, or honest King *Arthur*, will never displease a Souldier: but the quiddity of *Ens*, and *Prima materia*, will hardly agree with a Corslet: and therefore, as I said in the beginning, even Turks and Tartares are delighted with Poets. *Homer* a Greek, florished, before Greece florished. And if to a slight conjecture, a conjecture may be opposed:

truly it may seeme, that as by him, their learned men, tooke almost their first light of knowledge, so their active men, received their first notions of courage. Onlie *Alexanders* example may serve, who by *Plutarch* is accounted of such vertue, that Fortune was not his guide, but his foote-stoole: whose acts speake for him, though *Plutarch* did not: indeede, the Phœnix of warlike Princes. This *Alexander*, left his Schoole-maister, living *Aristotle*, behinde him, but tooke deade *Homer* with him: he put the Philosopher *Calisthenes* to death, for his seeming philosophicall, indeed mutinous stubburnnes. But the chiefe thing he ever was heard to wish for, was, that *Homer* had been alive. He well found he received more braverie of minde, bye the patterne of *Achilles*, then by hearing the definition of Fortitude: and therefore, if *Cato* misliked *Fulvius*, for carying *Ennius* with him to the fielde, it may be aun-swered, that if *Cato* misliked it, the noble *Fulvius* liked it, or els he had not doone it: for it was not the ex-cellent *Cato Uticensis*, (whose authority I would much more have reverenced,) but it was the former: in truth, a bitter punisher of faults, but else, a man that had never wel sacrificed to the Graces. Hee misliked and cryed out upon all Greeke learning, and yet being 80. yeeres olde, began to learne it. Be-like, fearing that *Pluto* understood not Latine. Indeede, the Romaine lawes allowed, no person to be carried to the warres, but hee that was in the Souldiers role: and therefore, though *Cato* misliked his unmustered person, hee misliked not his worke. And if hee had, *Scipio Nasica* judged by common consent, the best Romaine, loved him. Both the other *Scipio* Brothers, who had by their vertues no lesse surnames, then of *Asia*, and *Affrick*, so loved him, that they caused his body to be buried in their Sepulcher. So as *Cato*, his authoritie being but against his person, and that aunswered, with so farre greater then himselfe, is heerein of no validitie. But now indeede my burthen is great; now *Plato* his name is layde upon mee, whom I must confesse, of all Philosophers, I have ever esteemed most worthy of reverence, and with great reason: Sith of all Philosophers, he is the most poeticall. Yet if

AN APOLOGIE FOR POETRIE

he will defile the Fountaine, out of which his flowing streames have proceeded, let us boldly examine with what reasons hee did it. First truly, a man might maliciously object, that *Plato* being a Philosopher was a naturall enemie of Poets: for indeede, after the Philosophers, had picked out of the sweete misteries of Poetrie, the right discerning true points of knowledge, they forthwith putting it in method, and making a Schoole-arte of that which the Poets did onely teach, by a divine delightfulnes, beginning to spurne at their guides, like ungratefull Prentises, were not content to set up shops for themselves, but sought by all meanes to discredit their Maisters. Which by the force of delight being barred them, the lesse they could overthrow them, the more they hated them. For indeede, they found for *Homer*, seaven Cities strove, who should have him for their Citizen: where many Cities banished Philosophers, as not fitte members to live among them. For onely repeating certaine of *Euripides* verses, many *Athenians* had their lyves saved of the *Siracusians*: when the *Athenians* themselves, thought many Philosophers, unwoorthie to live.

Certaine Poets, as *Simonides*, and *Pindarus* had so prevailed with *Hiero* the first, that of a Tirant they made him a just King, where *Plato* could do so little with *Dionisius*, that he himselfe, of a Philosopher, was made a slave. But who should doe thus, I confesse, should requite the objections made against Poets, with like cavillation against Philosophers, as likewise one should doe, that should bid one read *Phædrus*, or *Symposium* in *Plato*, or the discourse of love in *Plutarch*, and see whether any Poet doe authorize abhominable filthines, as they doe. Againe, a man might aske out of what Commonwealth *Plato* did banish them? insooth, thence where he himselfe alloweth communitie of women: So as belike, this banishment grewe not for effeminate wantonnes, sith little should poeticall Sonnets be hurtfull, when a man might have what woman he listed. But I honor philosophicall instructions, and blesse the wits which bred them: so as they be not abused, which is likewise stretched to Poetrie.

S. *Paule* himselfe, (who yet for the credite of Poets) alledgeth twise two Poets, and one of them by the name of a Prophet, setteth a watch-word upon Philosophy, indeede upon the abuse. So dooth *Plato*, upon the abuse, not upon Poetrie. *Plato* found fault, that the Poets of his time, filled the worlde, with wrong opinions of the Gods, making light tales of that unspotted essence; and therefore, would not have the youth depraved with such opinions. Heerin may much be said, let this suffice: the Poets did not induce such opinions, but dyd imitate those opinions already induced. For all the Greek stories can well testifie, that the very religion of that time, stoode upon many, and many-fashioned Gods, not taught so by the Poets, but followed, according to their nature of imitation. Who list, may reade in *Plutarch*, the discourses of *Isis* and *Osiris*, of the cause why Oracles ceased, of the divine providence; and see, whether the Theologie of that nation, stood not upon such dreames, which the Poets indeed supersticiously observed, and truly, (sith they had not the light of Christ,) did much better in it then the Philosophers, who shaking off superstition, brought in Atheisme. *Plato* therefore, (whose authoritie I had much rather justly conster, then unjustly resist,) meant not in general of Poets, in those words of which *Julius Scaliger* saith *Qua authoritate, barbari quidam, atque hispidi, abuti velint, ad Poetas é republica exigendos:* but only meant, to drive out those wrong opinions of the Deitie (whereof now, without further law, Christianity hath taken away all the hurtful beliefe,) perchance (as he thought) norished by the then esteemed Poets. And a man need goe no further then to *Plato* himselfe, to know his meaning: who in his Dialogue called *Ion*, giveth high, and rightly divine commendation to Poetrie. So as *Plato*, banishing the abuse, not the thing, not banishing it, but giving due honor unto it, shall be our Patron, and not our adversarie. For indeed I had much rather, (sith truly I may doe it) shew theyr mistaking of *Plato*, (under whose Lyons skin they would make an Asse-like braying against Poesie,) then goe about to overthrow his authority, whom the wiser a man is, the more just cause he shall find to have in admiration : especially, sith he attributeth unto Poesie, more then my selfe doe ; namely, to be a very inspiring of a divine force, farre above mans wit ; as in the aforenamed Dialogue is apparent.

Of the other side, who wold shew the honors, have been by the best sort of judgements granted them, a whole Sea of examples woulde present themselves. *Alexanders*, *Cæsars*, *Scipios*, al favorers of Poets. *Lelius*, called the Romane *Socrates*, himselfe a Poet : so as part of *Heautontimorumenon* in *Terence*, was supposed to be made by him. And even the Greek *Socrates*, whom *Apollo* confirmed to be the onely wise man, is sayde to have spent part of his old tyme, in putting *Esops* fables into verses. And therefore, full evill should it become his scholler *Plato*, to put such words in his Maisters mouth, against Poets. But what need more ? *Aristotle* writes the Arte of Poesie : and why if it should not be written ? *Plutarch* teacheth the use to be gathered of them, and how if they should not be read ? And who reades *Plutarchs* eyther historie or philosophy, shall finde, hee trymmeth both theyr garments, with gards of Poesie. But I list not to defend Poesie, with the helpe of her underling, Historiography. Let it suffise, that it is a fit soyle for prayse to dwell upon : and what dispraise may set upon it, is eyther easily over-come, or transformed into just commendation. So that, sith the excellencies of it, may be so easily, and so justly confirmed, and the low-creeping objections, so soone troden downe ; it not being an Art of lyes, but of true doctrine : not of effeminatenes, but of notable stirring of courage : not of abusing mans witte, but of strengthning mans wit : not banished, but honored by *Plato :* let us rather plant more Laurels, for to engarland our Poets heads, (which honor of beeing laureat, as besides them, onely tryumphant Captaines weare, is a sufficient authority, to shewe the price they ought to be had in,) then suffer the ill-favouring breath of such wrong-speakers, once to blowe upon the cleere springs of Poesie.

But sith I have runne so long a careere in this matter,

me thinks, before I give my penne a fulle stop, it shal be but a little more lost time, to inquire, why England, (the Mother of excellent mindes,) shoulde bee growne so hard a step-mother to Poets, who certainly in wit ought to passe all other: sith all onely proceedeth from their wit, being indeede makers of themselves, not takers of others. How can I but exclaime,

> Musa mihi causas memora, quo numine læso.

Sweete Poesie, that hath aunciently had Kings, Emperors, Senators, great Captaines, such, as besides a thousand others, *David, Adrian, Sophocles, Germanicus*, not onely to favour Poets, but to be Poets. And of our neerer times, can present for her Patrons, a *Robert*, king of Sicil, the great king *Francis* of France, King *James* of Scotland. Such Cardinals as *Bembus*, and *Bibiena*. Such famous Preachers and Teachers, as *Beza* and *Melancthon*. So learned Philosophers, as *Fracastorius* and *Scaliger*. So great Orators, as *Pontanus* and *Muretus*. So piercing wits, as *George Buchanan*. So grave Counsellors, as besides many, but before all, that *Hospitall* of Fraunce: then whom, (I thinke) that Realme never brought forth a more accomplished judgement: more firmely builded upon vertue. I say these, with numbers of others, not onely to read others Poesies, but to poetise for others reading, that Poesie thus embraced in all other places, should onely finde in our time, a hard welcome in England, I thinke the very earth lamenteth it, and therefore decketh our Soyle with fewer Laurels then it was accustomed. For heertofore, Poets have in England also florished. And which is to be noted, even in those times, when the trumpet of *Mars* did sounde loudest. And now, that an overfaint quietnes should seeme to strew the house for Poets, they are almost in as good reputation, as the *Mountibancks* at *Venice*. Truly even that, as of the one side, it giveth great praise to Poesie, which like *Venus*, (but to better purpose) hath rather be troubled in the net with *Mars*, then enjoy the homelie quiet of *Vulcan:* so serves it for a peece of reason, why they are lesse gratefull to idle England, which nowe can scarce endure the payne of a pen. Upon this, necessarily followeth, that base men, with servile wits undertake it : who think it inough, if they can be rewarded of the Printer. And so as *Epaminondas* is sayd, with the honor of his vertue, to have made an office, by his exercising it, which before was contemptible, to become highly respected : so these, no more but setting their names to it, by their owne disgracefulnes, disgrace the most gracefull Poesie. For now, as if all the Muses were gotte with childe, to bring foorth bastard Poets, without any commission, they doe poste over the banckes of *Helicon*, tyll they make the readers more weary then Post-horses : while in the mean tyme, they

Queis meliore luto sinxit præcordia Titan,

are better content, to suppresse the out-flowing of their wit, then by publishing them, to bee accounted Knights of the same order. But I, that before ever I durst aspire unto the dignitie, am admitted into the company of the Paper-blurers, doe finde the very true cause of our wanting estimation, is want of desert : taking upon us to be Poets, in despight of *Pallas*. Nowe, wherein we want desert, were a thankeworthy labour to expresse : but if I knew, I should have mended my selfe. But I, as I never desired the title, so have I neglected the meanes to come by it. Onely over-mastred by some thoughts, I yeelded an inckie tribute unto them. Mary, they that delight in Poesie it selfe, should seeke to knowe what they doe, and how they doe ; and especially, looke themselves in an unflattering Glasse of reason, if they bee inclinable unto it. For Poesie, must not be drawne by the eares, it must bee gently led, or rather, it must lead. Which was partly the cause, that made the auncient-learned affirme, it was a divine gift, and no humaine skill ; sith all other knowledges, lie ready for any that hath strength of witte : A Poet, no industrie can make, if his owne *Genius* bee not carried unto it : and therefore is it an old Proverbe, *Orator fit ; Poeta nascitur*. Yet confesse I alwayes, that as the firtilest ground must bee manured, so must the highest flying wit, have a *Dedalus* to guide him. That *Dedalus*, they say, both in this, and in other, hath three wings, to beare it selfe up into the ayre of due commendation: that is, Arte, Imitation, and Exercise. But these, neyther artificiall rules, nor imitative patternes, we much cumber our selves withall. Exercise indeede wee doe, but that, very fore-backwardly: for where we should exercise to know, wee exercise as having knowne: and so is oure braine delivered of much matter, which never was begotten by knowledge. For, there being two principal parts, matter to be expressed by wordes, and words to expresse the matter, in neyther, wee use Arte, or Imitation, rightly. Our matter is *Quodlibet* indeed, though wrongly perfourming *Ovids* verse,

Quicquid conabar dicere versus erit:

never marshalling it into an assured rancke, that almost the readers cannot tell where to finde themselves.

Chaucer, undoubtedly did excellently in hys *Troylus* and *Cresseid*; of whom, truly I know not, whether to mervaile more, either that he in that mistie time, could see so clearely, or that wee in this cleare age, walke so stumblingly after him. Yet had he great wants, fitte to be forgiven, in so reverent antiquity. I account the *Mirrour of Magistrates*, meetely furnished of beautiful parts; and in the Earle of Surries *Liricks*, many things tasting of a noble birth, and worthy of a noble minde. The *Sheapheards Kalender*, hath much Poetrie in his Eglogues: indeede worthy the reading if I be not deceived. That same framing of his stile, to an old rustick language, I dare not alowe, sith neyther *Theocritus* in Greeke, *Virgill* in Latine, nor *Sanazar* in Italian, did affect it. Besides these, doe I not remember to have seene but fewe, (to speake boldely) printed, that have poeticall sinnewes in them: for proofe whereof, let but most of the verses bee put in Prose, and then aske the meaning: and it will be found, that one verse did but beget another, without ordering at the first, what should be at the last: which becomes a confused masse of words, with a tingling sound of ryme, barely accompanied with reason.

Our Tragedies, and Comedies, (not without cause cried

out against,) observing rules, neyther of honest civilitie, nor of skilfull Poetrie, excepting *Gorboduck*, (againe, I say, of those that I have seen,) which notwithstanding, as it is full of stately speeches, and well sounding Phrases, clyming to the height of *Seneca* his stile, and as full of notable moralitie, which it doth most delightfully teach; and so obtayne the very end of Poesie: yet in troth it is very defectious in the circumstaunces; which greeveth mee, because it might not remaine as an exact model of all Tragedies. For it is faulty both in place, and time, the two necessary companions of all corporall actions. For where the stage should alwaies represent but one place, and the uttermost time presupposed in it, should be, both by *Aristotles* precept, and common reason, but one day: there is both many dayes, and many places, inartificially imagined. But if it be so in *Gorboduck*, how much more in al the rest? where you shal have *Asia* of the one side, and *Affrick* of the other, and so many other under-kingdoms, that the Player, when he commeth in, must ever begin with telling where he is: or els, the tale wil not be conceived. Now ye shal have three Ladies, walke to gather flowers, and then we must beleeve the stage to be a Garden. By and by, we heare newes of shipwracke in the same place, and then wee are to blame, if we accept it not for a Rock.

Upon the backe of that, comes out a hidious Monster, with fire and smoke, and then the miserable beholders, are bounde to take it for a Cave. While in the meantime, two Armies flye in, represented with foure swords and bucklers, and then what harde heart will not receive it for a pitched fielde? Now, of time they are much more liberall, for ordinary it is that two young Princes fall in love. After many traverces, she is got with childe, delivered of a faire boy, he is lost, groweth a man, falls in love, and is ready to get another child, and all this in two hours space: which how absurd it is in sence, even sence may imagine, and Arte hath taught, and all auncient examples justified: and at this day, the ordinary Players in Italie, wil not erre in. Yet wil some bring in an example of *Eunuchus* in *Terence*, that containeth matter of two dayes, yet far short of twenty yeeres. True it is, and so was it to be playd in two daies, and so fitted to the time it set forth. And though *Plautus* hath in one place done amisse, let us hit with him, and not misse with him. But they wil say, how then shal we set forth a story, which containeth both many places, and many times? And doe they not knowe, that a Tragedie is tied to the lawes of Poesie, and not of Historie? not bound to follow the storie, but having liberty, either to faine a quite newe matter, or or to frame the history, to the most tragicall conveniencie. Againe, many things may be told, which cannot be shewed, if they knowe the difference betwixt reporting and representing. As for example, I may speake, (though I am heere) of *Peru*, and in speech, digresse from that, to the description of *Calicut:* but in action, I cannot represent it without *Pacolets* horse: and so was the manner the Aunciencts tooke, by some *Nuncius*, to recount thinges done in former time, or other place. Lastly, if they wil represent an history, they must not (as *Horace* saith) beginne *Ab ovo:* but they must come to the principall poynt of that one action, which they wil represent. By example this wil be best expressed. I have a story of young *Polidorus*, delivered for safeties sake, with great riches, by his Father *Priamus* to *Polimnestor* king of *Thrace*, in the Troyan war time: Hee after some yeeres, hearing the over-throwe of *Priamus*, for to make the treasure his owne, murthereth the child: the body of the child is taken up [by] *Hecuba:* shee the same day, findeth a slight to bee revenged most cruelly of the Tyrant: where nowe would one of our Tragedy writers begin, but with the delivery of the childe? Then should he sayle over into *Thrace*, and so spend I know not how many yeeres, and travaile numbers of places. But where dooth *Euripides?* Even with the finding of the body, leaving the rest to be tolde by the spirit of *Polidorus*. This need no further to be inlarged, the dullest wit may conceive it. But besides these grosse absurdities, how all theyr Playes be neither right Tragedies, nor right Comedies: mingling Kings and Clownes, not because the matter so carrieth it: but thrust in Clownes by head and shoulders, to play a part in majesticall matters, with neither decencie, nor discretion. So as neither the admiration and commiseration, nor the right sportfulnes, is by their mungrell Tragy-comedie obtained. I know *Apuleius* did some-what so, but that is a thing recounted with space of time, not represented in one moment: and I knowe, the Aunceints have one or two examples of Tragy-comedies, as *Plautus* hath *Amphitrio*: But if we marke them well, we shall find, that they never, or very daintily, match Horn-pypes and Funeralls. So falleth it out, that having indeed no right Comedy, in that comicall part of our Tragedy, we have nothing but scurrility, unwoorthy of any chast eares: or some extreame shew of doltishnes, indeed fit to lift up a loude laughter, and nothing els: where the whole tract of a Comedy, shoulde be full of delight, as the Tragedy shoulde be still maintained, in a well raised admiration. But our Comedians, thinke there is no delight without laughter, which is very wrong, for though laughter may come with delight, yet commeth it not of delight: as though delight should be the cause of laughter, but well may one thing breed both together: nay, rather in themselves, they have as it were, a kind of contrarietie; for delight we scarcely doe, but in things that have a conveniencie to our selves, or to the general nature: laughter, almost ever commeth, of things most disproportioned to our selves, and nature. Delight hath a joy in it, either permanent, or present. Laughter, hath onely a scornful tickling.

For example, we are ravished with delight to see a faire woman, and yet are far from being moved to laughter. We laugh at deformed creatures, wherein certainely we cannot delight. We delight in good chaunces, we laugh at mischaunces; we delight to heare the happines of our friends, or Country; at which he were worthy to be laughed at, that would laugh; wee shall contrarily laugh sometimes, to finde a matter quite mistaken, and goe downe the hill agaynst the byas, in the mouth of some such men, as for the respect of them, one shal be hartely sorry, yet he cannot chuse but laugh; and so is rather pained, then delighted with laughter. Yet deny I not, but that they may goe well together, for as in *Alexanders* picture well set out, wee delight without laughter, and in twenty mad Anticks we laugh without delight: so in *Hercules*, painted with his great beard, and furious countenance, in womans attire, spinning at *Omphales* commaundement, it breedeth both delight and laughter. For the representing of so strange a power in love, procureth delight: and the scornefulnes of the action, stirreth laughter. But I speake to this purpose, that all the end of the comicall part, bee not upon such scornefull matters, as stirreth laughter onely: but mixt with it, that delightful teaching which is the end of Poesie. And the great fault even in that point of laughter, and forbidden plainely by *Aristotle*, is, that they styrre laughter in sinfull things; which are rather execrable then ridiculous: or in miserable, which are rather to be pittied than scorned. For what is it to make folkes gape at a wretched Begger, or a beggerly Clowne? or against lawe of hospitality, to jest at straungers, because they speake not English so well as wee doe? what do we learne, sith it is certaine

(Nil habet infœlix paupertas durius in se,)
Quam quod ridiculos homines facit.———

But rather a busy loving Courtier, a hartles threatening *Thraso*. A selfe-wise-seeming schoolemaster. A awry-transformed Traveller. These, if we sawe walke in stage names, which wee play naturally, therein were delightfull laughter, and teaching delightfulnes: as in the other, the Tragedies of *Buchanan*, doe justly bring forth a divine admiration. But I have lavished out too many wordes of this play matter. I doe it because as they are excelling parts of Poesie, so is there none so much used in England, and none can be more pittifully abused. Which like an unmannerly Daughter, shewing a bad education, causeth her mother Poesies honesty, to bee called in question. Other sorts of Poetry almost have we none, but that Lyricall kind of Songs and Sonnets: which, Lord, if he gave us so good mindes, how well it might be imployed, and with howe heavenly fruite, both private and publique, in singing the prayses of the immortall beauty: the immortall goodnes of that God, who gyveth us hands to write, and wits to conceive, of which we might well want words, but never matter, of which, we could turne our eies to nothing, but we should ever have new budding occasions. But truely many of such writings, as come under the banner of unresistable love, if I were a Mistres, would never perswade mee they were in love: so coldely they apply fiery speeches, as men that had rather red Lovers writings; and so caught up certaine swelling phrases, which hang together, like a man which once tolde mee, the winde was at North, West, and by South, because he would be sure to name windes enowe: then that in truth they feele those passions, which easily (as I think) may be bewrayed, by that same forciblenes, or *Energia*, (as the Greekes cal it) of the writer. But let this bee a sufficient, though short note, that wee misse the right use of the materiall point of Poesie.

Now, for the out-side of it, which is words, or (as I may tearme it) *Diction*, it is even well worse. So is that honny-flowing Matron Eloquence, apparelled, or rather disguised, in a Curtizan-like painted affectation: one time with so farre sette words, they may seeme Monsters: but must seeme straungers to any poore English man. Another tyme, with coursing of a Letter, as if they were bound to followe the method of a Dictionary: an other tyme, with figures and flowers, extreamelie winter-starved. But I would this fault were only peculier to Versifiers, and had not as large possession among Prose-printers; and, (which is to be mervailed) among many Schollers, and, (which is to be pittied) among some Preachers. Truly I could wish, if at least I might be so bold, to wish in a thing beyond the reach of my capacity, the diligent imitators of *Tullie*, and *Demosthenes*, (most worthy to be imitated) did not so much keep, *Nizolian* Paper-bookes of their figures and phrases, as by attentive translation (as it were) devoure them whole, and make them wholly theirs: For nowe they cast Sugar and Spice, upon every dish that is served to the table; Like those Indians, not content to weare eare-rings at the fit and naturall place of the eares, but they will thrust Jewels through their nose, and lippes because they will be sure to be fine.

Tullie, when he was to drive out *Cateline*, as it were with a Thunder-bolt of eloquence, often used that figure of repitition, *Vivit vivit? imo Senatum venit &c.* Indeed, inflamed with a well-grounded rage, hee would have his words (as it were) double out of his mouth: and so doe that artificially, which we see men doe in choller naturally. And wee, having noted the grace of those words, hale them in sometime to a familier Epistle, when it were to too much choller to be chollerick. Now for similitudes, in certaine printed discourses, I thinke all Herbarists, all stories of Beasts, Foules, and Fishes, are rifled up, that they come in multitudes, to waite upon any of our conceits; which certainly is as absurd a surfet to the eares, as is possible: for the force of a similitude, not being to proove anything to a contrary Disputer, but onely to explane to a willing hearer, when that is done, the rest is a most tedious pratling: rather over-swaying the memory from the purpose whereto they were applyed, then any whit informing the judgement, already eyther satisfied, or by similitudes not to be satis-fied. For my part, I doe not doubt, when *Antonius* and *Crassus*, the great forefathers of *Cicero* in eloquence, the one (as *Cicero* testifieth of them) pretended not to know Arte, the other, not to set by it: because with a playne sensiblenes, they might win credit of popular eares; which credit, is the neerest step to perswasion: which perswasion, is the chiefe marke of Oratory; I doe not doubt (I say) but that they used these tracks very sparingly, which who doth generally use, any man may see doth daunce to his owne musick: and so be noted by the audience, more careful to speake curiously, then to speake truly.

Undoubtedly, (at least to my opinion undoubtedly,) I have found in divers smally learned Courtiers, a more sounde stile, then in some professors of learning: of which I can gesse no other cause, but that the Courtier following that which by practise hee findeth fittest to nature, therein, (though he know it not,) doth according to Art, though not by Art; where the other, using Art

AN APOLOGIE FOR POETRIE

to shew Art, and not to hide Art, (as in these cases he should doe) flyeth from nature, and indeede abuseth Art.

But what? me thinkes I deserve to be pounded, for straying from Poetrie to Oratorie: but both have such an affinity in this wordish consideration, that I thinke this digression, will make my meaning receive the fuller understanding: which is not to take upon me to teach Poets howe they should doe, but onely finding my selfe sick among the rest, to shewe some one or two spots of the common infection, growne among the most part of Writers: that acknowledging our selves somewhat awry, we may bend to the right use both of matter and manner; whereto our language gyveth us great occasion, beeing indeed capable of any excellent exercising of it. I know, some will say it is a mingled language. And why not so much the better, taking the best of both the other? Another will say it wanteth Grammer. Nay truly, it hath that prayse, that it wanteth not Grammer: for Grammer it might have, but it needes it not; beeing so easie of it selfe, and so voyd of those cumbersome differences of Cases, Genders, Moodes, and Tenses, which I thinke was a peece of the Tower of *Babilons* curse, that a man should be put to schoole to learne his mother-tongue. But for the uttering sweetly, and properly the conceits of the minde, which is the end of speech, that hath it equally with any other tongue in the world: and is particularly happy, in compositions of two or three words together, neere the Greeke, far beyond the Latine: which is one of the greatest beauties can be in a language.

Now, of versifying there are two sorts, the one Aunciennt, the other Moderne: the Aunciennt marked the quantitie of each silable, and according to that, framed his verse: the Moderne, observing onely number, (with some regarde of the accent,) the chiefe life of it, standeth in that lyke sounding of the words, which we call Ryme. Whether of these be the most excellent, would beare many speeches. The Aunciennt, (no doubt) more fit for Musick, both words and tune observing quantity, and more fit lively to expresse divers passions, by the low and lofty sounde of the well-weyed silable. The latter

likewise, with hys Ryme, striketh a certaine musick to
the eare: and in fine, sith it dooth delight, though by
another way, it obtaines the same purpose: there beeing
in eyther sweetnes, and wanting in neither majestie.
Truely the English, before any other vulgar language I
know, is fit for both sorts: for, for the Ancient, the
Italian is so full of Vowels, that it must ever be cumbred
with *Elisions*. The Dutch, so of the other side with
Consonants, that they cannot yeeld the sweet slyding,
fit for a Verse. The French, in his whole language, hath
not one word, that hath his accent in the last silable,
saving two, called *Antepenultima*, and little more hath
the Spanish: and therefore, very gracelesly may they
use *Dactiles*. The English is subject to none of these
defects.

Nowe, for the ryme, though wee doe not observe
quantity, yet wee observe the accent very precisely:
which other languages, eyther cannot doe, or will not
doe so absolutely. That *Cæsura*, or breathing place
in the middest of the verse, neither Italian nor Spanish
have, the French, and we, never almost fayle of.
Lastly, even the very ryme it selfe, the Italian cannot
put in the last silable, by the French named the Masculine
ryme, but still in the next to the last, which the French
call the Female; or the next before that, which the
Italians terme *Sdrucciola*. The example of the former, is
Buono, Suono, of the *Sdrucciola, Femina, Semina*. The
French, of the other side, hath both the Male, as *Bon,
Son*, and the Female, as *Plaise, Taise*. But the
Sdrucciola, hee hath not: where the English hath all
three, as *Due, True, Father, Rather, Motion, Potion;* with
much more which might be sayd, but that I finde already,
the triflingnes of this discourse, is much too much
enlarged. So that sith the ever-praise-worthy Poesie,
is full of vertue-breeding delightfulnes, and voyde of
no gyfte, that ought to be in the noble name of learning:
sith the blames laid against it, are either false, or feeble:
sith the cause why it is not esteemed in Englande, is the
fault of Poet-apes, not Poets: sith lastly, our tongue
is most fit to honor Poesie, and to bee honored by
Poesie, I conjure you all, that have had the evill lucke

to reade this incke-wasting toy of mine, even in the
name of the nyne Muses, no more to scorne the sacred
misteries of Poesie : no more to laugh at the name of
Poets, as though they were next inheritours to Fooles :
no more to jest at the reverent title of a Rymer : but to
beleeve with *Aristotle*, that they were the auncient
Treasurers, of the Græcians Divinity. To beleeve
with *Bembus*, that they were first bringers in of all
civilitie. To beleeve with *Scaliger*, that no Philosophers
precepts can sooner make you an honest man, then the
reading of *Virgill*. To beleeve with *Clauserus*, the
Translator of *Cornutus*, that it pleased the heavenly
Deitie, by *Hesiod* and *Homer*, under the vayle of fables,
to give us all knowledge, Logick, Rethorick, Philosophy,
naturall, and morall; and *Quid non?* To beleeve
with me, that there are many misteries contained in
Poetrie, which of purpose were written darkely, least
by prophane wits, it should bee abused. To beleeve
with *Landin*, that they are so beloved of the Gods, that
whatsoever they write, proceeds of a divine fury.
Lastly, to beleeve themselves, when they tell you they
will make you immortall, by their verses.

Thus doing, your name shal florish in the Printers
shoppes ; thus doing, you shall bee of kinne to many
a poeticall Preface ; thus doing, you shall be most fayre,
most ritch, most wise, most all, you shall dwell upon
Superlatives. Thus dooing, though you be *Libertino
patre natus*, you shall suddenly grow *Hercules proles :*

> Si quid mea carmina possunt.

Thus doing, your soul shal be placed with *Dantes
Beatrix*, or *Virgils Anchises*. But if, (fie of such a but)
you be borne so neere the dull making *Cataphract of
Nilus*, that you cannot heare the Plannet-like Musick
of Poetrie, if you have so earth-creeping a mind, that it
cannot lift it selfe up, to looke to the sky of Poetry :
or rather, by a certaine rusticall disdaine, will become
such a Mome, as to be a *Momus* of Poetry : then, though
I will not wish unto you, the Asses eares of *Midas*, nor
to bee driven by a Poets verses, (as *Bubonax* was) to
hang himselfe, nor to be rimed to death, as is sayd to

be doone in Ireland : yet thus much curse I must send you in the behalfe of all Poets, that while you live, you live in love, and never get favour, for lacking skill of a *Sonnet:* and when you die, your memory die from the earth, for want of an *Epitaph.*

THOMAS CAMPION

(*c.* 1575–1620)

OBSERUATIONS IN THE ART OF ENGLISH POESIE

Wherein it is demonstratively proved, and by example confirmed, that the English toong will receive eight severall kinds of numbers, proper to itself, which are all in this book set forth, and were never before this time by any man attempted. (First published in 1602.)

TO THE RIGHT NOBLE AND WORTHILY HONOURD, THE LORD BUCKHURST, LORD HIGH TREASURER OF ENGLAND.

IN two things (right honorable) it is generally agreed that man excels all other creatures, in reason, and speech: and in them by how much one man surpasseth an other, by so much the neerer he aspires to a celestiall essence.

Poesy in all kind of speaking is the chiefe beginner, and maintayner of eloquence, not only helping the eare with the acquaintance of sweet numbers, but also raysing the minde to a more high and lofty conceite. For this end haue I studyed to induce a true forme of versefying into our language: for the vulgar and vnarteficiall custome of riming hath I know deter'd many excellent wits from the exercise of English Poesy. The obseruations which I haue gathered for this purpose, I humbly present to your Lordship, as to the noblest iudge of Poesy, and the most honorable protector of all industrious learning; which if your Honour shall vouchsafe to receiue, who both in your publick, and priuate Poemes haue so deuinely crowned your fame, what man will dare to repine? or not striue to imitate them? VVherefore with all humility I subiect my selfe and them to your gratious fauour, beseeching you in the noblenes of your mind to take in worth so simple a present, which by some worke drawne from my more serious studies, I will hereafter endeauour to excuse.

Your Lordships humbly deuoted
THOMAS CAMPION.

THE WRITER TO HIS BOOKE.

Whether thus hasts my little booke so fast?
To Paules Churchyard; what in those cels to stād,
With one leafe like a riders cloke put vp

> *To catch a termer? or lye mustie there*
> *With rimes a terme set out, or two before?*
> *Some will redeeme me ; fewe ; yes, reade me too ;*
> *Fewer ; nay loue me ; now thou dot'st I see ;*
> *Will not our English Athens arte defend?*
> *Perhaps ; will lofty courtly wits not ayme*
> *Still at perfection?   If I graunt?   I flye ;*
> *Whether? to Pawles ; Alas poore booke I rue*
> *Thy rash selfe-loue, goe spread thy pap'ry wings,*
> *Thy lightnes can not helpe, or hurt my fame*

THE FIRST CHAPTER, INTREATING OF NUMBERS IN GENERALL.

THERE is no writing too breefe, that without obscuritie comprehends the intent of the writer. These my late obseruations in English Poesy I haue thus briefely gathered, that they might proue the lesse troublesome in perusing, and the more apt to be retayn'd in memorie. And I will first generally handle the nature of Numbers. Number is *discreta quantitas*, so that when we speake simply of number, we intend only the disseuer'd quantity ; But when we speake of a Poeme written in number, we consider not only the distinct number of the sillables, but also their value, which is contained in the length or shortnes of their sound. As in Musick we do not say a straine of so many notes, but so many sem'briefes (though sometimes there are no more notes then sem'briefes) so in a verse the numeration of the sillables is not so much to be obserued, as their waite, and due proportion. In ioyning of words to harmony there is nothing more offensiue to the eare then to place a long sillable with a short note, or a short sillable with a long note, though in the last the vowell often beares it out. The world is made by Simmetry and proportion, and is in that respect compared to Musick, and Musick to Poetry : for *Terence* saith speaking of Poets, *artem qui tractant musicam*, confounding musick and Poesy together. What musick can there be where there is no proportion obserued? Learning first flourished in *Greece*, from thence it was deriued vnto the *Romaines*, both diligent obseruers of the number, and quantity of sillables, not in their verses only, but likewise in their prose. Learning after the declining of the *Romaine* Empire, and the pollution of their language through the conquest of the *Barbarians*, lay most pitifully deformed, till the time of *Erasmus, Rewcline,* Sir *Thomas More,* and other learned men of that age, who brought the Latine toong againe to light, redeeming it with much labour out of the hands of the illiterate Monks and Friers: as a scoffing booke, entituled *Epistolæ obscurorum virorum,* may sufficiently testifie. In those lack-learning times, and in barbarized *Italy,* began that vulgar and easie kind of Poesie which is now in vse throughout most parts of Christendome, which we abusiuely call Rime, and Meeter, of *Rithmus* and *Metrum,* of which I will now discourse.

The second Chapter, declaring the vnaptnesse of Rime in Poesie.

I am not ignorant that whosoeuer shall by way of reprehension examine the imperfections of Rime, must encounter with many glorious enemies, and those very expert, and ready at their weapon, that can if neede be extempore (as they say) rime a man to death. Besides there is growne a kind of prescription in the vse of Rime, to forestall the right of true numbers, as also the consent of many nations, against all which it may seeme a thing almost impossible, and vaine to contend. All this and more can not yet deterre me from a lawful defence of perfection, or make me any whit the sooner adheare to that which is lame and vnbeseeming. For custome I alleage, that ill vses are to be abolisht, and that things naturally imperfect can not be perfected by vse. Old customes, if they be better, why should they not be recald, as the yet florishing custome of numerous poesy vsed among the *Romanes* and *Grecians:* But the vnaptnes of our toongs, and the difficultie of imitation dishartens vs; againe the facilitie & popularitie of Rime creates as many Poets, as a hot sommer flies. But let me now examine the nature of that which we call Rime. By Rime is vnderstoode that which ends in the like sound, so that verses in such maner composed, yeeld but a continual repetition of that Rhetoricall figure which we tearme *similiter desinentia*, and that being but *figura verbi*, ought (as *Tully* and all other Rhetoritians haue iudicially obseru'd) sparingly to be vsd, least it should offend the eare with tedious affectation. Such was that absurd following of the letter amõgst our English so much of late affected, but now hist out of Paules Churchyard: which foolish figuratiue repetition crept also into the Latine toong, as it is manifest in the booke of P^s cald *prælia porcorum*, and an other pamphlet all of F^s, which I haue seene imprinted; but I will leaue these follies to their owne ruine, and returne to the matter intended. The eare is a rationall sence, and a chiefe iudge of proportion, but in our kind of riming what proportion is there kept, where there remaines such a confused inequalitie of sillables? *Iambick* and *Trochaick* feete which are opposd by nature, are by all Rimers confounded, nay oftentimes they place in stead of an *Iambick* the foote *Pyrrychius*, consisting of two short sillables, curtalling their verse, which they supply in reading with a ridiculous, and vnapt drawing of their speech. As for example:

Was it my desteny, or dismall chaunce?

In this verse the two last sillables of the word, *Desteny*, being both short, and standing for a whole foote in the verse, cause the line to fall out shorter then it ought by nature. The like impure errors haue in time of rudenesse bene vsed in the Latine toong, as the *Carmina prouerbialia* can witnesse, and many other such reuerend bables. But the noble *Grecians* and *Romaines* whose skilfull monuments outliue barbarisme, tyed themselues to the strict obseruation of poeticall numbers, so abandoning the childish titillation of riming, that it was imputed a great error to *Ouid* for setting forth this one riming verse,

Quot cælum stellas tot habet tua Roma puellas.

For the establishing of this argument, what better

confirmation can be had, then that of Sir *Thomas Moore* in his booke of Epigrams, where he makes two sundry Epitaphs vpon the death of a singing man at *Westminster*, the one in learned numbers and dislik't, the other in rude rime and highly extold: so that he concludes, *tales lactucas talia labra petunt*, like lips, like lettuce. But there is yet another fault in Rime altogether intollerable, which is, that it inforceth a man oftentimes to abiure his matter, and extend a short conceit beyond all bounds of arte: for in *Quatorzens* me thinks the Poet handles his subiect as tyrannically as *Procrustes* the thiefe his prisoners, whom when he had taken, he vsed to cast vpon a bed, which if they were too short to fill, he would stretch thē longer, if too long, he would cut them shorter. Bring before me now any the most selfe-lou'd Rimer, & let me see if without blushing he be able to reade his lame halting rimes. Is there not a curse of Nature laid vpon such rude Poesie, when the Writer is himself asham'd of it, and the hearers in contempt call it Riming and Ballating? What Deuine in his Sermon, or graue Counseller in his Oration will alleage the testimonie of a rime? But the deuinity of the *Romaines* and *Gretians* was all written in verse: and *Aristotle*, *Galene*, and the bookes of all the excellent Philosophers are full of the testimonies of the old Poets. By them was laid the foundation of all humane wisedome, and from them the knowledge of all antiquitie is deriued. I will propound but one question, and so conclude this point. If the *Italians*, *Frenchmen* and *Spanyards*, that with commendation haue written in Rime, were demaunded whether they had rather the bookes they haue publisht (if their toong would beare it) should remaine as they are in Rime, or be translated into the auncient numbers of the *Greekes* and *Romaines*, would they not answere into numbers? What honour were it then for our English language to be the first that after so many yeares of barbarisme could second the perfection of the industrious *Greekes* and *Romaines*? which how it may be effected I will now proceede to demonstrate.

THE THIRD CHAPTER: OF OUR ENGLISH NUMBERS IN GENERALL.

There are but three feete, which generally distinguish the Greeke and Latine verses, the *Dactil* consisting of one long sillable and two short, as *vĭuĕrĕ* the *Trochy*, of one long and one short, as *vītă*, and the *Iambick* of one short and one long, as *ămōr*. The *Spondee* of two long, the *Tribrach* of three short, the *Anapæstick* of two short and a long, are but as seruants to the first. Diuers other feete I know are by the Grammarians cited, but to little purpose. The *Heroical* verse that is distinguisht by the *Dactile*, hath bene oftentimes attempted in our English toong, but with passing pitifull successe: and no wonder, seeing it is an attempt altogether against the nature of our language. For both the concurse of our monasillables make our verses vnapt to slide, and also if we examine our polysillables, we shall finde few of them by reason of their heauinesse, willing to serue in place of a *Dactile*. Thence it is, that the writers of English heroicks do so often repeate *Amyntas*, *Olympus*, *Auernus*, *Erinnis*, and such like borrowed words, to supply the defect of our hardly intreated *Dactile*. I could in this place set downe many ridiculous kinds of *Dactils* which they vse, but that it is not my purpose here to incite men to laughter. If we therefore reiect the *Dactil* as vnfit for our vse (which of necessity we are enforst to do) there remayne only the *Iambick* foote, of which the *Iambick* verse is fram'd, and the *Trochee*, frõ which the *Trochaick* numbers haue their originall. Let vs now then examine the property of these two feete, and try if they consent with the nature of our English sillables. And first for the *Iambicks*, they fall out so naturally in our toong, that if we examine our owne writers, we shall find they vnawares hit oftentimes vpon the true *Iambick* numbers, but alwayes ayme at them as far as their eare without the guidance of arte can attaine vnto, as it shall hereafter more euidently appeare. The *Trochaick* foote which is but an *Iambick* turn'd ouer and ouer, must of force in like manner accord in proportion with our Brittish sillables, and so produce an English *Trochaicall* verse. Then hauing these two principall kinds of verses, we may easily out of them deriue other formes, as the Latines and Greekes before vs haue done, whereof I will make plaine demonstration, beginning at the *Iambick* verse.

The fourth Chapter, of the Iambick verse.

I haue obserued, and so may any one that is either practis'd in singing, or hath a naturall eare able to time a song, that the Latine verses of sixe feete, as the *Heroick* and *Iambick*, or of fiue feete, as the *Trochaick* are in nature all of the same length of sound with our English verses of fiue feete; for either of them being tim'd with the hand *quinque perficiunt tempora*, they fill vp the quantity (as it were) of fiue sem'briefs, as for example, if any man will proue to time these verses with his hand.

A pure *Iambick*.
Suis & ipsa Roma viribus ruit.

A licentiate *Iambick*.
Ducunt volentes fata, nolentes trahunt.

An *Heroick* verse.
Tytere tu patulæ recubans sub tegmine fagi.

A *Trochaick* verse.
Nox est perpetua vna dormienda.

English *Iambicks* pure.
The more secure, the more the stroke we feele
Of vnpreuented harms; so gloomy stormes
Appeare the sterner if the day be cleere.

Th'English *Iambick* licentiate.
Harke how these winds do murmur at thy flight.

The English *Trochee*.
Still where Enuy leaues, remorse doth enter.

The cause why these verses differing in feete yeeld the same length of sound, is by reason of some rests which either the necessity of the numbers, or the heauines of the sillables do beget. For we find in musick, that oftentimes the straines of a song can not be reduct to true number without some rests prefixt in the beginning and middle, as also at the close if need requires. Besides, our English monasillables enforce many breathings which no doubt greatly lengthen a verse, so that it is no wonder if for these reasons our English verses of fiue feete hold pace with the *Latines* of sixe. The pure *Iambick* in English needes small demonstration, because it consists simply of *Iambick* feete, but our *Iambick licentiate* offers it selfe to a farther consideration; for in the third and fift place we must of force hold the *Iambick* foote, in the first, second, and fourth place we may vse a *Spondee* or *Iambick* and sometime a *Tribrack* or *Dactile*, but rarely an *Anapestick* foote, and that in the second or fourth place. But why an *Iambick* in the third place? I answere, that the forepart of the verse may the gentlier slide into his *Dimeter*, as for example sake deuide this verse: *Harke how these winds do murmure at thy flight*. *Harke how these winds*, there the voice naturally affects a rest, then *murmur at thy flight*, that is of it selfe a perfect number, as I will declare in the next Chapter, and therefore the other odde sillable betweene thẽ ought to be short, least the verse should hang too much betweene the naturall pause of the verse, and the *Dimeter* following, the which *Dimeter* though it be naturally *Trochaical*, yet it seemes to haue his originall out of the *Iambick* verse. But the better to confirme and expresse these rules, I will set downe a short Poeme in *Licentiate Iambicks*, which may giue more light to them that shall hereafter imitate these numbers.

Goe numbers boldly passe, stay not for ayde
Of shifting rime, that easie flatterer
Whose witchcraft can the ruder eares beguile;
Let your smooth feete enur'd to purer arte
True measures tread; what if your pace be slow?
And hops not like the Grecian elegies?

It is yet gracefull, and well fits the state
Of words ill-breathed, and not shap't to runne:
Goe then, but slowly till your steps be firme,
Tell them that pitty, or peruersely skorne
Poore English Poesie as the slaue to rime,
You are those loftie numbers that reuiue
Triumphs of Princes, and sterne tragedies:
And learne henceforth t'attend those happy sprights
Whose bounding fury, height, and waight affects,
Assist their labour, and sit close to them,
Neuer to part away till for desert
Their browes with great Apollos *bayes are hid.*
He first taught number, and true harmonye,
Nor is the lawrell his for rime bequeath'd,
Call him with numerous accents paisd by arte
He'le turne his glory from the sunny clymes,
The North-bred wits alone to patronise.
Let France their Bartas, *Italy* Tasso *prayse,*
Phæbus shuns none, but in their flight from him.

Though as I said before, the naturall breathing place of our English *Iambick* verse is in the last sillable of the second foote, as our *Trochy* after the manner of the Latine *Heroick* and *Iambick* rests naturally in the first of the third foote: yet no man is tyed altogether to obserue this rule, but he may alter it, after the iudgement of his eare, which Poets, Orators, and Musitions of all men ought to haue most excellent. Againe, though I said peremtorily before, that the third, and fift place of our licentiate *Iambick* must alwayes hold an *Iambick* foote, yet I will shew you example in both places where a *Tribrack* may be very formally taken, and first in the third place,

Some trade in Barbary, *some in* Turky *trade.*

An other example.
Men that do fall to misery, quickly fall

If you doubt whether the first of misery be naturally short or no, you may iudge it by the easie sliding of these two verses following:

The first.
Whome misery can not alter, time deuours,

The second.
What more vnhappy life, what misery more?

Example of the *Tribrack* in the fift place, as you may perceiue in the last foote of the fift verse.

> *Some from the starry throne his fame deriues,*
> *Some from the mynes beneath, from trees, or herbs,*
> *Each hath his glory, each his sundry gift,*
> *Renown'd in eu'ry art there liues not any.*

To proceede farther, I see no reason why the English *Iambick* in his first place may not as well borrow a foote of the *Trochy*, as our *Trochy* or the Latine *Hendicasillable* may in the like case make bold with the *Iambick*: but it must be done euer with this caueat, which is, that a *Sponde*, *Dactile* or *Tribrack* do supply the next place: for an *Iambick* beginning with a single short sillable, and the other ending before with the like, would too much drinke vp the verse if they came immediatly together.

The example of the *Sponde* after
the *Trochy*.

As the faire sonne the lightsome heau'n adorns.

The example of the *Dactil*.

Noble, ingenious, and discreetly wise.

The example of the *Tribrack*.

Beawty to ielosie brings ioy, sorrow, feare.

Though I haue set downe these second licenses as good and ayreable enough, yet for the most part my first rules are generall.

These are those numbers which Nature in our English destinates to the Tragick, and Heroik Poeme: for the subiect of them both being all one, I see no impediment why one verse may not serue for them both, as it appeares more plainely in the old comparison of the two Greeke writers, when they say, *Homerus est Sophocles heroicus*, and againe, *Sophocles est Homerus tragicus*, intimating that both *Sophocles* and *Homer* are the same in height and subiect, and differ onely in the kinde of their numbers.

The *Iambick* verse in like manner being yet made a

little more licentiate, that it may thereby the neerer imitate our common talke, will excellently serue for Comedies, and then may we vse a *Sponde* in the fift place, and in the third place any foote except a *Trochy*, which neuer enters into our *Iambick* verse, but in the first place, and then with his caueat of the other feete which must of necessitie follow.

THE FIFT CHAPTER, OF THE IAMBICK DIMETER, OR ENGLISH MARCH.

The *Dimeter* (so called in the former Chapter) I intend next of all to handle, because it seems to be a part of the *Iambick* which is our most naturall and auncient English verse. We may terme this our English march, because the verse answers our warlick forme of march in similitude of number. But call it what you please, for I will not wrangle about names, only intending to set down the nature of it and true structure. It consists of two feete and one odde sillable. The first foote may be made either a *Trochy*, or a *Spondee*, or an *Iambick* at the pleasure of the composer, though most naturally that place affects a *Trochy* or *Spondee*; yet by the example of *Catullus* in his *Hendicasillables*, I adde in the first place sometimes an *Iambick* foote. In the second place, we must euer insert a *Trochy* or *Tribrack*, and so leaue the last sillable (as in the end of a verse it is alwaies held) common. Of this kinde I will subscribe three examples, the first being a peece of a *Chorus* in a Tragedy.

> *Rauing warre begot*
> *In the thirstye sands*
> *Of the* Lybian *Iles*
> *Wasts our emptye fields,*
> *What the greedye rage*
> *Of fell wintrye stormes,*
> *Could not turne to spoile,*
> *Fierce* Bellona *now*
> *Hath laid desolate,*
> *Voyd of fruit, or hope.*
> *Th'eger thriftye hinde*
> *Whose rude ioyle reuin'd*
> *Our skie-blasted earth*
> *Himselfe is but earth,*

> *Left a skorne to fate*
> *Through seditious armes:*
> *And that soile, aliue*
> *Which he duly nurst,*
> *Which him duly fed,*
> *Dead his body feeds:*
> *Yet not all the glebe*
> *His tuffe hands manur'd*
> *Now one turfe affords*
> *His poore funerall.*
> *Thus still needy liues,*
> *Thus still needy dyes*
> *Th'vnknowne multitude.*

An example *Lyrical*.

> *Greatest in thy wars,*
> *Greater in thy peace*
> *Dread* Elizabeth;
> *Our muse only Truth*
> *Figments can not vse*
> *Thy ritch name to deck*
> *That it selfe adornes:*
> *But should now this age*
> *Let all poesye fayne,*
> *Fayning poesy could*
> *Nothing faine at all*
> *Worthy halfe thy fame.*

An example *Epigrammicall*.

> *Kind in euery kinde*
> *This deare Ned resolue,*
> *Neuer of thy prayse*
> *Be too prodigall;*
> *He that prayseth all*
> *Can praise truly none.*

THE SIXTH CHAPTER, OF THE ENGLISH TROCHAICK VERSE.

Next in course to be intreated of is the English *Trochaick*, being a verse simple, and of it selfe depending. It consists, as the Latine *Trochaick* of fiue feete, the first whereof may be a *Trochy*, a *Spondee*, or an *Iambick*, the other foure of necessity all *Trochyes*, still holding this rule authenticall, that the last sillable of a verse is alwayes common. The spirit of this verse most of all delights in *Epigrams*, but it may be diuersly vsed, as shall hereafter be declared. I haue written diuers light Poems in this kinde, which for the better satisfaction of the reader, I thought conuenient here in way of example to publish. In which though sometimes vnder a knowne name I haue shadowed a fain'd conceit, yet is it done without reference, or offence to any person, and only to make the stile appeare the more English.

The first *Epigramme*.

Lockly spits apace, the rhewme he cals it,
But no drop (though often vrged) he straineth
From his thirstie iawes, yet all the morning,
And all day he spits, in eu'ry corner,
At his meales he spits, at eu'ry meeting,
At the barre he spits before the Fathers,
In the Court he spits before the Graces,
In the Church he spits, thus all prophaning
With that rude disease, that empty spitting.
Yet no cost he spares, he sees the Doctors,
Keepes a strickt diet, precisely vseth
Drinks and bathes drying, yet all preuailes not.
'Tis not China (Lockly) Salsa Guacum,
Nor dry Sassafras can helpe, or ease thee;
'Tis no humor hurts, it is thy humor.

The second *Epigramme*.

Cease fond wretch to loue so oft deluded,
Still made ritch with hopes, still vnrelieued,
Now fly her delaies; she that debateth
Feeles not true desire, he that deferred
Others times attends, his owne betrayeth:
Learne t'affect thy selfe, thy cheekes deformed
With pale care reuiue by timely pleasure,
Or with skarlet heate them, or by paintings
Make thee louely, for such arte she vseth
Whome in vayne so long thy folly loued.

The third *Epigramme*.

Kate can fancy only berdles husbands,
Thats the cause she shakes off eu'ry suter,
Thats the cause she liues so stale a virgin,
For before her heart can heate her answer,
Her smooth youths she finds all hugely berded.

The fourth *Epigramme*.

All in sattin Oteny will be suted,
Beaten sattin (as by chaunce he cals it)
Oteny sure will haue the bastinado

The fift *Epigramme*.

Tosts as snakes or as the mortall Henbane
Hunks detests when huffcap ale he tipples,
Yet the bread he graunts the fumes abateth:
Therefore apt in ale, true, and he graunts it,
But it drinks vp ale, that Hunks detesteth.

The sixt *Epigramme*.

What though Harry *braggs, let him be noble,*
Noble Harry *hath not halfe a noble.*

The seauenth *Epigramme*.

Phæbe *all the rights* Elisa *claymeth,*
Mighty riuall, in this only diff'ring
That shees only true, thou only fayned.

The eight *Epigramme*.

Barnzy *stiffly vowes that hees no Cuckold,*
Yet the vulgar eu'ry where salutes him
With strange signes of hornes, from eu'ry corner,
Wheresoere he commes a sundry Cucco
Still frequents his eares, yet hees no Cuccold.
But this Barnzy *knowes that his* Matilda
Skorning him with Haruy *playes the wanton;*
Knowes it? nay desires it, and by prayers
Dayly begs of heau'n, that it for euer
May stand firme for him, yet hees no Cuccold:
And tis true, for Haruy *keeps* Matilda,
Fosters Barnzy, *and relieues his houshold,*
Buyes the Cradle, and begets the children,
Payes the Nurces eu'ry charge defraying,
And thus truly playes Matildas *husband:*
So that Barnzy *now becoms a cypher,*
And himselfe th'adultrer of Matilda.
Mock not him with hornes, the case is alterd,
Haruy *beares the wrong, he proues the Cuccold.*

The ninth *Epigramme*.

Buffe *loues fat vians, fat ale, fat all things,*
Keepes fat whores, fat offices, yet all men
Him fat only wish to feast the gallous.

The tenth *Epigramme*.

Smith *by sute diuorst, the knowne adultres*
Freshly weds againe; what ayles the mad-cap
By this fury? euen so theeues by frailty
Of their hempe reseru'd, againe the dismall
Tree embrace, againe the fatall halter.

The eleuenth *Epigramme*.

His late losse the Wiuelesse Higs *in order*
Eu'rywhere bewailes to friends, to strangers;
Tels them how by night a yongster armed
Saught his Wife (as hand in hand he held her)
With drawne sword to force, she cryed, he mainely
Roring ran for ayde, but (ah) returning
Fled was with the prize the beawty-forcer,
Whome in vaine he seeks, he threats, he followes.
Chang'd is Hellen, Hellen *hugs the stranger*
Safe as Paris *in the Greeke triumphing.*
Therewith his reports to teares he turneth,
Peirst through with the louely Dames remembrance;
Straight he sighes, he raues, his haire he teareth,
Forcing pitty still by fresh lamenting.
Cease vnworthy, worthy of thy fortunes,
Thou that couldst so faire a prize deliuer,
For feare vnregarded, vndefended,
Hadst no heart I thinke, I know no liuer.

The twelfth *Epigramme*.

Why droopst thou Trefeild? *will* Hurst *the Banker*
Make dice of thy bones? by heau'n he can not;
Can not? whats the reason? ile declare it,
Th'ar all growne so pockie, and so rotten.

THE SEAUENTH CHAPTER, OF THE ENGLISH ELEGEICK VERSE.

The *Elegeick* verses challenge the next place, as being of all compound verses the simplest. They are deriu'd out of our owne naturall numbers as neere the imitation of the *Greekes* and *Latines*, as our heauy sillables will permit. The first verse is a meere licentiate *Iambick*; the second is fram'd of two vnited *Dimeters*. In the first *Dimeter* we are tyed to make the first foote either a *Trochy* or a *Spondee*, the second a *Trochy*, and the odde sillable of it alwaies long. The second *Dimeter* consists of two *Trochyes* (because it requires more swiftness than the first) and an odde sillable, which being last, is euer common. I will giue you example both of *Elegye* and *Epigramme*, in this kinde.

An *Elegye*.

Constant to none, but euer false to me,
  Traiter still to loue through thy faint desires,
Not hope of pittie now nor vaine redresse
  Turns my griefs to teares, and renu'd laments

Too well thy empty vowes, and hollow thoughts
  Witnes both thy wrongs, and remorseles hart.
Rue not my sorrow, but blush at my name,
  Let thy bloudy cheeks guilty thoughts betray.
My flames did truly burne, thine made a shew,
  As fires painted are which no heate retayne,
Or as the glossy Pirop faines to blaze,
  But toucht cold appeares, and an earthy stone,
True cullours deck thy cheeks, false foiles thy brest,
  Frailer then thy light beawty is thy minde.
None canst thou long refuse, nor long affect,
  But turn'st feare with hopes, sorrow with delight,
Delaying, and deluding eu'ry way
  Those whose eyes are once with thy beawty chain'd.
Thrice happy man that entring first thy loue,
  Can so guide the straight raynes of his desires,
That both he can regard thee, and refraine :
  If grac't, firme he stands, if not, easely falls.

Example of *Epigrams*, in *Elegeick* verse.

The first *Epigramme*.

Arthure brooks only those that brooke not him,
  Those he most regards, and deuoutly serues :
But them that grace him his great brau'ry skornes,
  Counting kindnesse all duty, not desert :
Arthure wants forty pounds, tyres eu'ry friend,
  But finds none that holds twenty due for him.

The second *Epigramme*.

If fancy can not erre which vertue guides,
  In thee Laura then fancy can not erre.

The third *Epigramme*.

Drue feasts no Puritans, the churles he saith
  Thanke no men, but eate, praise God, and depart.

The fourth *Epigramme*.

A wiseman wary liues, yet most secure,
  Sorrowes moue not him greatly, nor delights.
Fortune and death he skorning, only makes
  Th'earth his sober Inne, but still heau'n his home.

The fift *Epigramme*.

Thou telst me Barnzy Dawson hath a wife,
  Thine he hath I graunt Dawson hath a wife.

The sixt *Epigramme*.

Drue *giues thee money, yet thou thankst not him,*
 But thankst God for him, like a godly man.
Suppose rude Puritan thou begst of him,
 And he saith God help, who's the godly man?

The seauenth *Epigramme*.

All wonders *Barnzy speakes, all grosely faind,*
 Speake some wonder once Barnzy, speake the truth.

The eight *Epigramme*.

None then should through thy beawty **Lawra** *pine,*
 Might sweet words alone ease a loue-sick heart :
But your sweet words alone that quit so well
 Hope of friendly deeds kill the loue-sick heart.

The ninth *Epigramme*.

At all thou frankly throwst, while Frank *thy wife*
 Bars not Luke *the mayn,* Oteny *barre the bye.*

THE EIGHT CHAPTER, OF DITTIES AND ODES.

To descend orderly from the more simple numbers to them that are more compounded, it is now time to handle such verses as are fit for *Ditties* or *Odes*; which we may call *Lyricall*, because they are apt to be soong to an instrument, if they were adorn'd with conuenient notes. Of that kind I will demonstrate three in this Chapter, and in the first we will proceede after the manner of the *Saphick* which is a *Trochaicall* verse as well as the *Hendicasillable* in Latine. The first three verses therefore in our English *Saphick* are meerely those *Trochaicks* which I handled in the sixt Chapter, excepting only that the first foote of either of them must euer of necessity be a *Spondee*, to make the number more graue. The fourth and last closing verse is compounded of three *Trochyes* together, to giue a more smooth farewell, as you may easily obscrue in this Poeme made vpon a Triumph at *Whitehall*, whose glory was dasht with an vnwelcome showre, hindring the people from the desired sight of her Maiestie.

The English *Sapphick*.

Faiths pure shield the Christian Diana
Englands *glory crowned with all deuinenesse,*
Liue long *with triumphs to blesse thy people*
  At *thy sight triumphing.*
Loe *they sound, the Knights in order armed*
Entring *threat the list, adrest to combat*
For *their courtly loues ; he, hees the wonder*
  Whome Eliza *graceth.*
Their *plum'd pomp the vulgar heaps detaineth,*
And *rough steeds, let vs the still deuices*
Close *obserue, the speeches and the musicks*
  Peacefull *arms adorning.*
But *whence showres so fast this angry tempest,*
Clowding *dimme the place ? behold* Eliza
This *day shines not here, this heard, the launces*
  And *thick heads do vanish.*

The second kinde consists of *Dimeter*, whose first foote may either be a *Sponde* or a *Trochy*: The two verses following are both of them *Trochaical*, and consist of foure feete, the first of either of them being a *Spondee* or *Trochy*, the other three only *Trochyes*. The fourth and last verse is made of two *Trochyes*. The number is voluble and fit to expresse any amorous conceit.

The Example.

Rose-cheekt Lawra *come*
Sing *thou smoothly with thy beawties*
Silent *musick, either other*
  Sweetely *gracing.*
Louely *formes do flowe*
From *concent deuinely framed,*
Heau'n *is musick, and thy beawties*
  Birth *is heauenly.*
These *dull notes we sing*
Discords *neede for helps to grace them,*
Only *beawty purely louing*
  Knowes *no discord :*
But *still mooues delight*
Like *cleare springs renu'd by flowing,*
Euer *perfet, euer in them-*
  selues *eternall.*

The third kind begins as the second kind ended, with a verse consisting of two *Trochy* feete, and then as the second kind had in the middle two *Trochaick*

THE ART OF ENGLISH POESIE 79

verses of foure feete, so this hath three of the same nature, and ends in a *Dimeter* as the second began. The *Dimeter* may allow in the first place a *Trochy* or a *Spondee*, but no *Iambick*.

The Example.

Iust beguiler,
Kindest loue, yet only chastest,
Royall in thy smooth denyals,
Frowning or demurely smiling
   Still my pure delight.

Let me view thee
With thoughts and with eyes affected,
And if then the flames do murmur,
Quench them with thy vertue, charme them
   With thy stormy browes.

Heau'n so cheerefull
Laughs not euer, hory winter
Knowes his season, euen the freshest
Sommer mornes from angry thunder
   Iet not still secure.

THE NINTH CHAPTER, OF THE ANACREONTICK VERSE.

If any shall demaund the reason why this number being in it selfe simple, is plac't after so many compounded numbers, I answere, because I hold it a number too licentiate for a higher place, and in respect of the rest imperfect, yet is it passing gracefull in our English toong, and will excellently fit the subiect of a *Madrigall*, or any other lofty or tragicall matter. It consists of two feete, the first may be either a *Sponde* or *Trochy*, the other must euer represent the nature of a *Trochy*, as for example:

Follow, followe
Though with mischiefe
Arm'd, like whirlewind
Now she flyes thee;
Time can conquer
Loues vnkindnes;
Loue can alter
Times disgraces;
Till death faint not
Then but followe.

> *Could I catch that*
> *Nimble trayter*
> *Skornefull* Lawra,
> *Swift foote* Lawra,
> *Soone then would I*
> *Seeke auengement;*
> *Whats th'auengement?*
> *Euen submissely*
> *Prostrate then to*
> *Beg for mercye*

Thus haue I briefly described eight seuerall kinds of English numbers simple or compound. The first was our *Iambick* pure and licentiate. The second, that which I call our *Dimeter*, being deriued either from the end of our *Iambick*, or from the beginning of our *Trochaick*. The third which I deliuered was our English *Trochaick* verse. The fourth our English *Elegeick*. The fift, sixt, and seauenth, were our English *Sapphick*, and two other *Lyricall* numbers, the one beginning with that verse which I call our *Dimeter*, the other ending with the same. The eight and last was a kind of *Anacreontick* verse, handled in this Chapter. These numbers which by my long obseruation I haue found agreeable with the nature of our sillables, I haue set forth for the benefit of our language, which I presume the learned will not only imitate, but also polish and amplifie with their owne inuentions. Some eares accustomed altogether to the fatnes of rime, may perhaps except against the cadences of these numbers, but let any man iudicially examine them, and he shall finde they close of themselues so perfectly, that the help of rime were not only in them superfluous, but also absurd. Moreouer, that they agree with the nature of our English it is manifest, because they entertaine so willingly our owne British names, which the writers in English Heroicks could neuer aspire vnto, and euen our Rimers themselues haue rather delighted in borrowed names then in their owne, though much more apt and necessary. But it is now time that I proceede to the censure of our sillables, and that I set such lawes vpon them as by imitation, reason, or experience, I can confirme. Yet before

THE ART OF ENGLISH POESIE

I enter into that discourse, I will briefly recite, and dispose in order all such feete as are necessary for composition of the verses before described. They are sixe in number, three whereof consist of two sillables, and as many of three.

Feete of two sillables.

Iambick :
Trochaick : } as { rĕuĕnge.
Sponde : Bĕawtĭe.
cōnstānt.

Feete of three sillables.

Tribrack :
Anapestick : } as { mĭsĕrĭe.
Dactile : mĭsĕrīes.
Dēstĕnĭe.

THE TENTH CHAPTER, OF THE QUANTITY OF ENGLISH SILLABLES.

The *Greekes* in the quantity of their sillables were farre more licentious then the *Latines*, as *Martiall* in his Epigramme of *Earinon* witnesseth, saying, *Musas qui colimus seueriores.* But the English may very well challenge much more licence then either of them, by reason it stands chiefely vpon monasillables, which in expressing with the voyce, are of a heauy cariage, and for that cause the *Dactil, Trybrack,* and *Anapestick* are not greatly mist in our verses. But aboue all the accent of our words is diligently to be obseru'd, for chiefely by the accent in any language the true value of the sillables is to be measured. Neither can I remember any impediment except position that can alter the accent of any sillable in our English verse. For though we accent the second of *Trumpington* short, yet is it naturally long, and so of necessity must be held of euery composer. Wherefore the first rule that is to be obserued, is the nature of the accent, which we must euer follow.

The next rule is position, which makes euery sillable long, whether the position happens in one or in two words, according to the manner of the *Latines*, wherein is to be noted that *h* is no letter.

Position is when a vowell comes before two consonants, either in one or two words. In one, as in *best*, *e* before *st*, makes the word *best* long by position. In two words, as in *setled loue*: *e* before *d* in the last sillable of the first word, and *l* in the beginning of the second makes *led* in *setlēd* long by position.

A vowell before a vowell is alwaies short, as, *flŭĭng*, *dĭĭng*, *gŏĭng*, vnlesse the accent alter it, as in *dĕnīing*.

The dipthong in the midst of a word is alwaies long, as *plaīing*, *deceīuing*.

The *Synalæphas* or *Elisions* in our toong are either necessary to auoid the hollownes and gaping in our verse as *to*, and *the*, *t'inchaunt*, *th'inchaunter*, or may be vsd at pleasure, as for *let vs*, to say *let's*, for *we will*, *wee'l*, for *euery*, *eu'ry*, for *they are*, *th'ar*, for *he is*, *hee's*, for *admired*, *admir'd*, and such like.

Also, because our English Orthography (as the French) differs from our common pronunciation, we must esteeme our sillables as we speake, not as we write, for the sound of them in a verse is to be valued, and not their letters, as for *follow*, we pronounce *follo*, for *perfect*, *perfet*, for *little*, *littel*, for *loue-sick*, *loue-sik*, for *honour*, *honor*, for *money*, *mony*, for *dangerous*, *dangerus*, for *raunsome*, *raunsum*, for *though*, *tho*, and their like.

Deriuatiues hold the quantities of their primatiues, as *dĕuōut*, *dĕuōutelĭe*, *prŏphāne*, *prŏphānelĭe*, and so do the compositiues, as *dĕsēru'd*, *ūndĕseru'd*.

In words of two sillables, if the last haue a full and rising accent that sticks long vpon the voyce, the first sillable is alwayes short, vnlesse position, or the dipthong doth make it long, as *dĕsīre*, *prĕsērue*, *dĕfīne*, *prŏphāne*, *rĕgārd*, *mănūre*, and such like.

If the like dissillables at the beginning haue double consonants of the same kind, we may vse the first sillable as common, but more naturally short, because in their pronunciation we touch but one of those double letters, as *ătĕnd*, *ăpēare*, *ŏpōse*. The like we may say when silent and melting consonants meete together, as *ădrēst*, *rĕdrēst*, *ŏprēst*, *rĕprēst*, *rĕtrĭu'd*, and such like.

Words of two sillables that in their last sillable

mayntayne a flat or falling accent, ought to hold their first sillable long, as *rīgŏr, glōrĭe, spīrĭt, fūrĭe, lābŏur*, and the like: *ăny, mănÿ, prĕty, hŏly*, and their like, are excepted.

One obseruation which leades me to iudge of the difference of these dissillables whereof I last spake, I take from the originall monasillable, which if it be graue, as *shāde*, I hold that the first of *shādĭe* must be long, so *trūe, trūlĭe, hāue, hāuĭng, tīre, tīrĭng*.

Words of three sillables for the most part are deriued from words of two sillables, and from them take the quantity of their first sillable, as *flōrĭsh, flōrĭshĭng* long, *hŏlĭe, hŏlĭnes* short, but *mi*, in *mīser* being long, hinders not the first of *mĭsery* to be short, because the sound of the *i* is a little altred.

De, di, and *pro*, in trisillables (the second being short) are long, as *dēsŏlāte, dīlĭgēnt, prōdĭgall*.

Re is euer short, as *rĕmĕdĭe, rĕfĕrēnce, rĕdŏlēnt, rĕuĕrēnd*.

Likewise the first of these trisillables is short, as the first of *bĕnĕfit, gĕnĕrall, hĭdĕous, mĕmŏrĭe, nŭmĕrous, pĕnĕtrāte, sĕpĕrat, tĭmĕrous, vărĭānt, vărĭous*, and so may we esteeme of all that yeeld the like quicknes of sound.

In words of three sillables the quantity of the middle sillable is lightly taken from the last sillable of the originall dissillable, as the last of *dĕuīne*, ending in a graue or long accent, makes the second of *dĕuīnĭng* also long, and so *ēspīe, ēspīĭng, dĕnīe, dĕnīĭng*: contrarywise it falles out if the last of the dissillable beares a flat or falling accent, as *glōrĭe, glōrĭĭng, ĕnuĭe, ēnuĭĭng*, and so forth.

Words of more sillables are eyther borrowed and hold their owne nature, or are likewise deriu'd, and so follow the quantity of their primatiues, or are knowne by their proper accents, or may be easily censured by a iudiciall eare.

All words of two or more sillables ending with a falling accent in *y* or *ye*, as *faīrelĭe, dĕmurelĭe, beawtĭe, pĭttĭe*; or in *ue*, as *vĕrtuĕ, rĕscuĕ*, or in *ow*, as *fŏllŏw, hŏllŏw*, or in *e*, as *parlĕ, Daphnĕ*, or in *a*, as *Mannă*, are naturally short in their last sıllables: neither let any man cauill at this licentiate abbreuiating of sillables, contrary to the custome of the *Latines*, which made all their last sillables that ended in *u* long, but let him consider that our verse of fiue feete, and for the most part but of ten sillables, must equall theirs of sixe feete and of many sillables, and therefore may with sufficient reason aduenture vpon this allowance. Besides, euery man may obserue what an infinite number of sillables both among the *Greekes* and *Romaines* are held as common. But words of two sillables ending with a rising accent in *y* or *ye*, as *denye, descrye*, or in *ue*, as *ensue*, or in *ee*, as *foresee*, or in *oe*, as *forgoe*, are long in their last sillables, vnlesse a vowell begins the next word.

All monasillables that end in a graue accent are euer long, as *wrāth, hāth, thēse, thōse, toōth, soōth, thrōugh, dāy, plāy, feāte, speēde, strīfe, flōw, grōw, shēw*.

The like rule is to be obserued in the last of dissillables, bearing a graue rising sound, as *deuine, delaie, retire, refuse, manure*, or a graue falling sound, as *fortune, pleasure, rampire*.

All such as haue a double consonant lengthning them, as *wārre, bārre, stārre, fūrre, mūrre*, appeare to me rather long then any way short.

There are of these kinds other, but of a lighter sound, that if the word following do begin with a vowell are short, as *doth, though, thou, now, they, two, too, flye, dye true, due, see, are, far, you, thee*, and the like.

These monasillables are alwayes short, as *ă, thĕ, thĭ, shĕ, wĕ, bĕ, hĕ, nŏ, tŏ, gŏ, sŏ, dŏ*, and the like.

But if *i*, or *y*, are ioyn'd at the beginning of a word with any vowell, it is not then held as a vowell, but as a consonant, as *Ielosy, iewce, iade, ioy, Iudas, ye, yet, yel, youth, yoke*. The like is to be obseru'd in *w*, as *winde, wide, wood*: and in all words that begin with *va, ve, vi, vo*, or *vu*, as *vacant, vew, vine, voide*, and *vulture*.

All Monasillables or Polysillables that end in single consonants, either written, or sounded with single consonants, hauing a sharp liuely accent and standing

THE ART OF ENGLISH POESIE

without position of the word following, are short in their last sillable, as *scăb, flĕd, pārtĕd, Gŏd, ŏf, ĭf, bāndŏg, āngŭïsh, sĭck, quĭck, rīuăl, wĭll, pēoplĕ, sĭmplĕ, comĕ, sŏme, hĭm, thĕm, frŏm, sŭmmŏn, thĕn, prŏp, prōspĕr, hōnoŭr, lāboŭr, thĭs, hĭs, spēchĕs, gōddĕsse, pērfĕct, bŭt, whăt, thăt,* and their like.

The last sillable of all words in the plurall number that haue two or more vowels before s, are long, as *vertūes, dutīes, miserīes, fellowēs.*

These rules concerning the quantity of our English sillables I haue disposed as they came next into my memory, others more methodicall, time and practise may produce. In the meane season, as the Grammarians leaue many sillables to the authority of Poets, so do I likewise leaue many to their iudgements; and withall thus conclude, that there is no Art begun and perfected at one enterprise.

SAMUEL DANIEL

(1562–1619)

A Defence of Ryme
Against a Pamphlet entituled "Obseruations in the Art of English Poesie."

Wherein is demonstratively proved, that Ryme is the fittest harmonie of words that comportes with our Language. 1602.

To all the Worthie Louers and learned Professors of Ryme, within his Maiesties Dominions, S: D.

Worthie Gentlemen, about a yeare since, vpon the great reproach giuen to the Professors of Rime, and the vse therof, I wrote a priuate letter, as a defence of mine owne vndertakings in that kinde, to a learned Gentleman a great friend of mine, then in Court. VVhich I did, rather to confirm my selfe in mine owne courses, and to hold him from being wonne from vs, then with any desire to publish the same to the world.

But now, seeing the times to promise a more regarde to the present condition of our writings, in respect of our Soueraignes happy inclination this way; whereby wee are rather to expect an incoragement to go on with what we do, then that any innouation should checke vs, with a shew of what it would do in an other kinde, and yet doe nothing but depraue: I haue now giuen a greater body to the same Argument. And here present it to your view, vnder the patronage of a Noble Earle, who in bloud and nature is interessed to take our parte in this cause, with others, who cannot, I know, but holde deare the monuments that haue beene left vnto the world in this manner of composition. And who I trust will take in good parte this my defence, if not as it is my particular, yet in respect of the cause I vndertake, which I heere inuoke you all to protect.

Sa: D.

To William Herbert Earle of Pembrooke.

The Generall Custome, and vse of Ryme in this kingdome, Noble Lord, hauing beene so long (as if from a Graunt of Nature) held vnquestionable; made me to imagine that it lay altogither out of the way of contradiction, and was become so natural, as we should neuer haue had a thought to cast it off into reproch, or be made to thinke that it ill-became our language. But now I see, when there is opposition made to all things in the world by wordes, wee must nowe at length likewise fall to contend for words themselues; and make a question, whether they be right or not. For we are tolde how that our measures goe wrong, all Ryming is grosse, vulgare, barbarous, which if it be so, we haue lost much labour to no purpose: and for mine owne particular, I cannot but blame the fortune of the times and mine owne Genius that cast me vppon so wrong a course, drawne with the current of custome, and an vnexamined example. Hauing beene first incourag'd or fram'd thereunto by your most Worthy and Honourable Mother, receiuing the first notion for the formall ordering of those compositions at *Wilton*, which I must euer acknowledge to haue beene my best Schoole, and thereof always am to hold a feeling and gratefull Memory. Afterward, drawne farther on by the well-liking and approbation of my worthy Lord, the fosterer of mee and my *Muse*, I aduentured to bestow all my whole powers therein, perceiuing it agreed so well, both with the complexion of the times, and mine owne constitution, as I found not wherein I might better imploy me. But yet now, vpon the great discouery of these new measures, threatning to ouerthrow the whole state of Ryme in this kingdom, I must either stand out to defend, or else be forced to forsake my selfe, and giue ouer all. And though irresolution and a selfe distrust be the most apparent faults of my nature, and that the least checke of reprehension, if it fauour of reason, will as easily shake my resolution as any mans liuing: yet in this case I know not how I am growne more resolued, and before I sinke, willing to examine what those powers of iudgement are, that must beare me downe, and beat me off from the station of my profession, which by the law of nature I am set to defend.

And the rather for that this detractor (whose commendable Rymes albeit now himselfe an enemy to ryme, haue giuen heretofore to the world the best notice of his worth) is a man of faire parts, and good reputation, and therefore the reproach forcibly cast from such a hand may throw downe more at once then the labors of many shall in long time build vp againe, specially vpon the slippery foundation of opinion, and the worlds inconstancy, which knowes not well what it would haue, and :

> *Discit enim citius, meminitque libentius illud*
> *Quod quis deridet quam quod probat & veneratur.*

And he who is thus, become our vnkinde aduersarie, must pardon vs if we be as iealous of our fame and reputation, as hee is desirous of credite by his new-old arte, and must consider that we cannot, in a thing that concernes vs so neere, but haue a feeling of the wrong done, wherein euery Rymer in this vniuersall Iland as well as my selfe, stands interressed. So that if his charitie had equally drawne with his learning hee would haue forborne to procure the enuie of so powerfull a number vpon him, from whom he cannot but expect the returne of a like measure of blame, and onely haue made way to his owne grace, by the proofe of his abilitie, without the disparaging of vs, who would haue bin glad to haue stood quietly by him, & perhaps commended his aduenture, seeing that euermore of one science an other may be borne, & that these Salies made out of the quarter of our set knowledges, are the gallant proffers onely of attemptiue spirits, and commendable though they worke no other effect than make a Brauado : and I know it were *Indecens, & morosum nimis, alienæ industriæ, modum ponere.* We could well haue allowed of his numbers had he not disgraced our Ryme ; Which both Custome and Nature doth most powerfully defend. Custome that is before all Law, Nature that is aboue all Arte. Euery language hath her proper number or measure fitted to vse and delight, which, Custome intertaining by the allowance of the Eare, doth indenize, and make naturall. All verse is but a frame of wordes confinde within certaine measure ; differing from the ordinarie speach, and introduced, the better to expresse mens conceipts, both for delight and memorie. Which frame of wordes consisting of *Rithmus* or *Metrum*, Number or Measure, are disposed into diuers fashions, according to the humour of the Composer and the set of the time; And these *Rhythmi* as *Aristotle* saith are familiar amongst all Nations, and *è naturali & sponte fusa compositione*: And they fall as naturally already in our language as euer Art can make them; being such as the Eare of it selfe doth marshall in their proper roomes, and they of themselues will not willingly be put out of their ranke; and that in such a verse as best comports with the Nature of our language. And for our Ryme (which is an excellencie added to this worke of measure, and a Harmonie, farre happier than any proportion Antiquitie could euer shew vs) dooth adde more grace, and hath more of delight than euer bare numbers, howsoeuer they can be forced to runne in our slow language, can possibly yeeld. Which, whether it be deriu'd of *Rhythmus*, or of *Romance* which were songs the *Bards* & *Druydes* about Rymes vsed, & thereof were caled *Remensi*, as some Italians hold; or howsoeuer, it is likewise number and harmonie of words, consisting of an agreeing sound in the last silables of seuerall verses, giuing both to the Eare an Eccho of a delightfull report & to the Memorie a deeper impression of what is deliuered therein. For as Greeke and Latine verse consists of the number and quantitie of sillables, so doth the English verse of measure and accent. And though it doth not strictly obserue long and short sillables, yet it most religiously respects the accent: and as the short and the long make number, so the Acute and graue accent yeelde harmonie: And harmonie is likewise number, so that the English verse then hath number, measure and harmonie in the best proportion of Musike. Which being more certain & more resounding, works that effect of motion with as happy successe as either the Greek or Latin. And so naturall a melody is it, & so vniuersall as it seems to be generally borne with al the nations of the world, as an hereditary eloquence proper to all mankind. The vniuersallitie argues the generall power of it: for if the Barbarian vse it, then it shews that it swais th'affection of the Barbarian, if ciuil nations practise it, it proues that it works vpon the harts of ciuil nations:

If all, then that it hath a power in nature on all. *Georgieuez de Turcarum moribus*, hath an example of the Turkish Rymes iust of the measure of our verse of eleuen sillables, in feminine Ryme: neuer begotten I am perswaded by any example in *Europe*, but borne no doubt in *Scythia*, and brought ouer *Caucasus* and *Mount Taurus*. The Sclauonian and Arabian tongs acquaint a great part of *Asia* and *Affrique* with it, the Moscouite, Polack, Hungarian, German, Italian, French, and Spaniard vse no other harmonie of words. The Irish, Briton, Scot, Dane, Saxon, English, and all the Inhabiters of this Iland, either haue hither brought, or here found the same in vse. And such a force hath it in nature, or so made by nature, as the Latine numbers notwithstanding their excellencie, seemed not sufficient to satitsfie the eare of the world thereunto accustomed, without this Harmonicall cadence: which made the most learned of all nations labour with exceeding trauaile to bring those numbers likewise vnto it: which many did with that happinesse, as neither their puritie of tongue, nor their materiall contemplations are thereby any way disgraced, but rather deserue to be reuerenced of all gratefull posteritie, with the due regard of their worth. And for *Schola Salerna*, and those *Carmina Prouerbialia*, who finds not therein more precepts for vse, concerning diet, health, and conuersation, then *Cato*, *Theognes*, or all the Greekes and Latines can shew vs in that kinde of teaching: and that in so few words, both for delight to the eare, and the hold of memorie, as they are to be imbraced of all modest readers that studie to know and not to depraue.

Me thinkes it is a strange imperfection, that men should thus ouer-runne the estimation of good things with so violent a censure, as though it must please none else, because it likes not them. Whereas *Oportet arbitratores esse non contradictores eos qui verum iudicaturi sunt*, saith *Arist.* though he could not obserue it himselfe. And milde Charitie tells vs:

——— non egc paucis
Offendor maculis quas aut incuria fudi.
Aut humana parum cauet natura.

For all men haue their errors, and we must take the best of their powers, and leaue the rest as not appertaining vnto vs.

Ill customes are to be left, I graunt it: but I see not howe that can be taken for an ill custome, which nature hath thus ratified, all nations receiued, time so long confirmed, the effects such as it performes those offices of motion for which it is imployed; delighting the eare, stirring the heart, and satisfying the iudgement in such sort as I doubt whether euer single numbers will do in our Climate, if they shew no more worke of wonder then yet we see. And if euer they prooue to become any thing, it must be by the approbation of many ages that must giue them their strength for any operation, or before the world will feele where the pulse, life, and enargie lies, which now we are sure where to haue in our Rymes, whose knowne frame hath those due staies for the minde, those incounters of touch as makes the motion certaine, though the varietie be infinite. Nor will the Generall sorte, for whom we write (the wise being aboue bookes) taste these laboured measures but as an orderly prose when wee haue all done. For this kinde acquaintance and continuall familiaritie euer had betwixt our eare and this cadence, is growne to so intimate a friendship, as it will nowe hardly euer be brought to misse it. For be the verse neuer so good, neuer so full, it seemes not to satisfie nor breede that delight as when it is met and combined with a like sounding accents. Which seemes as the iointure without which it hangs loose, and cannot subsist, but runnes wildely on, like a tedious fancie without a close: suffer then the world to inioy that which it knowes, and what it likes. Seeing that whatsoeuer force of words doth mooue, delight and sway the affections of men, in what Scythian sorte soeuer it be disposed or vttered: that is true number, measure, eloquence, and the perfection of speach: which I said, hath as many shapes as there be tongues or nations in the world, nor can with all the tyrannicall Rules of idle Rhetorique be gouerned otherwise then custome, and present obseruation will allow. And being now the trym, and fashion of the times, to sute a man otherwise cannot but giue a touch of singularity, for when hee hath all done, hee hath but found other clothes to the same body, and peraduenture not so fitting as the former. But could our Aduersary hereby set vp the musicke of our times to a higher note of iudgement and discretion, or could these new lawes of words better our imperfections, it were a happy attempt; but when hereby we shall but as it were change prison, and put off these fetters to receiue others, what haue we gained, as good still to vse ryme and a little reason, as neither ryme nor reason, for no doubt as idle wits will write, in that kinde, as do now in this, imitation wil after, though it breake her necke. *Scribimus indocti doctique poemata passim*. And this multitude of idle writers can be no disgrace to the good, for the same fortune in one proportion or other is proper in a like season to all States in their turne: and the same vnmeasureable confluence of Scriblers hapned, when measures were most in vse among the Romanes, as we finde by this reprehension,

> *Mutauit mentem populus leuis, & calet vno*
> *Scribendi studio, pueri, patrésque seueri,*
> *Fronde comas vincti cœnant, & carmina dictant.*

So that their plentie seemes to haue bred the same waste and contempt as ours doth now, though it had not power to disvalew what was worthy of posteritie, nor keep backe the reputation of excellencies, destined to continue for many ages. For seeing it is matter that satisfies the iudiciall, appeare it in what habite it will, all these pretended proportions of words, howsoeuer placed, can be but words, and peraduenture serue but to embroyle our vnderstanding, whilst seeking to please our eare, we inthrall our iudgement: to delight an exterior sense, wee smoothe vp a weake confused sense, affecting sound to be vnsound, and all to seeme *Seruum pecus*, onely to imitate the Greekes and Latines, whose felicitie, in this kind, might be something to themselues, to whome their owne *idioma* was naturall, but to vs it can yeeld no other commoditie then a sound. We admire them not for their smooth-gliding words, nor their measures, but for their inuentions: which treasure, if it were to be found in Welch, and Irish, we should hold those languages in the same estimation, and they may thanke their sword that made their tongues so famous and vniuersall as they are. For to say truth, their Verse is many times but a confused deliuerer of their excellent conceits, whose scattered limbs we are faine to looke out and ioyne together, to discerne the image of what they represent vnto vs. And euen the Latines, who professe not to be so licentious as the Greekes, shew vs many times examples but of strange crueltie, in torturing and dismembring of wordes in the middest, or disioyning such as naturally should be married and march together, by setting them as farre asunder, as they can possibly stand: that sometimes, vnlesse the kind reader, out of his owne good nature, wil stay them vp by their measure, they will fall downe into flatte prose, and sometimes are no other indeede in their naturall sound: and then againe, when you finde them disobedient to their owne Lawes, you must hold it to be *licentia poetica*, and so dispensable. The striuing to shew their changable measures in the varietie of their Odes, haue beene very painefull no doubt vnto them, and forced them thus to disturbe the quiet streame of their wordes, which by a naturall succession otherwise desire to follow in their due course.

But such affliction doth laboursome curiositie still lay vpon our best delights (which euer must be made strange and variable) as if Art were ordained to afflict Nature, and that we could not goe but in fetters. Euery science, euery profession, must be so wrapt vp in vnnecessary intrications, as if it were not to fashion, but to confound the vnderstanding, which makes me much to distrust man, and feare that our presumption goes beyond our abilitie, and our Curiositie is more than our Iudgement: laboring euer to seeme to be more than we are, or laying greater burthens vpon our mindes, then they are well able to beare, because we would not appeare like other men.

And indeed I haue wished there were not that multiplicitie of Rymes as is vsed by many in Sonets, which yet we see in some so happily to succeed, and hath beene so farre from hindering their inuentions, as it hath begot conceit beyond expectation, and comparable to the best inuentions of the world: for sure in an eminent spirit whome Nature hath fitted for that mysterie, Ryme is no impediment to his conceit, but rather giues him wings to mount and carries him, not out of his course, but as it were beyond his power to a farre happier flight. Al excellencies being sold vs at the hard price of labour, it followes, where we bestow most thereof, we buy the best successe: and Ryme being farre more laborious then loose measures (whatsoeuer is obiected) must needs, meeting with wit and industry, breed greater and worthier effects in our language. So that if our labours haue wrought out a manumission from bondage, and that wee goe at libertie, notwithstanding these ties, wee are no longer the slaues of Ryme, but we make it a most excellent instrument to serue vs. Nor is this certaine limit obserued in Sonnets, any tyrannicall bounding of the conceit, but rather a reducing it in *girum*, and a iust forme, neither too long for the shortest proiect, nor too short for the longest, being but onely imployed for a present passion. For the body of our imagination, being as an vnformed *Chaos* without fashion, without day, if by the diuine power of the spirit it be wrought into an Orbe of order and forme, is it not more pleasing to Nature, that desires a certaintie, and comports not with that which is infinite, to haue these clozes, rather than, not to know where to end, or how farre to goe, especially seeing our passions are often without measure: and wee finde the best of the latines many times, either not concluding, or els otherwise in the end then they began. Besides, is it not most delightfull to see much excellently ordred in a small-roome, or little, gallantly disposed and made to fill vp a space of like capacitie, in such sort, that the one would not appeare so beautifull in a larger circuite, nor the other do well in a lesse: which often we find to be so, according to the powers of nature, in the workeman. And these limited proportions, and rests of Stanzes: consisting of 6. 7. or 8. lines are of that happines, both for the disposition of the matter, the apt planting the sentence where it may best stand to hit, the certaine close of delight with the full body of a iust period well carried, is such, as neither the Greekes or Latines euer attained vnto. For their boundlesse running on, often so confounds the Reader, that hauing once lost himselfe, must either giue off vnsatisfied, or vncertainely cast backe to retriue the escaped sence, and to find way againe into his matter.

Me thinkes we should not so soone yeeld our consents captiue to the authoritie of Antiquitie, vnlesse we saw more reason: all our vnderstandings are not to be built by the square of *Greece* and *Italie*. We are the children of nature as well as they, we are not so placed out of the way of iudgement, but that the same Sunne of Discretion shineth vppon vs, wee haue our portion of the same vertues as well as of the same vices, *Et Catilinam Quocunque in populo videas, quocunque sub axe*. Time and the turne of things bring about these faculties according to the present estimation: and, *Res temporibus non tempora rebus seruire opportet*. So that we must neuer rebell against vse: *Quem penes arbitrium est, & vis & norma loquendi*. It is not the obseruing of *Trochaicques* nor their *Iambicques*, that wil make our writings ought the wiser: All their Poesie, all their Philosophie is nothing, vnlesse we bring the discerning light of conceipt with vs to apply it to vse. It is not bookes, but onely that great booke of the world, and the all-ouerspreading grace of heauen that makes men truely iudiciall. Nor can it be but a touch of arrogant ignorance, to hold this or that nation Barbarous, these or those times grosse, considering how this manifold creature man, wheresoeuer hee stand in the world, hath alwayes some disposition of worth, intertaines the order of societie, affects that which is most in vse, and is eminent in some one thing or other, that fits his humour and the times. The Grecians held all other nations barbarous but themselues, yet *Pirrhus* when he saw the well ordered marching of the Romanes, which made them see their presumptuous errour, could say it

was no barbarous maner of proceeding. The *Gothes*,
Vandales and *Longobards*, whose comming downe like
an inundation ouerwhelmed, as they say, al the glory
of learning in *Europe*, haue yet left vs still their lawes
and customes, as the originalls of most of the prouinciall
constitutions of Christendome; which well considered
with their other courses of gouernement, may serue to
cleere them from this imputation of ignorance. And
though the vanquished neuer yet spake well of the
Conquerour: yet euen thorow the vnsound couerings
of malediction appeare those monuments of trueth, as
argue wel their worth and proues them not without
iudgement, though without Greeke and Latine.

Will not experience confute vs, if wee shoulde say
the state of *China*, which neuer heard of Anapestiques,
Trochies, and Tribracques, were grosse, barbarous, and
vnciuile? And is it not a most apparant ignorance,
both of the succession of learning in *Europe*, and the
generall course of things, *to say, that all lay pittifully
deformed in those lacke-learning times from the declining
of the Romane Empire, till the light of the Latine tongue
was reuiued by* Rewcline, Erasmus *and* Moore. When
for three hundred yeeres before them about the comming downe of *Tamburlaine* into *Europe*, *Franciscus
Petrarcha* (who then no doubt likewise found whom to
imitate) shewed all the best notions of learning, in that
degree of excellencie, both in Latin, Prose and Verse,
and in the vulgare Italian, as all the wittes of posteritie
haue not yet much ouer-matched him in all kindes to
this day: his great Volumes written in Moral Philosophie, shew his infinite reading, and most happy power
of disposition: his twelue Æglogues, his *Affrica* containing nine Bookes of the last Punicke warre, with his
three Bookes of Epistles in Latine verse, shew all the
transformations of wit and inuention, that a Spirite
naturally borne to the inheritance of Poetrie & iudiciall
knowledge could expresse: All which notwithstanding
wrought him not that glory & fame with his owne
Nation, as did his Poems in Italian, which they esteeme
aboue al whatsoeuer wit could haue inuented in any
other forme then wherein it is: which questionles they

wil not change with the best measures, Greeks or Latins can shew them; howsoeuer our Aduersary imagines. Nor could this very same innouation in Verse, begun amongst them by *C. Tolomæi*, but die in the attempt, and was buried as soone as it came borne, neglected as a prodigious & vnnaturall issue amongst them: nor could it neuer induce *Tasso* the wonder of *Italy*, to write that admirable Poem of *Ierusalem*, comparable to the best of the ancients, in any other forme then the accustomed verse. And with *Petrarch* liued his scholer *Boccacius*, and neere about the same time, *Iohannis Rauenensis*, and from these *tanquam ex equo Troiano*, seemes to haue issued all those famous Italian Writers, *Leonardus Aretinus, Laurentius Valla, Poggius, Blondus*, and many others. Then *Emanuel Chrysolaras* a Constantinopolitan gentleman, renowmed for his learning and vertue, being imployed by *Iohn Paleologus* Emperour of the East, to implore the ayde of christian Princes, for the succouring of perishing *Greece*: and vnderstanding in the meane time, how *Baiazeth* was taken prisoner by *Tamburlan*, and his country freed from danger, stayed still at *Venice*, and there taught the Greeke tongue, discontinued before, in these parts the space of seauen hundred yeeres. Him followed *Bessarion, George Trapezantius, Theodore Gaza*, & others, transporting Philosophie beaten by the Turke out of *Greece* into christendome. Hereupon came that mightie confluence of Learning in these parts, which returning, as it were *per postliminium*, and heere meeting then with the new inuented stampe of Printing, spread it selfe indeed in a more vniuersall sorte then the world euer heeretofore had it. When *Pomponius Lætus, AEneas Syluius, Angelus Politianus, Hermolaus Barbarus, Iohannes Picus de Mirandula* the miracle & Phœnix of the world, adorned *Italie*, and wakened vp other Nations likewise with this desire of glory, long before it brought foorth, *Rewclen, Erasmus*, and *Moore*, worthy men I confesse, and the last a great ornament to this land, and a Rymer. And yet long before all these, and likewise with these, was not our Nation behind in her portion of spirite and worthinesse, but concurrent with the best of all this lettered worlde: witnesse venerable *Bede*, that flourished aboue a thousand yeeres since: *Aldelmus Durotelmus* that liued in the yeere 739. of whom we finde this commendation registred. *Omnium Poetarum sui temporis facilè primus, tantæ eloquentiæ, maiestatis & eruditionis homo fuit, vt nunquam satis admirari possim vnde illi in tam barbara ac rudi ætate facundia accreuerit, vsque adeo omnibus numeris tersa, elegans & rotunda, versus edidit cum antiquitate de palma contendentes.* Witnesse *Iosephus Deuonius*, who wrote *de bello Troiano*, in so excellent manner, and so neere resembling Antiquitie, as Printing his Worke beyond the Seas, they haue ascribed it to *Cornelius Nepos*, one of the Ancients.

What should I name *Walterus Mape, Gulielmus Nigellus, Geruasius Tilburiensis, Bracton, Bacon, Ockam*, and an infinite Catalogue of excellent men, most of them liuing about foure hundred yeares since, and haue left behinde them monuments of most profound iudgement and learning in all sciences. So that it is but the clowds gathered about our owne iudgement that makes vs thinke all other ages wrapt vp in mists, and the great distance betwixt vs, that causes vs to imagine men so farre off, to be so little in respect of our selues. We must not looke vpon the immense course of times past, as men ouer-looke spacious and wide countries, from off high Mountaines and are neuer the neere to iudge of the true Nature of the soyle, or the particular syte and face of those territories they see. Nor must we thinke, viewing the superficiall figure of a region in a Mappe that wee know strait the fashion and place as it is. Or reading an Historie (which is but a Mappe of men, and dooth no otherwise acquaint vs with the true Substance of Circumstances, than a superficiall Card dooth the Sea-man with a Coast neuer seene, which alwayes prooues other to the eye than the imagination forecast it) that presently wee know all the world, and can distinctly iudge of times, men and maners, iust as they were. When the best measure of man is to be taken by his owne foote, bearing euer the neerest proportion to himselfe, and is neuer so farre different and vnequall in his powers, that he hath all in perfection at one time, and nothing at an other. The distribution of giftes are vniuersall, and all seasons hath them in some sort. We must not thinke, but that there were *Scipioes, Cæsars, Catoes* and *Pompeies*, borne elsewhere then at *Rome*, the rest of the world hath euer had them in the same degree of nature, though not of state. And it is our weakenesse that makes vs mistake, or misconceiue in these deliniations of men the true figure of their worth. And our passion and beliefe is so apt to leade vs beyond truth, that vnlesse we try them by the iust compasse of humanitie, and as they were men, we shall cast their figures in the ayre when we should make their models vpon Earth. It is not the contexture of words, but the effects of Action that giues glory to the times: we finde they had *mercurium in pectore* though not *in lingua*, and in all ages, though they were not Ciceronians, they knew the Art of men, which onely is, *Ars Artium*, the great gift of heauen, and the chiefe grace and glory on earth, they had the learning of Gouernement, and ordring their State, Eloquence inough to shew their iudgements. And it seemes the best times followed *Lycurgus* councell: *Literas ad vsum saltem discebant, reliqua omnis disciplina erat, vt pulchre parerent vt labores perferrent &c.* Had not vnlearned *Rome* laide the better foundation, and built the stronger frame of an admirable state, eloquent *Rome* had confounded it vtterly, which we saw, ranne the way of all confusion, the plaine course of dissolution in her greatest skill: and though she had not power to vndoe her selfe, yet wrought she so that she cast her selfe quite away from the glory of a common-wealth, and fell vpon that forme of state she euer most feared and abhorred of all other: and then scarse was there seene any shadowe of pollicie vnder her first Emperours, but the most horrible and grosse confusion that could bee conceued, notwithstanding it stil indured, preseruing not only a Monarchie, locked vp in her own limits, but therewithall held vnder her obedience, so many Nations so farre distant, so ill affected, so disorderly commanded & vniustly conquerd, as it is not to be attributed to any other fate but to the first frame of that common-wealth, which was so strongly ioynted and with such infinite combinations interlinckt, as one naile or other euer held vp the Maiestie thereof. There is but one learning, which *omnes gentes habent scriptum in cordibus suis*, one and the selfe-same spirit that worketh in all. We haue but one body of Iustice, one body of Wisedome throughout the whole world, which is but apparaled according to the fashion of euery nation.

Eloquence and gay wordes are not of the Substance of wit, it is but the garnish of a nice time, the Ornaments that doe but decke the house of a State, *& imitatur publicos mores:* Hunger is as well satisfied with meat serued in pewter as siluer. Discretion is the best measure, the rightest foote in what habit soeuer it runne. *Erasmus, Rewcline* and *More*, brought no more wisdome into the world with all their new reuiued wordes then we finde was before, it bred not a profounder Diuine than Saint *Thomas*, a greater Lawyer than *Bartolus*, a more accute Logician than *Scotus*: nor are the effects of all this great amasse of eloquence so admirable or of that consequence, but that *impexa illa antiquitas* can yet compare with them. Let vs go no further, but looke vpon the wonderfull Architecture of this state of *England*, and see whether they were deformed times, that could giue it such a forme. Where there is no one the least piller of Maiestie, but was set with most profound iudgement and borne vp with the iust conueniencie of Prince and people. No Court of Iustice, but laide by the Rule and Square of Nature, and the best of the best commonwealths that euer were in the world. So strong and substantial, as it hath stood against al the storms of factions, both of beliefe & ambition, which so powerfully beat vpon it, and all the tempestuous alterations of humorous times whatsoeuer. Being continually in all ages furnisht with spirites fitte to maintaine the maiestie of her owne greatnes, and to match in an equall concurrencie all other kingdomes round about her with whome it had to incounter. But this innouation, like a Viper, must euer make way into the worlds opinion, thorow the bowelles of her owne breeding, & is alwayes borne with reproch in her mouth; the disgracing others is the best grace it can put on, to winne reputation of wit, and yet is it neuer so wise as it would seeme, nor doth the world euer get so much by it, as it imagineth: which being so often deceiued, and seeing it neuer performes so much as it promises, me thinkes men should neuer giue more credite vnto it. For, let vs change neuer so often, wee can not change man, our imperfections must still runne on with vs And therefore the wiser Nations haue taught menne alwayes to vse, *Moribus legibusque presentibus etiamsi deteriores sint.* The Lacedemonians, when a Musitian, thinckіng to winne him-selfe credite by his new inuention, and be before his fellowes, had added one string more to his Crowde, brake his fiddle, and banished him the Cittie, holding the Innouator, though in the least things, dangerous to a publike societie. It is but a fantastike giddinesse to forsake the way of other men, especially where it lies tollerable: *Vbi nunc est respublica, ibi simus potius quam dum illam veterem sequimur, simus in nulla.* But shal we not tend to perfection? Yes, and that euer best by going on in the course we are in, where we haue aduantage, being so farre onward, of him that is but now setting forth. For we shall neuer proceede, if wee be euer beginning, nor arriue at any certayne Porte, sayling with all windes that blow: *Non conualescit planta quæ sæpius transfertur*, and therefore let vs hold on in the course wee haue vndertaken, and not still be wandring. Perfection is not the portion of man, and if it were, why may wee not as well get to it this way as an other? and suspect these great vndertakers, lest they haue conspired with enuy to betray our proceedings, and put vs by the honor of our attempts, with casting vs backe vpon an other course, of purpose to ouerthrow the whole action of glory when we lay the fairest for it, and were so neere our hopes? I thanke God that I am none of these great Schollers, if thus their hie knowledges doe but giue them more eyes to looke out into vncertaintie and confusion, accounting my selfe, rather beholding to my ignorance, that hath set me in so lowe an vnder-roome of conceipt with other men, and hath giuen me as much distrust, as it hath done hope, daring not aduenture to goe alone, but plodding on the plaine tract I finde beaten by Custome and the Time, contenting me with what I see in vse. And surely mee thinkes these great wittes should rather seeke to adorne, than to disgrace the present, bring something to it, without taking from it what it hath. But it is euer the misfortune of Learning, to be wounded by her owne hand. *Stimulos dat emula virtus*, and when there is not abilitie to match what is, malice wil finde out ingines, either to disgrace or ruine it, with a peruerse incounter of some new impression: and which is the greatest misery, it must euer proceed from the powers of the best reputation, as if the greatest spirites were ordained to indanger the worlde, as the grosse are to dishonour it, and that we were to expect *ab optimis periculum, à pessimis dedecus publicum.* Emulation the strongest pulse that beates in high mindes, is oftentimes a winde, but of the worst effect: For whilst the Soule comes disappoynted of the obiect it wrought on, it presently forges an other, and euen cozins it selfe, and crosses all the world, rather than it wil stay to be vnder hir desires, falling out with all it hath, to flatter and make faire that which it would haue. So that it is the ill successe of our longings that with *Xerxes* makes vs to whippe the Sea, and send a cartel of defiance to mount *Athos:* and the fault laide vpon others weakenesse, is but a presumptuous opinion of our owne strength, who must not seeme to be maistered. But had our Aduersary taught vs by his owne proceedings, this way of perfection, and therein fram'd vs a Poeme of that excellencie as should haue put downe all, and beene the maisterpeece of these times, we should all haue admired him. But to depraue the present forme of writing, and to bring vs nothing but a few loose and vncharitable Epigrammes, and yet would make vs belieue those numbers were come to raise the glory of our language, giueth vs cause to suspect the performance, and to examine whether this new Arte, *constat sibi,* or, *aliquid sit dictum quod non sit dictum prius.*

First we must heere imitate the Greekes and Latines, and yet we are heere shewed to disobey them, euen in their owne numbers and quantities: taught to produce what they make short, and make short what they produce: made beleeue to be shewd measures in that forme we haue not seene, and no such matter: tolde that heere is the perfect Art of versifying, which in conclusion is yet confessed to be vnperfect, as if our Aduersary to be opposite to vs, were become vnfaithfull to himselfe, and seeking to leade vs out of the way of reputation, hath aduentured to intricate and confound him in his owne courses, running vpon most vn-euen groundes, with imperfect rules, weake proofes, and vnlawfull lawes. Whereunto the world, I am perswaded, is not so vnreasonable as to subscribe, considering the vniust authoritie of the Law-giuer. For who hath constituted him to be the *Radamanthus* thus to torture sillables, and adiudge them their perpetuall doome, setting his *Theta* or marke of condemnation vppon them, to indure the appoynted sentence of his crueltie, as hee shall dispose. As though there were that disobedience in our wordes, as they would not be ruled or stand in order without so many intricate Lawes, which would argue a great peruersenesse amongst them, according to that, *in pessima republica plurimæ leges*: or, that they were so farre gone from the quiet freedome of nature, that they must thus be brought backe againe by force. And now in what case were this poore state of words, if in like sorte another tyrant the next yeere should arise and abrogate these lawes and ordaine others cleane contrary according to his humor, and say that they were onely right, the others vniust, what disturbance were there here, to whome should we obey? Were it not farre better to hold vs fast to our old custome, than to stand thus distracted with vncertaine Lawes, wherein Right shal haue as many faces as it pleases Passion to make it, that wheresoeuer mens affections stand, it shall still looke that way. What trifles doth our vnconstant curiositie cal vp to contend for, what colours are there laid vpon indifferent things to make them seeme other then they are, as if it were but only to intertaine contestation amongst men; who standing according to the prospectiue of their owne humour, seeme to see the selfe same things to appeare otherwise to them, than either they doe to other, or are indeede in themselues, being but all one in nature. For what a doe haue we heere, what strange precepts of Arte about the framing of an Iambique verse in our language, which when all is done, reaches not by a foote, but falleth out to be the plaine ancient verse consisting of tenne sillables or fiue feete, which hath euer beene vsed amongest vs time out of minde. And for all this cunning and counterfeit name can or will be any other in nature then it hath beene euer heretofore: and this new *Dimeter* is but the halfe of this verse diuided in two, and no other then the *Cæsura* or breathing place in the middest thereof, and therefore it had bene as good to haue put two lines in one, but only to make them seeme diuerse. Nay it had beene much better for the true English reading and pronouncing thereof, without violating the accent, which now our Aduersarie hath heerein most vnkindely doone: for, being, as wee are to sound it, according to our English March, we must make a rest, and raise the last sillable, which falles out very vnnaturall in *Desolate, Funerall, Elizabeth, Prodigall*, and in all the rest sauing the Monosillables. Then followes the English *Trochaicke*, which is saide to bee a simple verse, and so indeede it is, being without Ryme; hauing here no other grace then that in sound it runnes like the knowne measure of our former ancient Verse, ending (as we terme it according to the French) in a feminine foote, sauing that it is shorter by one sillable at the beginning, which is not much missed, by reason it falles full at the last. Next comes the *Elegiacke*, being the fourth kinde, and that likewise is no other then our old accustomed measure of fiue feete, if there be any difference, it must be made in the reading, and therein wee must stand bound to stay where often we would not, and sometimes either breake the accent, or the due course of the word. And now for the other foure kinds of numbers, which are to be employed for *Odes*, they are either of the same measure, or such as haue euer beene familiarly vsed amongst vs. So that of all these eight seuerall kindes of new promised numbers you see what we haue. Onely what was our owne before, and the same but apparelled in forraine Titles, which had they come in their kinde and naturall attire of Ryme, wee should neuer haue suspected that they had affected to be other, or sought to degenerate into strange manners, which now we see was the cause why they were turned out of their proper habite, and brought in as Aliens, onely to induce men to admire them as farre-commers. But see the power of Nature, it is not all the artificiall couerings of wit that can hide their natiue and originall condition which breakes out thorow the strongest bandes of affectation, and will be it selfe, doe Singularitie what it can. And as for those imagined quantities of sillables, which haue bin euer held free and indifferent in our language, who can inforce vs to take knowledge of them, being *in nullius verba iurati*, & owing fealty to no forraine inuention; especially in such a case where there is no necessitie in Nature, or that it imports either the matter or forme, whether it be so, or otherwise. But euery Versifier that wel obserues his worke, findes in our language, without all these vnnecessary precepts, what numbers best fitte the Nature of her Idiome, and the proper places destined to such accents, as she will not let in, to any other roomes then into those for which they were borne. As for example, you cannot make this fall into the right sound of a Verse.

None thinkes reward rendred worthy his worth:

vnlesse you thus misplace the accent vppon *Rendrèd* and *Worthìe*, contrary to the nature of these wordes: which sheweth that two feminine numbers (or Trochies, if so you wil call them) will not succeede in the third and fourth place of the Verse. And so likewise in this case:

Though Death doth consume, yet Virtue preserues,

it will not be a Verse, though it hath the iust sillables, without the same number in the second, and the altering of the fourth place, in this sorte:

Though Death doth ruine, Virtue yet preserues.

Againe, who knowes not that we cannot kindely answere a feminine number with a masculine Ryme, or (if you will so terme it) a *Trochei* with a *Sponde*, as *Weakenes* with *Confesse*, *Nature* and *Indure*, onely for that thereby wee shall wrong the accent, the chiefe Lord and graue Gouernour of Numbers. Also you cannot in a Verse of foure feete, place a *Trochei* in the first, without the like offence, as,

Yearely out of his watry Cell,

for so you shall sound it *Yearelié* which is vnnaturall. And other such like obseruations vsually occurre, which Nature and a iudiciall eare, of themselues teach vs readily to auoyde.

But now for whom hath our Aduersary taken all this paines? For the Learned, or for the Ignorant, or for himselfe, to shew his owne skill? If for the Learned, it was to no purpose, for euerie Grammarian in this land hath learned his *Prosodia*, and alreadie knowes all this Arte of Numbers: if for the Ignorant, it was vaine: For if they become Versifiers, wee are like to haue leane Numbers, instede of fat Ryme: and if *Tully* would haue his Orator skilld in all the knowledges appertaining to God and man, what should they haue, who would be a degree aboue Orators? Why then it was to shew his owne skill, and what himselfe had obserued: so he might well haue done, without doing wrong to the fame of the liuing, and wrong to *England*, in seeking to lay reproach vppon her natiue ornaments, and to turne the faire streame and full course of her accents, into the shallow current of a lesse vncertaintie, cleane out of the way of her knowne delight. And I had thought it could neuer haue proceeded from the pen of a Scholler (who sees no profession free from the impure mouth of the scorner) to say the reproach of others idle tongues is the curse of Nature vpon us, when it is rather her curse vpon him, that knowes not how to vse his tongue. What, doth he think himselfe is now gotten so farre out of the way of contempt, that his numbers are gone beyond the reach of obloquie, and that how friuolous, or idle soeuer they shall runne, they shall be protected from disgrace, as though that light rymes and light numbers did not weigh all alike in the graue opinion of the wise. And that it is not Ryme, but our ydle Arguments that hath brought downe to so base a reckning, the price and estimation of writing in this kinde. When the few good things of this age, by comming together in one throng and presse with the many bad, are not discerned from them, but ouerlooked with them, and all taken to be alike. But when after-times shall make a quest of inquirie, to examine the best of this Age, peraduenture there will be found in the now contemned recordes of Ryme, matter not vnfitting the grauest Diuine, and seuerest Lawyer in this kingdome. But these things must haue the date of Antiquitie, to make them reuerend and authentical[1]: For euer in the collation of Writers, men rather weigh their age then their merite, *& legunt priscos cum reuerentia, quando coetaneos non possunt sine inuidia.* And let no writer in Ryme be any way discouraged in his endeuour by this braue allarum, but rather animated to bring vp all the best of their powers, and charge withall the strength of nature and industrie vpon contempt, that the shew of their reall forces may turne backe insolencie into her owne holde. For, be sure that innouation neuer workes any ouerthrow, but vpon the aduantage of a carelesse idlenesse. And let this make vs looke the better to our feete, the better to our matter, better to our maners. Let the Aduersary that thought to hurt vs, bring more profit and honor, by being against vs, then if he had stoode still on our side. For that (next to the awe of heauen) the best reine, the strongst hand to make men keepe their way, is that which their enemy beares vpon them: and let this be the benefite wee make by being oppugned, and the meanes to redeeme backe the good opinion, vanitie and idlenesse haue suffered to be wonne from vs; which, nothing but substance and matter can effect, for,

Scribendi rectè sapere est & principium & fons.

When we heare Musicke, we must be in our eare, in

[1] *Simplicius longè posita miramur.*

the vtter-roome of sense, but when we intertaine iudgement, we retire into the cabinet and innermost withdrawing chamber of the soule: And it is but as Musicke for the eare,

Verba sequi fidibus modulanda Latinis.

but it is a worke of power for the soule.

Numerósque modósque ediscere vitæ.

The most iudiciall and worthy spirites of this Land are not so delicate, or will owe so much to their eare, as to rest vppon the out-side of wordes, and be intertained with sound: seeing that both Number, Measure, and Ryme, is but as the ground or seate, whereupon is raised the work that commends it, and which may be easily at the first found out by any shallow conceipt: as wee see some fantasticke to beginne a fashion, which afterward grauity it selfe is faine to put on, because it will not be out of the weare of other men, and *Recti apud nos locum tenet error vbi publicus factus est.* And power and strength that can plant itselfe any where, hauing built within this compasse, and reard it of so high a respect, wee now imbrace it as the fittest dwelling for our inuention, and haue thereon bestowed all the substance of our vnderstanding to furnish it as it is: and therefore heere I stand foorth, onelie to make good the place we haue thus taken vp, and to defend the sacred monuments erected therein, which containe the honour of the dead, the fame of the liuing, the glory of peace, and the best power of our speach, and wherin so many honorable spirits haue sacrificed to Memorie their dearest passions, shewing by what diuine influence they haue beene moued, and vnder what starres they liued.

But yet now notwithstanding all this which I haue heere deliuered in the defence of Ryme, I am not so farre in loue with mine owne mysterie, or will seeme so froward, as to bee against the reformation, and the better setling these measures of ours. Wherein there be many things, I could wish were more certaine and better ordered, though my selfe dare not take vpon me to be a teacher therein, hauing so much neede to learne of others. And I must confesse, that to mine owne eare, those continuall cadences of couplets vsed in long and continued Poemes, are very tyresome, and vnpleasing, by reason that still, me thinks, they runne on with a sound of one nature, and a kinde of certaintie which stuffs the delight rather then intertaines it. But yet notwithstanding, I must not out of mine owne daintinesse, condemne this kinde of writing, which peraduenture to another may seeme most delightfull, and many worthy compositions we see to haue passed with commendation in that kinde. Besides, me thinkes sometimes, to beguile the eare, with a running out, and passing ouer the Ryme, as no bound to stay vs in the line where the violence of the matter will breake thorow, is rather gracefull then otherwise. Wherein I finde my *Homer-Lucan*, as if he gloried to seeme to haue no bounds, albeit hee were confined within his measures, to be in my conceipt most happy. For so thereby, they who care not for Verse or Ryme, may passe it ouer without taking notice thereof, and please themselues with a well-measured Prose. And I must confesse my Aduersary hath wrought this much vpon me, that I thinke a Tragedie would indeede best comporte with a blank Verse, and dispence with Ryme, sauing in the *Chorus* or where a sentence shall require a couplet. And to auoyde this ouerglutting the eare with that alwayes certaine, and ful incounter of Ryme, I haue assaid in some of my Epistles to alter the vsuall place of meeting, and to sette it further off by one Verse, to trie how I could disuse my owne eare and to ease it of this continuall burthen, which indeede seemes to surcharge it a little too much, but as yet I cannot come to please my selfe therein: this alternate or crosse Ryme holding still the best place in my affection.

Besides, to me this change of number in a Poem of one nature fits not so wel, as to mixe vncertainly, feminine Rymes with masculine, which, euer since I was warned of that deformitie by my kinde friend and countriman Maister *Hugh Samford*, I haue alwayes so auoyded it, as there are not aboue two couplettes in that kinde in all my Poem of the Ciuill warres: and I would willingly if I coulde, haue altered it in all the rest, holding feminine Rymes to be fittest for Ditties, and either to be set certaine, or else by themselues. But in these things, I say, I dare not take vpon mee to teach that they ought to be so, in respect my selfe holdes them to be so, or that I thinke it right; for indeede there is no right in these things that are continually in a wandring motion, carried with the violence of our vncertaine likings, being but onely the time that giues them their power. For if this right, or truth, should be no other thing then that wee make it, we shall shape it into a thousand figures, seeing this excellent painter Man, can so well lay the colours which himselfe grindes in his owne affections, as that hee will make them serue for any shadow, and any counterfeit. But the greatest hinderer to our proceedings, and the reformation of our errours, is this Selfe-loue, whereunto we Versifiers are euer noted to be especially subiect; a disease of all other, the most dangerous, and incurable, being once seated in the spirits, for which there is no cure, but onely by a spirituall remedy. *Multos puto, ad sapientiam potuisse peruenire, nisi putassent se peruenisse:* and this opinion of our sufficiencie makes so great a cracke in our iudgement, as it wil hardly euer holde any thing of worth. *Cæcus amor sui*, and though it would seeme to see all without it, yet certainely it discernes but little within. For there is not the simplest writer that will euer tell himselfe, he doth ill, but as if he were the parasite onely to sooth his owne doings, perswades him that his lines can not but please others, which so much delight himselfe:

> *Suffenus est quisque sibi.* —— *neque idem vnquam.*
> *Æque est beatus, ac poema cum scribit,*
> *Tam gaudet in se tamque se ipse miratur.*

And the more to shew that he is so, we shall see him euermore in all places, and to all persons repeating his owne compositions: and,

> *Quem vero arripuit, tenet occiditque legendo.*

A DEFENCE OF RYME

Next to this deformitie stands our affectation, wherein we always bewray our selues to be both vnkinde, and vnnaturall to our owne natiue language, in disguising or forging strange or vnvsuall wordes, as if it were to make our verse seeme an other kind of speach out of the course of our vsuall practise, displacing our wordes, or inuesting new, onely vpon a singularitie: when our owne accustomed phrase, set in the due place, would expresse vs more familiarly and to better delight, than all this idle affectation of antiquitie, or nouveltie can euer doe. And I can not but wonder at the strange presumption of some men that dare so audaciously aduenture to introduce any whatsoeuer forraine wordes, be they neuer so strange; and of themselues as it were, without a Parliament, without any consent, or allowance, establish them as Free-denizens in our language. But this is but a Character of that perpetuall reuolution which wee see to be in all things that neuer remaine the same, and we must heerein be content to submit our selues to the law of time, which in few yeeres wil make al that, for which we now contend, *Nothing*.

BEN JONSON

(1573–1637)

POETS AND POETRY.

From the "Discoveries upon Men and Matter."

The "Discoveries" were first published after Jonson's death, in 1641. They contain many scattered references to poetry; the passage that follows well represents Ben Jonson's sturdy feeling for the art of poetry, and for his fellow-poets.

What is a Poet?

A POET is that which by the Greeks is call'd κὰτ' ἐξοχήν, ὁ ποιητής, a Maker, or a fainer: his Art, an Art of imitation or faining; expressing the life of man in fit measure, numbers, and harmonye, according to Aristotle; from the word ποιεῖν, which signifies to make or fayne. Hence hee is called a Poet, not hee which writeth in measure only, but that fayneth and formeth a fable, and writes things like the truth. For the Fable and Fiction is, as it were, the forme and Soule of any Poeticall work or Poeme.

What meane you by a Poeme?

A Poeme is not alone any worke or composition of the Poets in many or few verses; but even one alone verse sometimes makes a perfect Poeme. As when Æneas[1] hangs up and consecrates the arms of Abas with this inscription:—

"Æneas hæc de Danais victoribus arma."

And calls it a Poeme or *Carmen*. Such are those in Martiall[2]:—

"Omnia, Castor, emis: sic fiet, ut omnia vendas."

---

[1] Virgilius Æneid, lib. 3.   [2] Martiall, lib. 8, epig. 19.

And—
> "Pauper videri Cinna vult, et est pauper."

So were Horace his odes call'd *Carmina*, his Lirik, Songs. And Lucretius designes a whole book in his sixt :—

> "Quod in primo quoque carmine claret."

And anciently all the Oracles were call'd *Carmina*; or whatever sentence was express'd, were it much or little, it was called an Epick, Dramatick, Lirik, Elegiake, or Epigrammatike Poeme.[1]

But how differs a Poeme from what wee call Poesy?

A Poeme, as I have told you, is the work of the Poet; the end and fruit of his labour and studye. Poesy is his skill or Crafte of making; the very Fiction it selfe, the reason or forme of the work. And these three voices differ, as the thing done, the doing, and the doer; the thing fain'd, the faining, and the fainer; so the Poeme, the Poesy, and the Poet. Now the Poesy is the habit or the Art; nay, rather the Queene of Arts, which had her Original from heaven, received thence from the 'Ebrewes, and had in prime estimation with the Greeks transmitted to the Latines and all nations that profess'd Civility. The study of it (if wee will trust Aristotle) offers to mankinde a certain rule and Patterne of living well and happily, disposing us to all Civill offices of Society. If wee will believe Tully, it nourisheth and instructeth our youth, delights our Age, adornes our prosperity, comforts our Adversity, entertaines us at home, keepes us company abroad, travailes with us, watches, devides the times of our earnest and sports, shares in our Country recesses and recreations; insomuch as the wisest and best learned have thought her the absolute Mistresse of manners and neerest of kin to Vertue. And wheras they entitle Philosophy to bee a rigid and austere Poesie, they have, on the contrary, stiled Poesy a dulcet and gentle philosophy, which leades on and guides us by the hand to action with a

[1] Epicum, Dramaticum, Liricum, Elegiacum, Epigrammat.

ravishing delight and incredible Sweetnes. But before wee handle the kindes of Poems, with their special differences, or make court to the Art itselfe, as a mistresse, I would leade you to the knowledge of our Poet by a perfect information what he is or should bee by nature, by exercise, by imitation, by Studie, and so bring him downe through the disciplines of Grammar, Logicke, Rhetoricke, and the Ethicks, adding somewhat out of all, peculiar to himselfe, and worthy of your admittance or reception.

1. *Ingenium.*—First, wee require in our Poet or maker (for that Title our Language affordes him elegantly with the Greeke) a goodnes of naturall wit. For whereas all other arts consist of doctrine and precepts, the Poet must be able by nature and instinct to pour out the Treasure of his minde, and as Seneca saith, *Aliquando secundum Anacreontem insanire jucundum esse;* by which hee understands the Poeticall Rapture. And according to that of Plato, *Frustra Poeticas fores sui compos pulsavit.* And of Aristotle, *Nullum magnum ingenium sine mixturâ dementiæ fuit. Nec potest grande aliquid, et supra cœteros loqui, nisi mota mens.* Then it riseth higher, as by a devine Instinct, when it contemnes common and knowne conceptions. It utters somewhat above a mortall mouth. Then it gets aloft and flies away with his Ryder, whether, before, it was doubtful to ascend. This the Poets understood by their Helicon, Pegasus, or Parnassus; and this made Ovid to boast,

"Est, Deus in nobis, agitante calescimus illo:
Sedibus æthereis spiritus ille venit."

And Lipsius to affirm, *Scio, Poetam neminem præstantem fuisse, sine parte quadam uberiore divinæ auræ.* And hence it is that the comming up of good Poets (for I mind not mediocres or *imos*) is so thinne and rare among us. Every beggerly corporation affoords the State a mayor or two bailiffs yearly; but *Solus rex, aut poeta, non quotannis nascitur.*

2. *Exercitatio.*—To this perfection of nature in our Poet, wee require Exercise of those parts, and frequent.

If his wit will not arrive soddainly at the dignitie of the
Ancients, let him not yet fall out with it, quarrell, or be
over hastily angry; offer, to turne it away from study in
a humor, but come to it againe upon better cogitation;
try another time, with labour. If then it succeed not,
cast not away the Quills yet, nor scratch the Waine-
scott, beate not the poor Deske, but bring all to the
forge, and file againe; tourne it anewe. There is
no statute Law of the Kingdome bidds you bee a poet
against your will; or the first quarter. If it come, in
a yeare or two, it is well. The common Rymers powre
forth Verses, such as they are, *ex tempore;* but there
never come from them one Sense, worth the life of a
Day. A Rymer, and a Poet, are two things. It is
said of the incomparable Virgil, that he brought forth
his verses like a Beare, and after form'd them with
licking. Scaliger, the father, writes it of him, that he
made a quantitie of verses in the morning, which afore
night hee reduced to a lesse number. But, that which
Valerius Maximus hath left recorded of Euripides, the
tragicke Poet, his answer to Alcestis, another Poet, is as
memorable, as modest; who, when it was told to
Alcestis that Euripides had in three daies brought
forth, but three verses, and those with some difficultie,
and throwes, Alcestis, glorying hee could with ease
have sent forth a hundred in the space, Euripides
roundly reply'd, "Like enough; but here is the difference: thy verses will not last those three daies, mine
will to all time." Which was, as to tell him; he could
not write a verse. I have met many of these rattles,
that made a noyse and buz'de. They had their humme,
and no more. Indeed, things wrote with labour deserve
to be so read, and will last their Age.

3. *Imitatio.*—The third requisite in our Poet, or
Maker, is Imitation, to bee able to convert the substance or Riches of another Poet to his owne use. To
make choice of one excellent man above the rest, and
so to follow him, till he grow very He, or so like him,
as the Copie may be mistaken for the Principal. Not
as a creature that swallowes what it takes in crude,
raw, or undigested, but that feedes with an Appetite,

and hath a Stomache to concoct, devide, and turne all into nourishment. Not to imitate servilely, as Horace saith, and catch at vices for vertue; but to draw forth out of the best and choicest flowers, with the Bee, and turn all into honey, worke it into one relish and savour; make our Imitation sweet; observe how the best writers have imitated, and follow them. How Virgil and Statius have imitated Homer; how Horace, Archilochus; how, Alcæus, and the other Liricks; and so of the rest.

4. *Lectio.*—But that which wee especially require in him is an exactnesse of Studie and multiplicity of reading, which maketh a full man, not alone enabling him to know the History or Argument of a Poeme and to report it, but so to master the matter and Stile, as to shew hee knowes how to handle, place, or dispose of either with Elegancie when need shall bee. And not thinke hee can leape forth suddainely a poet by dreaming hee hath been in Parnassus, or having washt his lips, as they say, in Helicon. There goes more to his making, then so; for to Nature, Exercise, Imitation, and Studie, Art must bee added to make all these perfect. And though these challenge to themselves much in the making up of our Maker, it is Art only can lead him to perfection, and leave him there in possession, as planted by her hand. It is the assertion of Tully, if to an excellent nature there happen an accession or confirmation of Learning and Discipline, there will then remaine somewhat noble and singular. For, as Simylus saith in Stobæus, Οὔτε φύσις ἱκανὴ γίνεται τέχνης ἄτερ, οὔτε πᾶν τέχνη μὴ φύσιν κεκτημένη, without Art, Nature can nere bee perfect; & without Nature, Art can clayme no being. But, our Poet must beware, that his Studie be not only to learn of himself; for hee that shall affect to doe that, confesseth his ever having a Foole to his master. Hee must read many, but ever the best and choisest; those that can teach him anything, hee must ever account his masters, and reverence. Among whom Horace and (hee that taught him) Aristotle, deserv'd to be the first in estimation. Aristotle was the first accurate Criticke and truest Judge—nay, the

greatest Philosopher the world ever had—for hee noted the vices of all knowledges in all creatures, and out of many mens perfections in a Science, hee formed still one Art. So hee taught us two offices together, how we ought to judge rightly of others, and what wee ought to imitate specially in ourselves. But all this in vaine, without a natural wit and a Poeticall nature in chiefe. For no man, so soone as hee knowes this or reades it, shall be able to write the better; but as he is adapted to it by Nature, he shall grow the perfecter Writer. Hee must have Civil prudence and Eloquence, and that whole; not taken up by snatches or peeces, in Sentences or remnants, when he will handle businesse or carry Counsells, as if he came then out of the Declamors Gallerie, or Shadowe, furnish'd but out of the body of the State, which commonly is the Schoole of men. . . .

JOHN MILTON
(1608-1674)

A School of Poetry

I. A Passage from "An Apology against a Pamphlet call'd Smectymnuus: a Modest Confutation."

The Treatise from which this passage is taken was published in 1642, in reply to Bishop Hall and his son's "Modest confutation against a Scandalous and Seditious Libel." With the dispute we have of course nothing to do, save in so far as it is the occasion of so noble a tribute to Poetry.

. . . I had my time Readers, as others have, who have good learning bestow'd upon them, to be sent to those places, where the opinion was, it might be soonest attain'd; and as the manner is, was not unstudied in those authors which are most commended; whereof some were grave Orators and Historians, whose matter methought I lov'd indeed, but as my age then was, so I understood them; others were the smooth Elegiack Poets, whereof the Schooles are not scarce, whom both for the pleasing sound of their numerous writing, which in imitation I found most easie, and most agreeable to natures part in me, and for their matter, which what it is, there be few who know not, I was so allur'd to read, that no recreation came to me better welcome. For that it was then those years with me which are excus'd, though they be least severe, I may be sav'd the labour to remember ye. Whence having deserv'd them to account it the chiefe glory of their wit, in that they were ablest to judge, to praise, and by that could esteeme themselves worthiest to love those high perfections, which under one or other name they took to celebrate, I thought with myselfe by every instinct and presage of nature which is not wont to be false, that what imbolden'd them to this task, might with such diligence as they us'd imbolden me; and that what judgment, wit, or elegance was my share would herein best appeare, and best value itselfe, by how much more wisely, and with more love of vertue I should choose (let rude eares be absent) the object of not unlike praises. For albeit these thoughts to some will seeme vertuous and commendable, to others only pardonable, to a third sort perhaps idle; yet the mentioning of them now will end in serious. Nor blame it, Readers, in those years to propose to themselves such a reward, as the noblest dispositions above other things in this life have sometimes preferr'd: Whereof not to be sensible when good and faire in one person meet, argues both a grosse and shallow judgment, and withall an ungentle and swainish brest: for by the firme setling of these perswasions, I became, to my best memory, so much a proficient, that if I found those authors anywhere speaking unworthy things of themselves, or unchaste of those names which before they had extoll'd; this effect it wrought with me, from time forward their Art I still applauded, but the men I deplor'd; and above them all, preferr'd the two famous renowners of Beatrice and Laura, who never write but honour of them to whom they devote their verse, displaying sublime and pure thoughts without transgression. And long it was not after, when I was confirm'd in this opinion, that he who would not be frustrate of his hope to write well hereafter in laudable things, ought himself to bee a true Poem; that is, a composition and patterne of the best and honourablest things; not presuming to sing high praises of heroick men or famous Cities, unlesse he have in himself the experience and the practice of all that which is praise worthy. These reasonings, together with a certain nicenesse of nature, an honest haughtinesse, and self-esteem either of what I was, or what I might be, (which let envie call pride,) and lastly that modesty, whereof though not in the Title-page, yet here I may be excus'd to make some beseeming profession; all these uniting the supply of their naturall aid together, kept me still above those low descents of minde, beneath which he must deject and plunge himself, that can agree to salable and unlawfull prostitutions. Next, (for hear me out now, Readers,) that I may tell ye whether my younger feet wander'd; I betook me among those lofty Fables and Romances, which recount in solemne canto's the deeds of Knighthood founded by our victorious Kings, and from hence had in renowne over all Christendome. There I read it in the oath of every Knight, that he should defend to the expence of his best blood, or of his life, if it so befell him, the honour and chastity of Virgin or Matron; from whence even then I learnt what a noble vertue chastity sure must be, to the defence of which so many worthies, by such a deare adventure of themselves, had sworne. And if I found in the story afterward, any of them, by word or deed, breaking that oath, I judg'd it the same fault of the Poet, as that which is attributed to Homer, to have written undecent things of the gods. Only this my minde gave me, that every free and gentle spirit, without that oath, ought to be borne a knight, nor needed to expect the guilt spurre, or the laying of a sword upon his shoulder to stirre him up both by his counsell and by his arme, to secure and protect the weaknesse of any attempted chastity. So that even those books, which to many others have been the fuell of wantonnesse and loose living, I cannot thinke how, unless by divine indulgence, prov'd to me so many incitements, as you have heard, to the love and stedfast observation of that vertue which abhorres the society of Bordello's. Thus from the Laureat fraternity of Poets, riper yeares and the ceaselesse round of study and reading led me to the shady spaces of philosophy; but chiefly to the divine volumes of Plato, and his equall Xenophon: where, if I should tell ye what I learnt of chastity and love, I meane that which is truly so, whose charming cup is only vertue, which she bears in her hand to those who are worthy. The rest are cheated with a thick intoxicating potion, which a certain Sorceresse, the abuser of loves name, carries about; and how the chiefest office of love begins and ends in the soule, producing those happy twins

A SCHOOL OF POETRY

of her divine generation, knowledge and vertue; with such abstracted sublimities as these, it might be worth your listning, Readers, as I may one day hope to have ye in a still time, when there shall be no chiding; not in these noises, the adversary, as ye know, barking at the doore, or searching for me at the Burdello's, where it may be he has lost himselfe, and raps up without pitty the sage and rheumatick old prelatesse, with all her young Corinthian Laity, to inquire for such a one.

II. A Passage from Milton's Letter to Master Samuel Hartlib, published as a tractate, "Of Education."

The letter was published in 1644, the same year when the "Areopagitica" appeared. It outlines a remarkable scheme of education, to be carried on in " a spacious house and ground about it fit for an academy, and big enough to lodge a hundred and fifty persons." "This place," it is added, " should be at once both school and university"; and the students are to be of ages ranging from twelve to twenty-one. At the point referred to in the following passage, they are supposed to be at an advanced stage, well read in law, religion, literature, and even in " Orpheus, Hesiod, Theocritus, . . . and in Latin, Lucretius, Manilius, and the rural part of Virgil."

WHEN all these employments are well conquer'd, then will the choice Histories, Heroic Poems, and Attic Tragedies of stateliest and most regal argument, with all the famous Political Orations, offer themselves; which, if they were not only read, but some of them got by memory, and solemnly pronounc't with right accent and grace, as might be taught, would endue them even with the spirit and vigour of Demosthenes or Cicero, Euripides, or Sophocles. And now, lastly, will be the time to read with them those organic arts, which inable men to discourse and write perspicuously, elegantly, and according to the fitted stile of lofty, mean, or lowly. Logic, therefore, so much as is useful, is to be referr'd to this due place with all her well-couch't Heads and Topics, untill it be time to open her contracted palm into a graceful and ornate Rhetoric taught out of the rule of Plato, Aristotle, Phalereus, Cicero, Hermogenes, Longinus. To which Poetry would be made subsequent, or indeed rather precedent, as being less suttle and fine, but more simple, sensuous, and passionate. I mean not here the prosody of a verse, which they could not but have hit on before among the rudiments of Grammar; but that sublime Art which in Aristotles Poetics, in Horace, and the Italian Commentaries of Castelvetro, Tasso, Mazzoni, and others, teaches what the laws are of a true Epic Poem, what of a Dramatic, what of a Lyric, what Decorum is, which is the grand masterpiece to observe. This would make them soon perceive what despicable creatures our common Rimers and Play-writers be: and shew them what religious, what glorious and magnificent use might be made of Poetry, both in divine and humane things. From hence, and not till now, will be the right season of forming them to be able Writers and Composers in every excellent matter, when they shall be thus fraught with an universal insight into things.

JOHN DRYDEN

(1631-1700)

Heroic Poetry and Poetic Licence

The Author's Apology prefixed to " The State of Innocence and Fall of Man," an Opera (1677).

To satisfy the curiosity of those who will give themselves the trouble of reading the ensuing poem, I think myself obliged to render them a reason why I publish an opera which was never acted. In the first place, I shall not be ashamed to own that my chiefest motive was the ambition which I acknowledged in the Epistle. I was desirous to lay at the feet of so beautiful and excellent a Princess a work which, I confess, was unworthy her, but which, I hope, she will have the goodness to forgive. I was also induced to it in my own defence; many hundred copies of it being dispersed abroad without my knowledge or consent: so that every one gathering new faults, it became at length a libel against me; and I saw, with some disdain, more nonsense than either I, or as bad a poet, could have crammed into it at a month's warning; in which time 'twas wholly written, and not since revised. After this, I cannot, without injury to the deceased author of *Paradise Lost*, but acknowledge that this poem has received its entire foundation, part of the design, and many of the ornaments, from him. What I have borrowed will be so easily discerned from my mean productions, that I shall not need to point the reader to the places: and truly I should be sorry, for my own sake, that any one should take the pains to compare them together; the original being undoubtedly one of the greatest, most noble, and most sublime poems which either this age or nation has produced. And though I could not refuse the partiality of my friend, who is pleased to commend me in his verses, I hope they will rather be esteemed the effect of his love to me, than of his deliberate and sober judgment. His genius is able to make beautiful what he pleases: yet, as he has been too favourable to me, I doubt not but he will hear of his kindness from many of our contemporaries; for we are fallen into an age of illiterate, censorious, and detracting people, who, thus qualified, set up for critics.

In the first place, I must take leave to tell them, that they wholly mistake the nature of criticism who think its business is principally to find fault. Criticism, as it was first instituted by Aristotle, was meant a standard of judging well; the chiefest part of which is, to observe those excellencies which should delight a reasonable reader. If the design, the conduct, the thoughts, and the expression of a poem, be generally such as proceed from a true genius of Poetry, the critic ought to pass his judgment in favour of the author. 'Tis malicious and unmanly to snarl at the little lapses of a pen, from which Virgil himself stands not exempted. Horace acknowledges that honest Homer nods sometimes: he is not equally awake in every line; but he leaves it also as a standing measure for our judgments,

> Non, ubi plura nitent in carmine, paucis
> Offendi maculis, quas aut incuria fudit,
> Aut humana parum cavit natura. . . .

And Longinus, who was undoubtedly, after Aristotle, the greatest critic amongst the Greeks, in his twenty-seventh chapter ΠΕΡΙ ὙΨΟΥΣ, has judiciously preferred the sublime genius that sometimes errs, to the middling or indifferent one, which makes few faults, but seldom or never rises to any excellence. He compares the first to a man of large possessions, who has not leisure to consider of every slight expense, will not debase himself to the management of every trifle: particular sums are not laid out, or spared, to the greatest advantage in his economy; but are sometimes suffered to run to waste, while he is only careful of the main. On the other side, he likens the mediocrity of wit to one of a mean fortune, who manages his store with extreme frugality, or rather parsimony; but who, with fear of running into profuseness, never arrives to the magnificence of living. This kind of genius writes indeed correctly. A wary man he is in grammar, very nice as to solecism or barbarism, judges to a hair of little decencies, knows better than any man what is not to be written, and never hazards himself so far as to fall, but plods on deliberately, and, as a grave man ought, is sure to put his staff before him; in short, he sets his heart upon it, and with wonderful care makes his business sure; that is, in plain English, neither to be blamed nor praised.—I could, says my author, find out some blemishes in Homer; and am perhaps as naturally inclined to be disgusted at a fault as another man; but, after all, to speak impartially, his failings are such as are only marks of human frailty: they are little mistakes, or rather negligences, which have escaped his pen in the fervour of his writing; the sublimity of his spirit carries it with me against his carelessness; and though Apollonius his *Argonauts*, and Theocritus his *Eidullia*, are more free from errors, there is not any man of so false a judgment who would choose rather to have been Apollonius or Theocritus than Homer.

'Tis worth our consideration a little, to examine how much these hypercritics of English poetry differ from the opinion of the Greek and Latin judges of antiquity; from the Italians and French, who have succeeded them; and, indeed, from the general taste and approbation of all ages. Heroic Poetry, which they condemn, has ever been esteemed, and ever will be, the greatest work of human nature: in that rank has Aristotle placed it; and Longinus is so full of the like expressions, that he abundantly confirms the other's testimony. Horace as plainly delivers his opinion, and particularly praises Homer in these verses—

> Trojani Belli scriptorem, maxime Lolli,
> Dum tu declamas Romæ, Præneste relegi:
> Qui quid sit pulchrum, quid turpe, quid utile, quid non,
> Plenius ac melius Chrysippo et Crantore dicit.

And in another place, modestly excluding himself from

the number of poets, because he only writ odes and satires, he tells you a poet is such an one,

> cui mens divinior, atque os
> Magna sonaturum.

Quotations are superfluous in an established truth; otherwise I could reckon up, amongst the moderns, all the Italian commentators on Aristotle's book of poetry; and, amongst the French, the greatest of this age, Boileau and Rapin; the latter of which is alone sufficient, were all other critics lost, to teach anew the rules of writing. Any man who will seriously consider the nature of an Epic Poem, how it agrees with that of Poetry in general, which is to instruct and to delight, what actions it describes, and what persons they are chiefly whom it informs, will find it a work which indeed is full of difficulty in the attempt, but admirable when it is well performed. I write not this with the least intention to undervalue the other parts of poetry: for Comedy is both excellently instructive, and extremely pleasant; satire lashes vice into reformation, and humour represents folly so as to render it ridiculous. Many of our present writers are eminent in both these kinds; and, particularly, the author of the *Plain Dealer*, whom I am proud to call my friend, has obliged all honest and virtuous men, by one of the most bold, most general, and most useful satires which has ever been presented on the English theatre. I do not dispute the preference of Tragedy; let every man enjoy his taste: but 'tis unjust that they, who have not the least notion of heroic writing, should therefore condemn the pleasure which others receive from it, because they cannot comprehend it. Let them please their appetites in eating what they like; but let them not force their dish on all the table. They who would combat general authority with particular opinion, must first establish themselves a reputation of understanding better than other men. Are all the flights of Heroic Poetry to be concluded bombast, unnatural, and mere madness, because they are not affected with their excellencies? It is just as reasonable as to conclude there is no day, because a blind man cannot distinguish of light and colours. Ought they not rather, in modesty, to doubt of their own judgments, when they think this or that expression in Homer, Virgil, Tasso, or Milton's *Paradise* to be too far strained, than positively to conclude that 'tis all fustian, and mere nonsense? 'Tis true, there are limits to be set betwixt the boldness and rashness of a poet; but he must understand those limits who pretends to judge as well as he who undertakes to write: and he who has no liking to the whole, ought, in reason, to be excluded from censuring of the parts. He must be a lawyer before he mounts the tribunal; and the judicature of one court, too, does not qualify a man to preside in another. He may be an excellent pleader in the Chancery who is not fit to rule the Common Pleas. But I will presume for once to tell them, that the boldest strokes of poetry, when they are managed artfully, are those which most delight the reader.

Virgil and Horace, the severest writers of the severest age, have made frequent use of the hardest metaphors, and of the strongest hyperboles; and in this case the best authority is the best argument; for generally to have pleased, and through all ages, must bear the force of universal tradition. And if you would appeal from thence to right reason, you will gain no more by it in effect, than, first, to set up your reason against those authors; and, secondly, against all those who have admired them. You must prove why that ought not to have pleased, which has pleased the most learned, and the most judicious; and, to be thought knowing, you must first put the fool upon all mankind. If you can enter more deeply than they have done into the causes and resorts of that which moves pleasure in a reader, the field is open, you may be heard: but those springs of human nature are not so easily discovered by every superficial judge: it requires Philosophy, as well as Poetry, to sound the depth of all the passions; what they are in themselves, and how they are to be provoked: and in this science the best poets have excelled. Aristotle raised the fabric of his *Poetry* from observation of those things in which Euripides, Sophocles, and Æschylus pleased: he considered how they raised the passions, and thence has drawn rules for our imitation. From hence have sprung the tropes and figures, for which they wanted a name, who first practised them, and succeeded in them. Thus I grant you that the knowledge of nature was the original rule; and that all poets ought to study her, as well as Aristotle and Horace, her interpreters. But then this also undeniably follows, that those things which delight all ages, must have been an imitation of Nature; which is all I contend. Therefore is Rhetoric made an art; therefore the names of so many tropes and figures were invented; because it was observed they had such and such effect upon the audience. Therefore catachreses and hyperboles have found their place amongst them; not that they were to be avoided, but to be used judiciously, and placed in poetry, as heightenings and shadows are in painting, to make the figure bolder, and cause it to stand off to sight.

> Nec retia cervis
> Ulla dolum meditantur

says Virgil in his *Eclogues*: and speaking of Leander, in his *Georgics*,

> Nocte natat cæca, serus freta, quem super ingens
> Porta tonat coeli, et scopulis illisa reclamant
> Æquora;

In both of these, you see, he fears not to give voice and thought to things inanimate.

Will you arraign your master, Horace, for his hardness of expression, when he describes the death of Cleopatra, and says she did *asperos tractare serpentes, ut atrum corpore combiberet venenum*, because the body, in that action, performs what is proper to the mouth?

As for hyperboles, I will neither quote Lucan, nor Statius, men of an unbounded imagination, but who often wanted the poise of judgment. The divine Virgil was not liable to that exception; and yet he describes Polyphemus thus—

> Graditurque per quoræ
> Jam medium; necdum fluctus latera ardua tinxit.

HEROIC POETRY AND POETIC LICENCE

In imitation of this place, our admirable Cowley thus paints Goliath—

> The valley, now, this monster seem'd to fill;
> And we, methought, look'd up to him from our hill:

where the two words, *seemed* and *methought*, have mollified the figure; and yet if they had not been there, the fright of the Israelites might have excused their belief of the giant's stature.

In the eighth of the Æneids, Virgil paints the swiftness of Camilla thus:

> Illa vel intactæ segetis per summa volaret
> Gramina, nec teneras cursu læsisset aristas;
> Vel mare per medium, fluctu suspensa tumenti,
> Ferret iter, celeres nec tingeret æquore plantas.

You are not obliged, as in History, to a literal belief of what the poet says; but you are pleased with the image, without being cozened by the fiction.

Yet even in History, Longinus quotes Herodotus on this occasion of hyperboles. The Lacedemonians, says he, at the straits of Thermopylæ, defended themselves to the last extremity; and when their arms failed them, fought it out with their nails and teeth; till at length (the Persians shooting continually upon them) they lay buried under the arrows of their enemies. It is not reasonable (continues the critic) to believe that men could defend themselves with their nails and teeth from an armed multitude; nor that they lay buried under a pile of darts and arrows; and yet there wants not probability for the figure: because the hyperbole seems not to have been made for the sake of the description, but rather to have been produced from the occasion.

'Tis true, the boldness of the figures is to be hidden sometimes by the address of the poet; that they may work their effect upon the mind, without discovering the art which caused it. And therefore they are principally to be used in passion; when we speak more warmly and with more precipitation than at other times: for then, *si vis me flere, dolendum est primum ipsi tibi;* the poet must put on the passion he endeavours to represent: a man in such an occasion is not cool enough, either to reason rightly, or to talk calmly. Aggravations are then in their proper places; interrogations, exclamations, hyperbata, or a disordered connection of discourse, are graceful there, because they are natural. The sum of all depends on what before I hinted, that this boldness of expression is not to be blamed, if it be managed by the coolness and discretion which is necessary to a poet.

Yet before I leave this subject, I cannot but take notice how disingenuous our adversaries appear: all that is dull, insipid, languishing, and without sinews, in a poem, they call an imitation of Nature: they only offend our most equitable judges who think beyond them; and lively images and elocution are never to be forgiven.

What fustian, as they call it, have I heard these gentlemen find out in Mr. Cowley's *Odes!* I acknowledge myself unworthy to defend so excellent an author, neither have I room to do it here; only in general I will say, that nothing can appear more beautiful to me than the strength of those images which they condemn.

Imaging is, in itself, the very height and life of Poetry. It is, as Longinus describes it, a discourse, which, by a kind of enthusiasm, or extraordinary emotion of the soul, makes it seem to us that we behold those things which the poet paints, so as to be pleased with them, and to admire them.

If poetry be imitation, that part of it must needs be best which describes most lively our actions and passions; our virtues and our vices; our follies and our humours: for neither is Comedy without its part of imaging; and they who do it best are certainly the most excellent in their kind. This is too plainly proved to be denied. But how are poetical fictions, how are hippocentaurs and chimeras, or how are angels and immaterial substances to be imaged; which, some of them, are things quite out of nature; others, such whereof we can have no notion? This is the last refuge of our adversaries; and more than any of them have yet had the wit to object against us. The answer is easy to the first part of it: the fiction of some beings which are not in nature (second notions, as the logicians call them) has been founded on the conjunction of two natures, which have a real separate being. So hippocentaurs were imaged by joining the natures of a man and horse together; as Lucretius tells us, who has used this word of *image* oftener than any of the poets—

> Nam certe ex vivo centauri non fit imago,
> Nulla fuit quoniam talis natura animai:
> Verum ubi equi atque hominis, casu, convenit imago,
> Hærescit facile extemplo, etc.

The same reason may also be alleged for chimeras and the rest. And poets may be allowed the like liberty for describing things which really exist not, if they are founded on popular belief. Of this nature are fairies, pigmies, and the extraordinary effects of magic; for 'tis still an imitation, though of other men's fancies: and thus are Shakspeare's *Tempest*, his *Midsummer Night's Dream*, and Ben Jonson's *Masque of Witches* to be defended. For immaterial substances, we are authorised by Scripture in their description: and herein the text accommodates itself to vulgar apprehension, in giving angels the likeness of beautiful young men. Thus, after the pagan divinity, has Homer drawn his gods with human faces: and thus we have notions of things above us, by describing them like other beings more within our knowledge.

I wish I could produce any one example of excellent imaging in all this poem. Perhaps I cannot; but that which comes nearest it is in these four lines, which have been sufficiently canvassed by my well-natured censors:

> Seraph and cherub, careless of their charge,
> And wanton, in full ease now live at large:
> Unguarded leave the passes of the sky,
> And all dissolved in hallelujahs lie

I have heard (says one of them) of anchovies dissolved in sauce; but never of an angel in hallelujahs. A mighty witticism! (if you will pardon a new word), but there is some difference between a laugher and a critic. He might have burlesqued Virgil too, from whom I took the image: *Invadunt urbem, somno vinoque sepultam.* A city's being buried, is just as proper on occasion, as an angel's being dissolved in ease, and songs of triumph. Mr. Cowley lies as open, too, in many places—

> Where their vast courts the mother waters keep, etc.

For if the mass of waters be the mothers, then their daughters, the little streams, are bound, in all good manners, to make courtesy to them, and ask them blessing. How easy 'tis to turn into ridicule the best descriptions, when once a man is in the humour of laughing, till he wheezes at his own dull jest! But an image, which is strongly and beautifully set before the eyes of the reader, will still be poetry when the merry fit is over, and last when the other is forgotten.

I promised to say somewhat of Poetic Licence, but have in part anticipated my discourse already. Poetic Licence I take to be the liberty which poets have assumed to themselves, in all ages, of speaking things in verse, which are beyond the severity of prose. 'Tis that particular character which distinguishes and sets the bounds betwixt *oratio soluta* and poetry. This, as to what regards the thought or imagination of a poet, consists in fiction: but then those thoughts must be expressed; and here arise two other branches of it; for if this licence be included in a single word, it admits of tropes; if in a sentence or proposition, of figures; both which are of a much larger extent, and more forcibly to be used in verse than prose. This is that birthright which is derived to us from our great forefathers, even from Homer down to Ben; and they who would deny it to us, in plain terms, the fox's quarrel to the grapes—they cannot reach it.

How far these liberties are to be extended, I will not presume to determine here, since Horace does not. But it is certain that they are to be varied, according to the language and age in which an author writes. That which would be allowed to a Grecian poet, Martial tells you, would not be suffered in a Roman. And 'tis evident that the English does more nearly follow the strictness of the latter than the freedoms of the former. Connection of epithets, or the conjunction of two words in one, are frequent and elegant in the Greek, which yet Sir Philip Sidney, and the translator of Du Bartas, have unluckily attempted in the English; though this, I confess, is not so proper an instance of poetic licence as it is of variety of idiom in languages.

Horace a little explains himself on this subject of *Licentia Poetica*, in these verses—

> Pictoribus atque Poetis
> Quidlibet audendi semper fuit æqua potestas: . . .
> Sed non, ut placidis coeant immitia, non ut
> Serpentes avibus geminentur, tigribus hædi.

He would have a poem of a piece; not to begin with one thing and end with another: he restrains it so far that thoughts of an unlike nature ought not to be joined together. That were indeed to make a chaos. He taxed not Homer, nor the divine Virgil, for interesting their gods in the wars of Troy and Italy; neither, had he now lived, would he have taxed Milton, as our false critics have presumed to do, for his choice of a supernatural argument; but he would have blamed my author, who was a Christian, had he introduced into his poem heathen deities, as Tasso is condemned by Rapin on the like occasion; and as Camoëns, the author of the *Lusiads*, ought to be censured by all his readers, when he brings in Bacchus and Christ into the same adventure of his fable.

From that which has been said, it may be collected, that the definition of Wit (which has been so often attempted, and even unsuccessfully by many poets) is only this: that it is a propriety of thoughts and words; or, in other terms, thoughts and words elegantly adapted to the subject. If our critics will join issue on this definition, that we may *convenire in alique tertio;* if they will take it as a granted principle, it will be easy to put an end to this dispute. No man will disagree from another's judgment concerning the dignity of style in Heroic Poetry; but all reasonable men will conclude it necessary, that sublime subjects ought to be adorned with the sublimest, and consequently often with the most figurative expressions. In the meantime I will not run into their fault of imposing my opinions on other men, any more than I would my writings on their taste: I have only laid down, and that superficially enough, my present thoughts; and shall be glad to be taught better by those who pretend to reform our Poetry.

ALEXANDER POPE
(1688–1744)

THE LYRIC STYLE

From the Preface to Homer's Iliad, 1715.

WE acknowledge Homer the father of poetical diction, the first who taught that *language of the Gods* to men. His expression is like the colouring of some great masters, which discovers itself to be laid on boldly, and executed with rapidity. It is indeed the strongest and most glowing imaginable, and touched with the greatest spirit. Aristotle had reason to say, He was the only poet who had found out *living words;* there are in him more daring figures and metaphors than in any good author whatever. An arrow is *impatient* to be on the wing, a weapon *thirsts* to drink the blood of an enemy, and the like. Yet his expression is never too big for the sense, but justly great in proportion to it.

A STYLE OF SOUND

From a Letter to Walsh, October 22, 1706.

IT is not enough that nothing offends the ear, but a good poet will adapt the very sounds, as well as words, to the things he treats of. So that there is (if one may express it so) a style of sound.

THOMAS GRAY

(1716-1771)

METRUM: OBSERVATIONS ON ENGLISH METRE.

PUTTENHAM, in his *Art of Poetry*, addressed to Queen Elizabeth in 1587, tells us, l. 2. c. 4, that "Chaucer, Lydgate, and others used *cesures* either very seldom, or not at all, or else very licentiously; and many times made their meetres (they called them *riding ryme*) of such unshapely words as would allow no convenient cesure; and therefore did let their rymes run out at length, and never staid till they came to the end; which manner, though it were not to be misliked in some sort of meetre, yet in every long verse the cesure ought to be kept precisely, if it were but to serve as a law to correct the licentiousness of rymers. Besides that, it pleaseth the eare better, and sheweth more cunning in the maker by following the rule of his restraint, for a rymer that will be tied by no rules at all, but range as he list, may utter what he will; but such maner of poesy is called in our vulgar,[1] '*ryme dogrell*,' with which

---

[1] It appears from Alderman Fabian's prologue to the second volume of his *Chronicle*, written in Henry the Seventh's reign, that the free verse, where no exact number of syllables was observed, was then called *doggrell*.. Thus,

> "Now would I fayne
> In wordes plaine
> Some honour sayne,
>   And bring to mynde
> Of that aunciente citye,
> That so goodly is to se,
> And full trewe ever hath be,
>   And also full kynde, etc.
> For though I shuld all day tell,
> Or that with my *ryme dogerell*
> Myght I not yet halfe do spell
>   This townes great honour, etc.

[Continued on p 137.

OBSERVATIONS ON ENGLISH METRE 137

rebuke we will that in no case our Maker shall be touched."

Then Puttenham gives rules for the cæsura, which he tells us, " In a verse of twelve syllables should always divide it exactly in the middle ; in one of ten, it should fall on the fourth, in one of eight on the same, in one of seven on the same, or on none at all," etc. I mention no [1] more than these, as they are now the only measures admitted into our serious poetry, and I shall consider how his rules hold in modern practice.

Alexandrines,[2] or verses of twelve syllables, it is true, though Spenser sometimes does otherwise, must, if they would strike the ear agreeably, have their pause in the middle, as—

    And after toilsome days | a soft repose at night.

Or—

    He both her warlike Lords | outshined in Helen's eyes.

And this uniformity in the cæsura is just the reason why we no longer use them but just to finish a lyric stanza : they are also sometimes interspersed arbitrarily among

    To the reader.
   Whoso hym liketh these versys to rede,
   Wyth favour I pray he wyll theym spell,
   Let not the rudeness of them hym lede
   For to desprave this *ryme dogerell*," etc.

[1] Lines of six, five, or four syllables are intermixed in lyric compositions, but, as Puttenham says, " they need no cesure, because the breath asketh no relief."

[2] Puttenham says, " The Alexandrine is with our modern rhymers most usual, with the auncyent makers it was not so. For before Sir Thomas Wyatt's time they were not used in our vulgar : they be for grave and stately matters fitter, than for any other ditty of pleasure. If the cesure be just in the middle, and that ye suffer the verse to run at full length, and do not (as common rimers do, or their printer, for sparing of paper) cut them off in the middest, wherein they make in two verses but halfe rime, they do very wel." (*Art of Poesie*, l. ii. c. 3.) The poets of Henry the Eighth's time mixed it with the line of fourteen syllables alternately, which is so tiresome, that we have long since quite banished it. Thus many things of Wyatt's and Lord Surrey's are written, and those of Queen Elizabeth on the Queen of Scots.

verses of ten syllables. This is an odd custom, but it is confirmed by the sanction which Dryden and Pope have given to it, for they soon tire the ear with this sameness of sound; and the French seemed to have judged ill in making them their heroic [1] measure.

Verses of *eight* syllables are so far from being obliged to have their cæsura on the fourth, that Milton, the best example of an exquisite ear that I can produce, varies it continually, as—

To live with her, | and live with thee	On the 4th.
In unreproved | pleasures free	——— 5th.
To hear the lark | begin his flight	——— 4th.
And singing | startle the dŭll nīght	——— 3d.
Whĕre thĕ grēat sūn | bĕgĭns hĭs stāte	——— 4th.
The clouds | in thousand liveries dight	——— 2d.
With masque | and antique pageantry	——— 2d.

The more we attend to the composition of Milton's harmony, the more we shall be sensible how he loved to vary [2] his pauses, his measures, and his feet, which gives that enchanting air of freedom and wildness to his versification, unconfined by any rules but those which

---

[1] They were not so till towards the end of the sixteenth century. "Quant aux vers de *douze* syllabes, que nous appellons Alexandrins, combien qu'ils proviennent d'une longue ancienneté, toutefois nous en avions perdu l'usage. Car, lorsque Marot insere quelques uns dedans ses Epigrammes ou Tombeaux, c'est avec cette suscription, Vers Alexandrins; comme si c'étoit chose nouvelle et inaccoustumée d'en user.—Le premier des nôtres, qui les mit en crédit, fut Baïf en ses *Amours de Francine*, suivy depuis par Du Bellay au livre de ses Regrets, et par Ronsard en ses Hymnes, et finalement par Du Bartas, qui semble vouloir renvier sur tous les autres en ses deux Semaines." (See Pasquier, l. vii. c. 8 and 11). Yet Ronsard, in his *Art of Poetry*, continues to call the decasyllabic measure only *heroic verse*, and uses it in his *Franciade* and other long compositions.

[2] Lord Surrey (who was Puttenham's example for sweetness and proportion of metre) generally, though not always, makes his cæsura on the fourth; as,

"True wisdom join'd | with simpleness,
The night | discharged of all care,   On the 2d.
Where wine the wit | may not oppresse
The faithful wife | without debate,
Such slepes | as may beguile the night,
Content thyself | with thine estate,
Ne wish for death, | ne feare his might."

OBSERVATIONS ON ENGLISH METRE

his own feeling and the nature of his subject demanded. Thus he mixes the line of eight syllables with that of seven, the trochee and the spondee with the iambic foot, and the single rhyme with the double. He changes the cæsura as frequently in the heptasyllabic measure, as,

Oft ŏn ă plăt | of rising ground	(Octosyll.)	
I hear | the far-off curfew sound,	(Oct:—)	On the 2d.
Over some | wide-water'd shore		——— 3d.
Swinging slow | with sullen roar:		——— 3d.
Or if the air | will not permit, etc.	(Oct:—)	——— 4th.
Far from all resort | of mirth		——— 5th.
Save the cricket | on the hearth		——— 4th.
Or the bellman's | drowsy charm		——— 4th.

But the greatest confinement which Puttenham would lay on our verse is that of making the cæsur- constantly fall on the fourth syllable of our decasyllabic measure, which is now become our only heroic [1] metre for all poems of any length. This restraint Wyatt and Lord Surrey submitted to, though here and there you find an instance of their breaking through it, though rarely. So,

> From these hye hilles \| as when a spring doth falle,
> It trilleth down \| with still and subtle course,
> Of this and that \| it gathers aye, and shall

---

[1] We probably took it from the Italians. Their heroic measure has indeed eleven syllables, because of the rhyme, which is double; but as our language requires single rhyme, the verse was reduced to ten syllables; the run of it is the same to the ear. The Italians borrowed it from the Provençals, there being verses extant still of this kind by Arnauld Daniel, who died in 1189, and is celebrated by Petrarch, under the title of "Gran Maestro d'amor," and of Arnauld de Merveille, who flourished about 1190, as,

> "Fazes auzir vostras castas preguieras
> Tant doussament, qu'a pietat sia moguda
> De s'inclinar a ma justa demanda," etc.
> *Crescimbeni Istor. della Volg. Poesia*, l. i. p. 6.

Dante judges it the best adapted of any metre to noble subjects. "Quorum omnium Endecasyllabum videtur esse snperbius, tam temporis occupatione quam capacitate sententiæ, constructionis, et vocabulorum, etc.—at omnes hoc Doctores perpendisse videntur, Cantiones illustres principientes ab illo." *De Vulgari Eloquentiâ*, l. ii. c. 5

> Till it have just | downe flowed to stream and force:
> So fareth Love, | when he hath ta'en a course;
> Rage is his raine; | resistance 'vaileth none;
> The first eschue | is remedy alone.
>
> WYATT.

And these verses of Surrey:

> In active games | of nimbleness and strength
> Where we did strain, | trained with swarms of youth,
> Our tender limbs, | which yet shot up in length:
> The secret groves, | which oft we made resound
> Of plesaunt plaint, | and of our Lady's praise,
> Recording oft, | what grace each one had found,
> What hope of speed, | what dread of long delays;
> The wild forèst, | the clothed holts with green,
> With reines availed, | and swift-ybreathed horse,
> With cry of hound, | and merry blasts between,
> Where we did chase | the fearful hart of force, etc.

But our poets have long since got loose from these fetters. Spenser judiciously shook them off; Milton, in his *Paradise Lost*, is ever changing and mingling his pauses, and the greatest writers after him have made it their study to avoid what Puttenham regarded as a rule of perfect versification.

These reflections may serve to shew us, that Puttenham, though he lived within about one hundred and fifty years of Chaucer's time, must have been mistaken with regard to what the old writers called their *riding rhyme;* for the *Canterbury Tales*, which he gives as an example of it, are as exact in their measure and in their pause as in the "Troilus and Cresseide," where he says, "*the metre is very grave and stately;*" and this not only in the "Knight's Tale," but in the comic introduction and characters; as,

> A monke ther was | fair for the maistery,
> An outrider | that loved venery,[1]
> A manly man, | to ben an abbot able,
> Many a dainty horse | had he in stable;   (On the 6th.)
> And when he rode, | men might his bridle heare,
> Gingiling in a whistling wind, | as cleare   (On the 8th.)
> And eke as loud, as doth the chapell-bell, etc.

I conclude, that he was misled by the change which

---

[1] Venerie. Fr. hunting.

OBSERVATIONS ON ENGLISH METRE 141

words had undergone in their accents since the days of Chaucer, and by the seeming defects of measure which frequently occur in the printed copies. I cannot pretend to say what it was they called *riding rhyme*, but perhaps it might be such as we see in the northern " Tale of Sir Thopas " in Chaucer.

> Sir Thopas was | a doughty swaine,
> White was his face, | as pain [1] de maine,[2]
> His lippis red as rose, |
> His rudd [3] is like | scarlet in graine,
> And I you tell | in gode certaine
> He had a seemly nose. | Etc.

But nothing can be more regular than this sort of stanza, the pause always falling just in the middle of those verses which are of eight syllables, and at the end of those of six. I imagine that it was this very regularity which seemed so tedious to *mine host of the Tabbarde*, as to make him interrupt Chaucer in the middle of his story, with

> " No more of this for Goddis dignitè—
> Mine earès akin of thy draftie [4] speeche,
> Now such a rime the Devil I beteeche,[5]
> This may well be clepe *Rime Dogrell*, quoth he," etc.

Hence too we see that Puttenham is mistaken in the sense of *rhyme dogrell*, for so far was it *from being tied to no rule at all*, that it was consistent with the greatest exactness in the cæsura and in the measure ; but as he himself has said very well in another place (b. ii. ch. ix), " the over busie and too speedie returne of one manner of tune doth too much annoy and, as it were, glut the eare, unless it be in small and popular musickes, sung

---

[1] " When thou beholdest before thy Lord *peyne-mayne :*
   A baker chosen, and waged well forthe,
   That only he should that ubsinesse applye," etc.
                               Alexander Barclay's *Eclogues*,
        Written in the beginning of Henry ye 8's reign
[2] The whitest bread.
[3] *Rudu*, Sax. colour of the cheek.
[4] *Tedious*, from *drof*, Sax. dirty, filthy.
[5] Betæcan, Sax. to give, or commit to.

by these Cantabanqui [1] upon benches and barrels-heads, where they have none other audience than boys and country fellows, that pass by them in the street; or else by blind harpers or such like tavern-minstrels, that give a fit of mirth for a groat; and their matters being for the most part stories of old time, as the *Tale of Sir Thopas*, the *Reportes of Bevis* [2] *of Southampton*,

[1] Doubtless the degenerate successors of those ancient *Jongleurs* in Provence, Italy, and other countries described by Crescimbeni, where he is speaking of the old romances. "Or questi Romanzi non v' ha dubbio che si cantavano, e forse non s' ingannò colui, che fu di parere, che i Romanzatori in panca vendessero l' opere loro cantando, imperocchè fioriva anticamente in Francia un' arte detta de' Giuglari, i quali erano faceti e spiritosi uomini, che solevano andar cantando i loro versi per le corte alle mense de' grandi, colla viuola, o' coll' arpa, o' con altro stromento.—Molti de' poeti Provenzali de' primi tempi questa stessa esercitarono ed anco de' nostri Italiani, che in quella lingua poetarono." (*Comentarj del Crescimbeni*, l. v. c. 5, p. 333.) And he cites on this occasion these verses in a romance composed about the year 1230:

"Quand les tables ostées furent
Cil Jugleur en pies esturent,
S' ont Vielles et Harpes prises;
Chansons, sons, vers, et reprises,
Et de Gestes chanté nos ont," etc.

These verses are in the *Tournoyement d' Antichrist*, by Huon de Mari, a monk of St. Germain. Fauchet, l. i. ch. 8.

And Huon de Villeneuve, a writer of the same age, addresses himself to the company whom he is going to entertain in these words:

"Gardez, qu' il n'i ait noise, ne tabor, ne criée,
Il est ensinc coustume en la vostre contrée.
Quant uns Chanterres vient entre gent honorée
Et il a en droit soi la Vielle attrempée;
Ja tant n'aura mantel, ne cotte desramée,
Que sa premiere * laisse ne soit bien escoutée:
Puis font chanter avant, se de riens lor agrée,
Ou tost sans vilenie puet recoillir s'estrée," etc.
* *Couple, ou* Entrée.

[2] The English romance, so called, is in rude verse, seemingly of great antiquity. The Italians have one which is named *Buovo d' Antona*, probably on the same story, mentioned by Gio. Villani, who died in 1348. See *Crescimbeni Comentarj*, l. v. c. 6.

This English romance is in free octasyllabic rhyme, written, as Mr. Thomas Warton observes (in his *Observations on the Fairy Queen*, Lond. 1754, 8vo) in that short measure which was

Adam Bell, and *Clymme of the Clough*, and such other old romances and historical rhymes, made on purpose for the recreation of the common people at Christmas dinners and bride-ales in taverns and alehouses, and such other places of base resort," etc. This was before *dogrell*, whose frequent return of rhyme and similarity of sound easily imprinted it in the memory of the vulgar; and, by being applied of old to the meanest uses of poetry, it was grown distasteful to the ears of the better sort.

But the *riding rhyme* I rather take to be that which is confined to one measure, whatever that measure may be, but not to one rhythm; having sometimes more, sometimes fewer syllables, and the pause hardly distinguishable, such as the *Prologue and History of Beryn*, found in some MSS. of Chaucer, and the Cook's *Tale of Gamelyn*, where the verses have twelve, thirteen, or fourteen syllables, and the cæsura on the sixth, seventh, or eighth, as it happens. This having an air of rusticity, Spenser has very well adapted it to pastoral poetry, and in his hands it has an admirable effect, as in the eclogue called *March*, which is in the same metre as Chaucer's *Tale of Sir Thopas;* and in *February* and *May*, where the two fables of the Oak and Bryer, and the Fox and Kid, for humour and expression are equal to anything in our language. The measure, like our usual verse of eight syllables, is dimeter-iambic, but admits of a trochee, spondee, amphybrachys, anapæst, etc., in almost every place. Thus,

Sēēst hŏw brāg yon bullock bears . .	Trochee in the 1st.
So smirk, so smooth, his pricked ears ? .	Pure Iambic.
His horns bēen ăs brāde, as rainbow bent,	Anapæst in the 2d.
Hĭs dēwlăp ăs līthe, as Lass of Kent !	. . . The same.
Seē hŏw hĕ vēntĕth īntŏ thē wīnd . .	Anapæst in the last.
Wĕenĕst, ŏf lŏve is not in his mind ? etc.	Trochee in the 1st.

frequently sung to the harp in Queen Elizabeth's days, a custom which descended from the ancient bards. Bevis is supposed to have been Earl of Southampton about the time of the Norman Invasion; his residence was at Duncton in Wiltshire; his sword, called *Morglay*, is kept as a relic in Arundel Castle, not equalling in length that of Edward the Third at Westminster. See Selden's notes on Drayton's *Polyolbion*, canto iii.

And,

Though marked him, with melting eyes,	Pure Iambic.
A thrilling throb frŏm hĕr heãrt did rise,	Anapæst in the 4th.
And ĭntĕrrŭptĕd ăll hĕr ŏthĕr spēech	Amphibrachys in the 2d. Tribrachys in the 3d.
Wĭth sōme ōld sŏrrŏw, thăt māde ă nĕw brēach,	
Sēemĕd shĕ sāw ĭn hĕr yŏunglĭng's fāce	Trochee in the 1st. Anapæst in the 3d.
The' ōld lĭnĕămĕnts ŏf hĭs Fāther's grace	Anapæst in 2d. and 3d.

In these last six lines, the first has eight syllables, and the second nine, the third and fourth ten, the fifth nine, and the last ten: and this is the only English measure which has such a liberty of choice allowed in its feet, of which Milton has taken some little advantage, in using here and there a trochee in his octosyllabics, and in the first foot only of his heroic verses. There are a very few instances of his going farther for the sake of some particular expression, as in that line,

> Bŭrnt āftĕr thĕm tŏ thĕ bōttŏmlĕss pīt,

where there is a spondee in the first place, a pyrrhic in the third, and a trochee in the fourth, and that line,

> Wĭth ĭmpētŭoŭs recoil and jarring sound,

with an anapæst in the first place, etc.

Spenser has also given an instance [1] of the decasyllabic measure with an unusual liberty in its feet, in the beginning of his pastoral called *August*, thus,

> Thĕn lŏ, Pĕrĭgōt, thĕ plēdge whĭch I plīght,
> Ă māzĕr ywroŭght ŏf thĕ māplĕ wāre,
> Whĕreĭn ĭs ĕnchāsĕd mānў ă faĭr sĭght
> Of beãrs ănd tўgĕrs, thăt mākĕn fiĕrce wār, etc.

where there are trochees, etc., in every foot but the last. I do not doubt that he had some ancient examples of

---

[1] And after him Dr. Donne (in his satires) observes no regularity in the pause, or in the feet of his verse, only the number of syllables is equal throughout. I suppose he thought this rough uncouth measure suited the plain familiar style of satirical poetry.

this rhythm in his memory, when he wrote it. Bishop Douglas in his Prologue to the Eighth *Æneid*, written about eighty years before Spenser's *Calendar*, has something of the same kind.

I make no mention of the hexameter, sapphic, and other measures which Sir Philip Sidney and his friends [1] attempted to introduce in Queen Elizabeth's reign, because they soon dropped into oblivion. The same thing had happened in France a little before, where, in 1553, Etienne Jodelle began to write in this way, and was followed by Baïf, Passerat, Nicholas Rapin, and others, but without success. (See Pasquier, *Recherches*, l. vii. c. 12.) And in Italy this was attempted by Claudio Tolomei,[2] and other men of learning, to as little purpose. (See *Crescimbeni Coment.*, vol. i. p. 21.)

---

[1] We see from Spenser's *Letters*, that he himself, his friend Mr. Harvey, and Mr. Dyer, one of his patrons, approved of this method and practised it. Mr. Drant (he says) had derived the rules and principles of the art, which were enlarged with Mr. Sydney's own judgment, and augmented with his (Spenser's) "Observations." This was in 1580.

[2] Bishop of Corsola; he flourished in 1540. He was five years ambassador from the Republic of Sienna in France, and died soon after his return in 1557.

ROBERT BURNS

(1759-1796)

Songs and Song Writing.

From his Scrap Book.

THERE is certainly some connection between love, and music, and poetry; and, therefore, I have always thought it a fine touch of nature, that passage in a modern love-composition:

> "As towards her cott he jogg'd along,
> Her name was frequent in his song."

For my own part I never had the least thought or inclination of turning poet till I got heartily in love, and then rhyme and song were, in a manner, the spontaneous language of my heart. The following composition was the first of my performances, and done at an early period of life, when my heart glowed with honest warm simplicity; unacquainted, and uncorrupted with the ways of a wicked world. The performance is, indeed, very puerile and silly; but I am always pleased with it, as it recalls to my mind those happy days when my heart was yet honest, and my tongue was sincere. The subject of it was a young girl who really deserved all the praises I have bestowed on her. I not only had this opinion of her then—but I actually think so still, now that the spell is long since broken, and the enchantment at an end.

> *Tune.*—" I am a man unmarried."
>
> O once I lov'd a bonnie lass,
> Ay, and I love her still,
> And whilst that honor warms my breast
> I'll love my handsome Nell.
>   *Fal lal de ral.*

> As bonnie lasses I hae seen,
>   And mony full as braw,
> But for a modest gracefu' mien
>   The like I never saw.
>
> A bonnie lass I will confess,
>   Is pleasant to the e'e,
> But without some better qualities
>   She's no a lass for me.
>
> But Nelly's looks are blythe and sweet,
>   And what is best of a',
> Her reputation is complete,
>   And fair without a flaw.
>
> She dresses ay sae clean and neat,
>   Both decent and genteel:
> And then there's something in her gait
>   Gars ony dress look weel.
>
> A gaudy dress and gentle air
>   May slightly touch the heart,
> But it's innocence and modesty
>   That polishes the dart.
>
> 'Tis this in Nelly pleases me,
>   'Tis this enchants my soul;
> For absolutely in my breast
>   She reigns without control.
>   *Fal lal de ral.*

Lest my works should be thought below criticism; or meet with a critic who, perhaps, will not look on them with so candid and favourable an eye; I am determined to criticize them myself.

The first distich of the first stanza is quite too much in the flimsy strain of our ordinary street ballads; and on the other hand, the second distich is too much in the other extreme. The expression is a little awkward, and the sentiment too serious. Stanza the second I am well pleased with; and I think it conveys a fine idea of that amiable part of the sex—the agreeables; or what in our Scotch dialect we call a *sweet sonsy lass*. The third stanza has a little of the flimsy turn in it; and the third line has rather too serious a cast. The fourth stanza is a very indifferent one; the first line is, indeed, all in the strain of the second stanza, but the rest is most expletive. The thoughts in the fifth stanza come finely up to my favourite idea—a *sweet sonsy lass*: the last line, however, halts a little. The same sentiments are kept up with equal spirit and tenderness in the sixth stanza: but the second and fourth lines ending with short syllables hurt the whole. The seventh stanza has several minute faults; but I remember I composed it in a wild enthusiasm of passion, and to this hour I never recollect it, but my heart melts, my blood sallies at the remembrance.

However, I am pleased with the works of our Scotch poets, particularly the excellent Ramsay, and the still more excellent Fergusson, yet I am hurt to see other places of Scotland, their towns, rivers, woods, haughs, etc., immortalized in such celebrated performances, while my dear native country, the ancient bailieries of Carrick, Kyle, and Cunningham, famous both in ancient and modern times for a gallant and warlike race of inhabitants; a country where civil, and particularly religious, liberty have ever found their first support, and their last asylum; a country, the birth-place of many famous philosophers, soldiers, and statesmen, and the scene of many important events recorded in Scottish history, particularly a great many of the actions of the glorious Wallace, the Saviour of his country; yet, we have never had one Scotch poet of any eminence to make the fertile banks of Irvine, the romantic woodlands and sequestered scenes on Aire, and the heathy mountainous source, and winding sweep of Doon, emulate Tay, Forth, Ettrick, Tweed, etc. This is a complaint I would gladly remedy, but alas! I am far unequal to the task, both in native genius and education. Obscure I am, and obscure I must be, though no young poet, nor young soldier's heart, ever beat more fondly for fame than mine.

There is a great irregularity in the old Scotch songs, a redundancy of syllables with respect to that exactness of accent and measure that the English poetry requires, but which glides in, most melodiously, with the respective tunes to which they are set. For instance, the fine old song of *The Mill, Mill, O!* to give it a plain prosaic reading it halts prodigiously out of measure; on the other hand, the song set to the same tune in Bremner's collection of Scotch songs, which begins *To Fanny fair could I impart*, etc., it is most exact measure, and yet, let them both be sung before a real critic, one above the biases of prejudice, but a thorough judge of nature,—how flat and spiritless will the last appear, how trite, and lamely methodical, compared with the wild-warbling cadence, the heart-moving melody of the first. This is particularly the case with all those airs which end with a hypermetrical syllable. There is a degree of wild irregularity in many of the compositions and fragments which are daily sung to them by my compeers, the common people—a certain happy arrangement of old Scotch syllables, and yet, very frequently, nothing, not even *like* rhyme, or sameness of jingle, at the ends of the lines. This has made me sometimes imagine that, perhaps it might be possible for a Scotch poet, with a nice judicious ear, to set compositions to many of our most favourite airs, particularly that class of them mentioned above, independent of rhyme altogether.

There is a noble sublimity, a heart-melting tenderness, in some of the ancient ballads, which shew them to be the work of a masterly hand: and it has often given me many a heartache to reflect, that such glorious old bards—bards who very probably owed all their talents to native genius, yet have described the exploits of heroes, the pangs of disappointment, and the meltings of love, with such fine strokes of nature—that their very names (O how mortifying to a bard's vanity!) are now "buried among the wreck of things which were."

O ye illustrious names unknown! who could feel so strongly and describe so well; the last, the meanest of the muses' train—one who, though far inferior to your flights, yet eyes your path, and with trembling wing would sometimes soar after you—a poor rustic bard unknown, pays this sympathetic pang to your memory! Some of you tell us, with all the charms of verse, that you have been unfortunate in the world—unfortunate in love: *he*, too, has felt the loss of his little fortune, the loss of friends, and, worse than all, the loss of the woman he adored. Like you, all his consolation was his muse: she taught him in rustic measures to complain. Happy could he have done it with your strength of imagination and flow of verse! May the turf lie lightly on your bones! and may you now enjoy that solace and rest which this world rarely gives to the heart tuned to all the feelings of poesy and love!

The following fragment is done, something in imitation of the manner of a noble old Scottish piece called *M'Millan's Peggy*, and sings to the tune of *Galla Water*. —My Montgomerie's Peggy was my deity for six or eight months. She had been bred (though, as the world says, without any just pretence for it) in a style of life rather elegant—but as Vanburgh says in one of his comedies, My " d——d star found me out," there too; for though I began the affair merely in a *gaieté de cœur*, or to tell the truth, which will scarcely be believed, a vanity of shewing my parts in courtship, particularly my abilities at a *Billet-doux*, which I always piqued myself upon, made me lay siege to her; and when, as I always do in my foolish gallantries, I had battered myself into a very warm affection for her, she told me, one day, in a flag of truce, that her fortress had been for some time before the rightful property of another; but, with the greatest friendship and politeness, she offered me every alliance except actual possession. I found out afterwards that what she told me of a pre-engagement was really true; but it cost me some heartache to get rid of the affair.

I have even tried to imitate, in this extempore thing, that irregularity in the rhyme, which, when judiciously done, has such a fine effect on the ear.—

Gallawater. *Tune:* Gallawater.

Altho' my bed were in yon muir,
   Amang the heather, in my plaidie,
Yet happy, happy would I be
   Had I my dear Montgomerie's Peggy. . . .

> When o'er the hill beat surly storms,
>   And winter nights were dark and rainy;
> I'd seek some dell, and in my arms
>   I'd shelter dear Montgomerie's Peggy.
>
> Were I a Baron proud and high
>   And horse and servants waiting ready,
> Then a' twad gie o' joy to me,
>   The sharin't with Montgomerie's Peggy. . . .

There is another fragment in imitation of an old Scotch song, well known among the country inglesides. . . . I cannot tell the name, neither of the song nor the tune, but they are in fine unison with one another. By the way, these old Scottish airs are so nobly sentimental, that when one would compose to them; to *south the tune*, as our Scotch phrase is, over and over, is the readiest way to catch the inspiration and raise the bard into that glorious enthusiasm so strongly characteristic of our old Scotch poetry. I shall here set down one verse of the piece mentioned above, both to mark the song and tune I mean, and likewise as a debt I owe to the author, as the repeating of that verse has lighted up my flame a thousand times.—

> When clouds in skies do come together
>   To hide the brightness of the sun,
> There will surely be some pleasant weather
>   When a' their storms are past and gone.
>
> Though fickle fortune has deceiv'd me,
>   She promis'd fair and perform'd but ill;
> Of mistress, friends, and wealth bereav'd me,
>   Yet I bear a heart shall support me still.
>
> I'll act with prudence as far's I'm able,
>   But if success I must never find,
> Then come misfortune, I bid thee welcome,
>   I'll meet thee with an undaunted mind.

The above was an extempore, under the pressure of a heavy train of misfortunes, which, indeed, threatened to undo me altogether. It was just at the close of that dreadful period mentioned on page viii, and though the weather has brightened up a little with me, yet there has always been since a tempest brewing round me in the grim sky of futurity, which I pretty plainly see will some time or other, perhaps, ere long, overwhelm me, and drive me into some doleful dell, to pine in solitary, squalid wretchedness. . . . However, as I hope my poor country muse, who, all rustic, awkward, and unpolished as she is, has more charms for me than any other of the pleasures of life beside—as I hope she will not then desert me, I may even then learn to be, if not happy, at least easy, and *south a song* to sooth my misery.

'Twas at the same time I set about composing an air in the old Scotch style. . . . I am not musical scholar enough to prick down my tune properly, so it can never see the light, and perhaps 'tis no great matter; but the following were the verses I composed to suit it.

> O raging fortune's withering blast
>   Has laid my leaf full low! O
> O raging fortune's withering blast
>   Has laid my leaf full low! O.
> My stem was fair, my bud was green,
>   My blossom sweet did blow; O
> The dew fell fresh, the sun rose mild,
>   And made my branches grow; O.
> But luckless fortune's northern storms
>   Laid a' my blossoms low, O
> But luckless fortune's northern storms
>   Laid a' my blossoms low, O.

The tune consisted of three parts, so that the above verses just went through the whole air.

SIR WALTER SCOTT

(1771–1832)

On Ballad Poetry

From "Introductory remarks on Popular Poetry and on the various collections of Ballads of Britain, particularly those of Scotland," originally prefixed to "The Minstrelsy of the Scottish Border," 1820.

It would be throwing away words to prove, what all must admit, the general taste and propensity of nations in their early state, to cultivate some species of rude poetry. When the organs and faculties of a primitive race have developed themselves, each for its proper and necessary use, there is a natural tendency to employ them in a more refined and regulated manner for purposes of amusement. The savage, after proving the activity of his limbs in the chase or the battle, trains them to more measured movements, to dance at the festivals of his tribe, or to perform obeisance before the altars of his deity. From the same impulse, he is disposed to refine the ordinary speech which forms the vehicle of social communication betwixt him and his brethren, until, by a more ornate diction, modulated by certain rules of rhythm, cadence, assonance of termination, or recurrence of sound or letter, he obtains a dialect more solemn in expression, to record the laws or exploits of his tribe, or more sweet in sound, in which to plead his own cause to his mistress.

This primeval poetry must have one general character in all nations, both as to its merits and its imperfections. The earlier poets have the advantage, and it is not a small one, of having the first choice out of the stock of materials which are proper to the art; and thus they compel later authors, if they would avoid slavishly imitating the fathers of verse, into various devices, often more ingenious than elegant, that they may establish, if not an absolute claim to originality, at least a visible distinction betwixt themselves and their predecessors. Thus it happens, that early poets almost uniformly display a bold, rude, original cast of genius and expression. They have walked at free-will, and with unconstrained steps, along the wilds of Parnassus, while their followers move with constrained gestures and forced attitudes, in order to avoid placing their feet where their predecessors have stepped before them. The first bard who compared his hero to a lion, struck a bold and congenial note, though the simile, in a nation of hunters, be a very obvious one; but every subsequent poet who shall use it, must either struggle hard to give his lion, as heralds say, with a *difference*, or lie under the imputation of being a servile imitator.

It is not probable that, by any researches of modern times, we shall ever reach back to an earlier model of poetry than Homer; but as there lived heroes before Agamemnon, so, unquestionably, poets existed before the immortal Bard who gave the King of kings his fame; and he whom all civilized nations now acknowledge as the Father of Poetry, must have himself looked back to an ancestry of poetical predecessors, and is only held original because we know not from whom he copied. Indeed, though much must be ascribed to the riches of his own individual genius, the poetry of Homer argues a degree of perfection in an art which practice had already rendered regular, and concerning which, his frequent mention of the bards, or chanters of poetry, indicates plainly that it was studied by many, and known and admired by all.

It is indeed easily discovered, that the qualities necessary for composing such poems are not the portion of every man in the tribe; that the bard, to reach excellence in his art, must possess something more than a full command of words and phrases, and the knack of arranging them in such form as ancient examples have fixed upon as the recognised structure of national verse. The tribe speedily become sensible, that besides this degree of mechanical facility, which (like making what are called at school nonsense verses) may be attained by dint of memory and practice, much higher qualifications are demanded. A keen and active power of observation, capable of perceiving at a glance the leading circumstances from which the incident described derives its character; quick and powerful feelings, to enable the bard to comprehend and delineate those of the actors in his piece; and a command of language, alternately soft and elevated, and suited to express the conceptions which he had formed in his mind, are all necessary to eminence in the poetical art.

Above all, to attain the highest point of his profession, the poet must have that original power of embodying and detailing circumstances, which can place before the eyes of others a scene which only exists in his own imagination. This last high and creative faculty, namely, that of impressing the mind of the hearers with scenes and sentiments having no existence save through their art, has procured for the bards of Greece the term of Ποιητης, which, as it singularly happens, is literally translated by the Scottish epithet for the same class of persons, whom they termed the *Makers*. The French phrase of Trouveurs, or Troubadours, namely, the Finders, or Inventors, has the same reference to the quality of original conception and invention proper to the poetical art, and without which it can hardly be said to exist to any pleasing or useful purpose.

The mere arrangement of words into poetical rhythm, or combining them according to a technical rule or measure, is so closely connected with the art of music, that an alliance between these two fine arts is very soon closely formed. It is fruitless to enquire which of them has been first invented, since doubtless the precedence is accidental; and it signifies little whether the musician adapts verses to a rude tune, or whether the primitive poet, in reciting his productions, falls naturally into a chant or song. With this additional accomplishment, the poet becomes ἀοιδος, or the man of song, and his character is complete when the additional accompaniment of a lute or harp is added to his vocal performance.

Here, therefore, we have the history of early poetry

in all nations. But it is evident that, though poetry seems a plant proper to almost all soils, yet not only is it of various kinds, according to the climate and country in which it has its origin, but the poetry of different nations differs still more widely in the degree of excellence which it attains. This must depend in some measure, no doubt, on the temper and manners of the people, or their proximity to those spirit-stirring events which are naturally selected as the subject of poetry, and on the more comprehensive or energetic character of the language spoken by the tribe. But the progress of the art is far more dependent upon the rise of some highly-gifted individual, possessing in a pre-eminent and uncommon degree the powers demanded, whose talents influence the taste of a whole nation, and entail on their posterity and language a character almost indelibly sacred. In this respect Homer stands alone and unrivalled, as a light from whose lamp the genius of successive ages, and of distant nations, has caught fire and illumination; and who, though the early poet of a rude age, has purchased for the era he has celebrated, so much reverence, that, not daring to bestow on it the term of barbarous, we distinguish it as the heroic period.

No other poet (sacred and inspired authors excepted) ever did, or ever will, possess the same influence over posterity, in so many distant lands, as has been acquired by the blind old man of Chios; yet we are assured that his works, collected by the pious care of Pisistratus, who caused to be united into their present form those divine poems, would otherwise, if preserved at all, have appeared to succeeding generations in the humble state of a collection of detached ballads, connected only as referring to the same age, the same general subjects, and the same cycle of heroes, like the metrical poems of the Cid in Spain, or of Robin Hood in England.

In other countries, less favoured, either in language or in picturesque incident, it cannot be supposed that even the genius of Homer could have soared to such exclusive eminence, since he must at once have been deprived of the subjects and themes so well adapted for his muse, and of the lofty, melodious, and flexible language in which he recorded them. Other nations, during the formation of their ancient poetry, wanted the genius of Homer, as well as his picturesque scenery and lofty language. Yet the investigation of the early poetry of every nation, even the rudest, carries with it an object of curiosity and interest. It is a chapter in the history of the childhood of society, and its resemblance to, or dissimilarity from, the popular rhymes of other nations in the same stage, must needs illustrate the ancient history of states; their slower or swifter progress towards civilisation; their gradual or more rapid adoption of manners, sentiments, and religion. The study, therefore, of lays rescued from the gulf of oblivion, must in every case possess considerable interest for the moral philosopher and general historian.

The historian of an individual nation is equally or more deeply interested in the researches into popular poetry, since he must not disdain to gather from the tradition conveyed in ancient ditties and ballads, the information necessary to confirm or correct intelligence collected from more certain sources. And although the poets were a fabling race from the very beginning of time, and so much addicted to exaggeration, that their accounts are seldom to be relied on without corroborative evidence, yet instances frequently occur where the statements of poetical tradition are unexpectedly confirmed.

To the lovers and admirers of poetry as an art, it cannot be uninteresting to have a glimpse of the National Muse in her cradle, or to hear her babbling the earliest attempts at the formation of the tuneful sounds with which she was afterward to charm posterity. And I may venture to add, that among poetry, which, however rude, was a gift of Nature's first fruits, even a reader of refined taste will find his patience rewarded, by passages in which the rude minstrel rises into sublimity or melts into pathos. These were the merits which induced the classical Addison[1] to write an elaborate commentary upon the ballad of *Chevy Chase*, and which

[1] See *The Spectator*, Nos. 70 and 74.

roused, like the sound of a trumpet, the heroic blood of Sir Philip Sidney.[1]

It is true, that passages of this high character occur seldom; for during the infancy of the art of poetry, the bards have been generally satisfied with a rude and careless expression of their sentiments; and even when a more felicitous expression, or loftier numbers, have been dictated by the enthusiasm of the composition, the advantage came unsought for, and perhaps unnoticed, either by the minstrel or the audience.

Another cause contributed to the tenuity of thought and poverty of expression, by which old ballads are too often distinguished. The apparent simplicity of the ballad stanza carried with it a strong temptation to loose and trivial composition. The collection of rhymes, accumulated by the earliest of the craft, appear to have been considered as forming a joint stock for the common use of the profession; and not mere rhymes only, but verses and stanzas, have been used as common property, so as to give an appearance of sameness and crudity to the whole series of popular poetry. Such, for instance, is the salutation so often repeated,

> Now Heaven thee save, thou brave young knight,
> Now Heaven thee save and see.

And such the usual expression for taking counsel with,

> Rede me, rede me, brother dear,
> My rede shall rise at thee.

Such also is the unvaried account of the rose and the brier, which are said to spring out of the grave of the hero and heroine of these metrical legends, with little effort at a variation of the expressions in which the incident is prescriptively told. The least acquaintance with the subject will recall a great number of commonplace verses, which each ballad-maker has unceremoniously appropriated to himself; thereby greatly

---

[1] I never heard the old song of *Percie and Douglas*, that I found not my heart moved more than with the sound of a trumpet; and yet it is sung but by some blind crowder, with no rougher voice than rude style.—SIDNEY.

ON BALLAD POETRY

facilitating his own task, and at the same time degrading his art by his slovenly use of over-scutched phrases. From the same indolence, the ballad-mongers of most nations have availed themselves of every opportunity of prolonging their pieces, of the same kind, without the labour of actual composition. If a message is to be delivered, the poet saves himself a little trouble, by using exactly the same words in which it was originally couched, to secure its being transmitted to the person for whose ear it was intended. The bards of ruder climes, and less favoured languages, may indeed claim the countenance of Homer for such repetitions; but whilst, in the Father of Poetry, they give the reader an opportunity to pause, and look back upon the enchanted ground over which they have travelled, they afford nothing to the modern bard, save facilitating the power of stupefying the audience with stanzas of dull and tedious iteration.

Another cause of the flatness and insipidity, which is the great imperfection of ballad poetry, is to be ascribed less to the compositions in their original state, when rehearsed by their *authors*, than to the ignorance and errors of the reciters or transcribers, by whom they have been transmitted to us. The more popular the composition of an ancient poet, or *Maker*, became, the greater chance there was of its being corrupted; for a poem transmitted through a number of reciters, like a book reprinted in a multitude of editions, incurs the risk of impertinent interpolations from the conceit of one rehearser, unintelligible blunders from the stupidity of another, and omissions equally to be regretted, from the want of memory in a third. This sort of injury is felt very early, and the reader will find a curious instance in the Introduction to the *Romance of Sir Tristrem*. Robert de Brunne there complains, that though the *Romance of Sir Tristrem* was the best which had ever been made, if it could be recited as composed by the author, Thomas of Erceldoune; yet that it was written in such an ornate style of language, and such a difficult strain of versification, as to lose all value in the mouths of ordinary minstrels, who could scarcely repeat one stanza without omitting some part of it, and marring, consequently, both the sense and the rhythm of the passage.[1] This deterioration could not be limited to one author alone; others must have suffered from the same cause, in the same or a greater degree. Nay, we are authorized to conclude, that in proportion to the care bestowed by the author upon any poem, to attain what his age might suppose to be the highest graces of poetry, the greater was the damage which it sustained by the inaccuracy of reciters, or their desire to humble both the sense and diction of the poem to their powers of recollection, and the comprehension of a vulgar audience. It cannot be expected that compositions subjected in this way to mutilation and corruption, should continue to present their original sense or diction; and the accuracy of our editions of popular poetry, unless in the rare event of recovering original or early copies, is lessened in proportion.

But the chance of these corruptions is incalculably increased, when we consider that the ballads have been, not in one, but innumerable instances of transmission, liable to similar alterations, through a long course of centuries, during which they have been handed from one ignorant reciter to another, each discarding whatever original words or phrases time or fashion had, in his opinion, rendered obsolete, and substituting anachronisms by expressions taken from the customs of his own day. And here it may be remarked, that the desire of the reciter to be intelligible, however natural and laudable, has been one of the greatest causes of the deterioration of ancient poetry. The minstrel who endeavoured to recite with fidelity the words of the author, might indeed fall into errors of sound and sense, and substitute corruptions for words he did not understand. But the ingenuity of a skilful critic could

[1] "That thou may hear in Sir Tristrem:
Over gestes it has the steem,
Over all that is or was,
If men it sayd as made Thomas:
But I hear it no man so say—
But of some copple some is away," etc

often, in that case, revive and restore the original meaning; while the corrupted words became, in such cases, a warrant for the authenticity of the whole poem.[1]

In general, however, the later reciters appear to have been far less desirous to speak the author's words, than to introduce amendments and new readings of their own, which have always produced the effect of modernizing, and usually that of degrading and vulgarizing, the rugged sense and spirit of the antique minstrel. Thus, undergoing from age to age a gradual process of alteration and recomposition, our popular and oral minstrelsy has lost, in a great measure, its original appearance; and the strong touches by which it had been formerly characterized, have been generally smoothed down and destroyed by a process similar to that by which a coin, passing from hand to hand, loses in circulation all the finer marks of the impress.

The very fine ballad of *Chevy Chase* is an example of this degrading species of alchymy, by which the ore of antiquity is deteriorated and adulterated. While Addison, in an age which had never attended to popular poetry, wrote his classical criticism on that ballad, he naturally took for his text the ordinary stall-copy, although he might, and ought to have suspected, that a ditty couched in the language nearly of his own time, could not be the same with that which Sir Philip Sidney, more than one hundred years before, had spoken of, as being "evil apparelled in the dust and cobwebs of an uncivilized age." The venerable Bishop Percy was the first to correct this mistake, by producing a copy of the song, as old at least as the reign of Henry VII, bearing the name of the author, or transcriber, Richard

---

[1] An instance occurs in the valuable old ballad, called *Auld Maitland*. The reciter repeated a verse, descriptive of the defence of a castle, thus:

"With *spring-wall*, stanes, and goads of airn
Among them fast he threw."

Spring-wall, is a corruption of *springald*, a military engine for casting darts or stones; the restoration of which reading gives a precise and clear sense to the lines.

Sheale.[1] But even the Rev. Editor himself fell under the mistake of supposing the modern *Chevy Chase* to be a new copy of the original ballad, expressly modernized by some one later bard. On the contrary, the current version is now universally allowed to have been produced by the gradual alterations of numerous reciters, during two centuries, in the course of which the ballad has been gradually moulded into a composition bearing only a general resemblance to the original—expressing the same events and sentiments in much smoother language, and more flowing and easy versification; but losing in poetical fire and energy, and in the vigour and pithiness of the expression, a great deal more than it has gained in suavity of diction. Thus:—

> The Percy owt of Northumberland,
> And a vowe to God mayd he,
> That he wolde hunte in the mountayns
> Off Cheviot within dayes thre,
> In the mauger of doughty Dougles,
> And all that ever with him be,

becomes,

> The stout Earl of Northumberland
> A vow to God did make,
> His pleasure in the Scottish woods
> Three summer days to take, etc.

From this, and other examples of the same kind, of which many might be quoted, we must often expect to find the remains of Minstrel poetry, composed originally for the courts of princes and halls of nobles, disguised in the more modern and vulgar dialect in which they have been of late sung to the frequenters of the rustic ale-bench. It is unnecessary to mention more than one other remarkable and humbling instance, printed in the curious collection entitled, *A Ballad Book*, where we find, in the words of the ingenious Editor,[2] a stupid ballad printed as it was sung in Annandale, founded on the well-known story of the Prince of Salerno's daughter, but with the uncouth change of

---

[1] See *Percy's Reliques*, vol. i. p. 2.
[2] Charles Kirkpatrick Sharpe. The *Ballad Book* was printed in 1823, and inscribed to Sir Walter Scott.

Dysmal for Ghismonda, and Guiscard transformed into a greasy kitchen-boy.

> To what base uses may we not return!

Sometimes a still more material and systematic difference appears between the poems of antiquity, as they were originally composed, and as they now exist. This occurs in cases where the longer metrical romances, which were in fashion during the Middle Ages, were reduced to shorter compositions, in order that they might be chanted before an inferior audience. A ballad, for example, of Thomas of Erceldoune, and his intrigues with the Queen of Faery-Land, is, or has been, long current in Teviotdale, and other parts of Scotland. Two ancient copies of a poem, or romance, on the same subject, and containing very often the same words and turns of expression, are preserved in the libraries of the Cathedral of Lincoln and Peterborough. We are left to conjecture whether the originals of such ballads have been gradually contracted into their modern shape by the impatience of later audiences, combined with the lack of memory displayed by more modern reciters, or whether, in particular cases, some ballad-maker may have actually set himself to work to retrench the old details of the minstrels, and regularly and systematically to modernize, and if the phrase be permitted, to balladize, a metrical romance. We are assured, however, that *Roswal and Lilian* was sung through the streets of Edinburgh two generations since; and we know that the *Romance of Sir Eger, Sir Grime, and Sir Greysteil*, had also its own particular chant, or tune. The stall-copies of both these romances, as they now exist, are very much abbreviated, and probably exhibit them when they were undergoing, or had nearly undergone, the process of being cut down into ballads.

Taking into consideration the various indirect channels by which the popular poetry of our ancestors has been transmitted to their posterity, it is nothing surprising that it should reach us in a mutilated and degraded state, and that it should little correspond with the ideas we are apt to form of the first productions of national genius; nay, it is more to be wondered at that we possess so many ballads of considerable merit, than that the much greater number of them which must have once existed, should have perished before our time.

Having given this brief account of ballad poetry in general, the purpose of the present prefatory remarks will be accomplished, by shortly noticing the popular poetry of Scotland, and some of the efforts which have been made to collect and illustrate it.

It is now generally admitted that the Scots and Picts, however differing otherwise, were each by descent a Celtic race; that they advanced in a course of victory somewhat farther than the present frontier between England and Scotland, and about the end of the eleventh century subdued and rendered tributary the Britons of Strathcluyd, who were also a Celtic race like themselves. Excepting, therefore, the provinces of Berwickshire and the Lothians, which were chiefly inhabited by an Anglo-Saxon population, the whole of Scotland was peopled by different tribes of the same aboriginal race,—a race passionately addicted to music, as appears from the kindred Celtic nations of Irish, Welsh, and Scottish, preserving each to this day a style and character of music peculiar to their own country, though all three bear marks of general resemblance to each other. That of Scotland, in particular, is early noticed and extolled by ancient authors, and its remains, to which the natives are passionately attached, are still found to afford pleasure even to those who cultivate the art upon a more refined and varied system.

This skill in music did not, of course, exist without a corresponding degree of talent for a species of poetry, adapted to the habits of the country, celebrating the victories of triumphant clans, pouring forth lamentations over fallen heroes, and recording such marvellous adventures as were calculated to amuse individual families around their household fires, or the whole tribe when regaling in the hall of the chief. It happened, however, singularly enough, that while the music continued to be Celtic in its general measure, the language of Scotland, most commonly spoken, began to be that of their neighbours the English, introduced by the multitude of Saxons who thronged to the court of Malcolm Canmore and his successors; by the crowds of prisoners of war, whom the repeated ravages of the Scots in Northumberland carried off as slaves to their country; by the influence of the inhabitants of the richest and most populous provinces in Scotland, Berwickshire, namely, and the Lothians, over the more mountainous; lastly, by the superiority which a language like the Anglo-Saxon, considerably refined, long since reduced to writing, and capable of expressing the wants, wishes, and sentiments of the speakers, must have possessed over the jargon of various tribes of Irish and British origin, limited and contracted in every varying dialect, and differing, at the same time, from each other. This superiority being considered, and a fair length of time being allowed, it is no wonder that, while the Scottish people retained their Celtic music, and many of their Celtic customs, together with their Celtic dynasty, they should nevertheless have adopted, throughout the Lowlands, the Saxon language, while in the Highlands they retained the Celtic dialect, along with the dress, arms, manners, and government of their fathers.

There was, for a time, a solemn national recognisance that the Saxon language and poetry had not originally been that of the royal family. For at the coronations of the kings of Scotland, previous to Alexander III, it was a part of the solemnity, that a Celtic bard stepped forth, so soon as the king assumed his seat upon the fated stone, and recited the genealogy of the monarch in Celtic verse, setting forth his descent, and the right which he had by birth to occupy the place of sovereignty. For a time, no doubt, the Celtic songs and poems remained current in the Lowlands, while any remnant of the language yet lasted. The Gaelic or Irish bards, we are also aware, occasionally strolled into the Lowlands, where their music might be received with favour, even after their recitation was no longer understood. But though these aboriginal poets showed themselves at festivals and other places of public resort, it does not appear that, as in Homer's time, they were honoured with high places at the board, and savoury morsels of the chine; but they seem rather to have been accounted fit company for the feigned fools and sturdy beggars, with whom they were ranked by a Scottish statute.[1]

Time was necessary wholly to eradicate one language and introduce another; but it is remarkable that, at the death of Alexander the Third, the last Scottish king of the pure Celtic race, the popular lament for his death was composed in Scoto-English, and, though closely resembling the modern dialect, is the earliest example we have of that language, whether in prose or poetry.[2] About the same time flourished the celebrated Thomas the Rhymer, whose poem, written in English, or Lowland Scottish, with the most anxious attention both to versification and alliteration, forms, even as it now exists, a very curious specimen of the early romance. Such complicated construction was greatly too concise for the public ear, which is best amused by a looser diction, in which numerous repetitions, and prolonged descriptions, enable the comprehension of the audience to keep up with the voice of the singer or reciter, and supply the gaps which in general must have taken place, either through a failure of attention in the hearers, or of voice and distinct enunciation on the part of the minstrel.

The usual stanza which was selected as the most natural to the language and the sweetest to the ear, after the complex system of the more courtly measures, used by Thomas of Erceldoune, was laid aside, was that which, when originally introduced, we very often find arranged in two lines, thus:—

Earl Douglas on his milk-white steed, most like a baron bold,
Rode foremost of his company, whose armour shone like gold;

---

[1] A curious account of the reception of an Irish or Celtic bard at a festival, is given in Sir John Holland's *Buke of the Houlat*, Bannatyne ed., p. liii.

[2] "Whan Alexander our king was ded,
  Wha Scotland led in luve and lee,
Away was sons of ale and bred,
  Of wine and wax, of game and glee."

ON BALLAD POETRY

but which, after being divided into four, constitutes what is now generally called the ballad stanza,—

> Earl Douglas on his milk-white steed,
> Most like a baron bold,
> Rode foremost of his company,
> Whose armour shone like gold.

The breaking of the lines contains a plainer intimation, how the stanza ought to be read, than every one could gather from the original mode of writing out the poem, where the position of the cæsura, or inflection of voice, is left to the individual's own taste. This was sometimes exchanged for a stanza of six lines, the third and sixth rhyming together. For works of more importance and pretension, a more complicated versification was still retained, and may be found in the tale of *Ralph Coilzear*, the *Adventures of Arthur at the Tarn-Wathelyn*, *Sir Gawain*, and *Sir Gologras*, and other scarce romances. A specimen of this structure of verse has been handed down to our times in the stanza of *Christ Kirk on the Green*, transmitted by King James I to Allan Ramsay and to Burns. The excessive passion for alliteration, which formed a rule of the Saxon poetry, was also retained in the Scottish poems of a more elevated character, though the more ordinary minstrels and ballad-makers threw off the restraint.

The varieties of stanza thus adopted for popular poetry were not, we may easily suppose, left long unemployed. In frontier regions, where men are continually engaged in active enterprise, betwixt the task of defending themselves and annoying their neighbours, they may be said to live in an atmosphere of danger, the excitation of which is peculiarly favourable to the encouragement of poetry. Hence, the expressions of Lesly the historian, in which he paints the delight taken by the Borderers in their peculiar species of music, and the rhyming ballads in which they celebrated the feats of their ancestors, or recorded their own ingenious stratagems in predatory warfare.

WILLIAM WORDSWORTH

(1770–1850)

Observations Prefixed to the Second Edition of "Lyrical Ballads."

This most famous of poets' prefaces was first published in 1800, in the volume of poems of that year. The Appendix on "Poetic Diction" was added two years later, when the Third Edition of the volume appeared.

It is supposed, that by the act of writing in verse an Author makes a formal engagement that he will gratify certain known habits of association; that he not only thus apprises the Reader that certain classes of ideas and expressions will be found in his book, but that others will be carefully excluded. This exponent or symbol held forth by metrical language must in different eras of literature have excited very different expectations: for example, in the age of Catullus, Terence, and Lucretius, and that of Statius or Claudian; and in our own country, in the age of Shakspeare and Beaumont and Fletcher, and that of Donne and Cowley, or Dryden, or Pope. I will not take upon me to determine the exact import of the promise which by the act of writing in verse an Author, in the present day, makes to his Reader; but I am certain it will appear to many persons that I have not fulfilled the terms of an engagement thus voluntarily contracted. They who have been accustomed to the gaudiness and inane phraseology of many modern writers, if they persist in reading this book to its conclusion, will, no doubt, frequently have to struggle with feelings of strangeness and awkwardness: they will look round for poetry, and will be induced to inquire by what species of courtesy these attempts can be permitted to assume that title. I hope therefore the Reader will not censure me, if I attempt to state what I have proposed to myself to perform; and also (as far as the limits of this notice will permit) to explain some of the chief reasons which have determined me in the choice of my purpose: that at least he may be spared any unpleasant feeling of disappointment, and that I myself may be protected from the most dishonourable accusation which can be brought against an Author, namely, that of an indolence which prevents him from endeavouring to ascertain what is his duty, or, when his duty is ascertained, prevents him from performing it.

The principal object, then, which I proposed to myself in these Poems was to chuse incidents and situations from common life, and to relate or describe them, throughout, as far as was possible, in a selection of language really used by men, and, at the same time, to throw over them a certain colouring of imagination, whereby ordinary things should be presented to the mind in an unusual way; and, further, and above all, to make these incidents and situations interesting by tracing in them, truly though not ostentatiously, the primary laws of our nature: chiefly, as far as regards the manner in which we associate ideas in a state of excitement. Low and rustic life was generally chosen, because, in that condition, the essential passions of the heart find a better soil in which they can attain their maturity, are less under restraint, and speak a plainer and more emphatic language; because in that condition of life our elementary feelings co-exist in a state of greater simplicity, and, consequently, may be more accurately contemplated, and more forcibly communicated; because the manners of rural life germinate from those elementary feelings; and from the necessary character of rural occupations, are more easily comprehended, and are more durable; and, lastly, because in that condition the passions of men are incorporated with the beautiful and permanent forms of nature. The language, too, of these men is adopted (purified indeed from what appears to be its real defects, from all lasting and rational causes of dislike or disgust) because such men hourly communicate with the best objects from which the best part of language is originally derived; and because, from their rank in society and the sameness and narrow circle of their intercourse, being less under the influence of social vanity, they convey their feelings and notions in simple and unelaborated expressions. Accordingly, such a language, arising out of repeated experience and regular feelings, is a more permanent, and a far more philosophical language, than that which is frequently substituted for it by Poets, who think that they are conferring honour upon themselves and their art, in proportion as they separate themselves from the sympathies of men, and indulge in arbitrary and capricious habits of expression, in order to furnish food for fickle tastes, and fickle appetites, of their own creation.[1]

I cannot, however, be insensible of the present outcry against the triviality and meanness, both of thought and language, which some of my contemporaries have occasionally introduced into their metrical compositions; and I acknowledge that this defect, where it exists, is more dishonourable to the Writer's own character than false refinement or arbitrary innovation, though I should contend at the same time, that it is far less pernicious in the sum of its consequences. From such verses the Poems in these volumes will be found distinguished at least by one mark of difference, that each of them has a worthy *purpose*. Not that I mean to say, I always began to write with a distinct purpose formally conceived; but my habits of meditation have so formed my feelings, as that my descriptions of such objects as strongly excite those feelings, will be found to carry along with them a *purpose*. If in this opinion I am mistaken, I can have little right to the name of a Poet. For all good poetry is the spontaneous overflow of powerful feelings: and though this be true, Poems to which any value can be attached were never produced on any variety of subjects but by a man, who, being possessed of more than usual organic sensibility, had also thought long and deeply. For our continued influxes of feeling are modified and directed by

[1] It is worth while here to observe, that the affecting parts of Chaucer are almost always expressed in language pure and universally intelligible even to this day.

our thoughts, which are indeed the representatives of all our past feelings; and, as by contemplating the relation of these general representatives to each other, we discover what is really important to men, so, by the repetition and continuance of this act, our feelings will be connected with important subjects, till at length, if we be originally possessed of much sensibility, such habits of mind will be produced, that, by observing blindly and mechanically the impulses of those habits, we shall describe objects, and utter sentiments, of such a nature, and in such connection with each other, that the understanding of the being to whom we address ourselves, if he be in a healthful state of association, must necessarily be in some degree enlightened, and his affections ameliorated.

I have said that each of these poems has a purpose. I have also informed my Reader what this purpose will be found principally to be: namely, to illustrate the manner in which our feelings and ideas are associated in a state of excitement. But, speaking in language somewhat more appropriate, it is to follow the fluxes and refluxes of the mind when agitated by the great and simple affections of our nature. This object I have endeavoured in these short essays to attain by various means; by tracing the maternal passion through many of its more subtle windings, as in the poems of the *Idiot Boy* and the *Mad Mother;* by accompanying the last struggles of a human being, at the approach of death, cleaving in solitude to life and society, as in the Poem of the *Forsaken Indian;* by showing, as in the Stanzas entitled *We are Seven*, the perplexity and obscurity which in childhood attend our notion of death, or rather our utter inability to admit that notion; or by displaying the strength of fraternal, or, to speak more philosophically, of moral attachment when early associated with the great and beautiful objects of nature, as in *The Brothers;* or, as in the Incident of *Simon Lee*, by placing my Reader in the way of receiving from ordinary moral sensations another and more salutary impression than we are accustomed to receive from them. It has also been part of my general purpose to attempt to sketch characters under the influence of less impassioned feelings, as in *The Two April Mornings, The Fountain, The Old Man Travelling, The Two Thieves*, etc., characters of which the elements are simple, belonging rather to nature than to manners, such as exist now, and will probably always exist, and which from their constitution may be distinctly and profitably contemplated. I will not abuse the indulgence of my Reader by dwelling longer upon this subject; but it is proper that I should mention one other circumstance which distinguishes these Poems from the popular Poetry of the day; it is this, that the feeling therein developed gives importance to the action and situation, and not the action and situation to the feeling. My meaning will be rendered perfectly intelligible by referring my Reader to the Poems entitled *Poor Susan* and the *Childless Father*, particularly to the last Stanza of the latter Poem.

I will not suffer a sense of false modesty to prevent me from asserting, that I point my Reader's attention to this mark of distinction, far less for the sake of these particular Poems than from the general importance of the subject. The subject is indeed important! For the human mind is capable of being excited without the application of gross and violent stimulants; and he must have a very faint perception of its beauty and dignity who does not know this, and who does not further know, that one being is elevated above another in proportion as he possesses this capability. It has therefore appeared to me, that to endeavour to produce or enlarge this capability is one of the best services in which, at any period, a Writer can be engaged; but this service, excellent at all times, is especially so at the present day. For a multitude of causes, unknown to former times, are now acting with a combined force to blunt the discriminating powers of the mind, and unfitting it for all voluntary exertion, to reduce it to a state of almost savage torpor. The most effective of these causes are the great national events which are daily taking place, and the increasing accumulation of men in cities, where the uniformity of their occupations produces a craving for extraordinary incident, which the rapid communication of intelligence hourly gratifies. To this tendency of life and manners the literature and theatrical exhibitions of the country have conformed themselves. The invaluable works of our elder writers, I had almost said the works of Shakspeare and Milton, are driven into neglect by frantic novels, sickly and stupid German Tragedies, and deluges of idle and extravagant stories in verse.—When I think upon this degrading thirst after outrageous stimulation, I am almost ashamed to have spoken of the feeble effort with which I have endeavoured to counteract it; and, reflecting upon the magnitude of the general evil, I should be oppressed with no dishonourable melancholy, had I not a deep impression of certain inherent and indestructible qualities of the human mind, and likewise of certain powers in the great and permanent objects that act upon it, which are equally inherent and indestructible; and did I not further add to this impression a belief, that the time is approaching when the evil will be systematically opposed, by men of greater powers, and with far more distinguished success.

Having dwelt thus long on the subjects and aim of these Poems, I shall request the Reader's permission to apprise him of a few circumstances relating to their *style*, in order, among other reasons, that I may not be censured for not having performed what I never attempted. The Reader will find that personifications of abstract ideas rarely occur in these volumes: and, I hope, are utterly rejected, as an ordinary device to elevate the style, and raise it above prose. I have proposed to myself to imitate, and, as far as is possible, to adopt the very language of men; and assuredly such personifications do not make any natural or regular part of that language. They are, indeed, a figure of speech occasionally prompted by passion, and I have made use of them as such; but I have endeavoured utterly to reject them as a mechanical device of style, or as a family language which Writers in metre seem to lay claim to by prescription. I have wished to keep my Reader in the company of flesh and blood, persuaded that by so doing I shall interest him. I am, however, well aware that others who pursue a different track may interest him likewise; I do not interfere with their claim, I only wish to prefer a different claim of my own. There will also be found in these pieces little of what is usually called poetic diction; I have taken as much pains to avoid it as others ordinarily take to produce it; this I have done for the reason already alleged, to bring my language near to the language of men, and further, because the pleasure which I have proposed to myself to impart, is of a kind very different from that which is supposed by many persons to be the proper object of poetry. I do not know how, without being culpably particular, I can give my Reader a more exact notion of the style in which I wished these poems to be written, than by informing him that I have at all times endeavoured to look steadily at my subject, consequently, I hope that there is in these Poems little falsehood of description, and that my ideas are expressed in language fitted to their respective importance. Something I must have gained by this practice, as it is friendly to one property of all good poetry, namely, good sense; but it has necessarily cut me off from a large portion of phrases and figures of speech which from father to son have long been regarded as the common inheritance of Poets. I have also thought it expedient to restrict myself still further, having abstained from the use of many expressions, in themselves proper and beautiful, but which have been foolishly repeated by bad Poets, till such feelings of disgust are connected with them as it is scarcely possible by any art of association to overpower.

If in a poem there should be found a series of lines, or even a single line, in which the language, though naturally arranged, and according to the strict laws of metre, does not differ from that of prose, there is a numerous class of critics, who, when they stumble upon these prosaisms, as they call them, imagine that they have made a notable discovery, and exult over the Poet as over a man ignorant of his own profession. Now these men would establish a canon of criticism which the Reader will conclude he must utterly reject, if he wishes to be pleased with these pieces. And it would be a most easy task to prove to him, that not only the language of a large portion of every good poem, even of the most elevated character, must necessarily, except with reference to the metre, in no respect differ from that of good prose, but likewise that some of the most interesting parts of the best poems will be found to be strictly the language of prose, when prose is well written. The truth of this assertion might be demonstrated by innumerable passages from almost all the poetical writings, even of Milton himself. I have not space for much quotation; but, to illustrate the subject in a general manner, I will here adduce a short composition of Gray, who was at the head of those who, by their reasonings, have attempted to widen the space of separation betwixt Prose and Metrical composition, and was more than any other man curiously elaborate in the structure of his own poetic diction.

> In vain to me the smiling mornings shine,
> And reddening Phœbus lifts his golden fire;
> The birds in vain their amorous descant join,
> Or cheerful fields resume their green attire.
> These ears, alas! far other notes repine;
> *A different object do these eyes require;*
> *My lonely anguish melts no heart but mine;*
> *And in my breast the imperfect joys expire:*
> Yet morning smiles the busy race to cheer,
> And new-born pleasure brings to happier men;
> The fields to all their wonted tribute bear;
> To warm their little loves the birds complain.
> *I fruitless mourn to him that cannot hear,*
> *And weep the more because I weep in vain.*

It will easily be perceived, that the only part of this Sonnet which is of any value is the lines printed in Italics; it is equally obvious, that, except in the rhyme, and in the use of the single word "fruitless" for fruitlessly, which is so far a defect, the language of these lines does in no respect differ from that of prose.

By the foregoing quotation I have shown that the language of Prose may yet be well adapted to Poetry; and I have previously asserted, that a large portion of the language of every good poem can in no respect differ from that of good Prose. I will go further. I do not doubt that it may be safely affirmed, that there neither is, nor can be, any essential difference between the language of prose and metrical composition. We are fond of tracing the resemblance between Poetry and Painting, and, accordingly, we call them Sisters: but where shall we find bonds of connection sufficiently strict to typify the affinity betwixt metrical and prose composition? They both speak by and to the same organs; the bodies in which both of them are clothed may be said to be of the same substance, their affections are kindred, and almost identical, not necessarily differing even in degree; Poetry [1] sheds no tears " such as Angels weep" but natural and human tears; she can boast of no celestial Ichor that distinguishes her vital juices from those of prose; the same human blood circulates through the veins of them both.

If it be affirmed that rhyme and metrical arrangement of themselves constitute a distinction which overturns what I have been saying on the strict affinity of metrical language with that of prose, and paves the way for other artificial distinctions which the mind voluntarily admits, I answer that the language of such Poetry as I am recommending is, as far as is possible, a selection of the language really spoken by men; that this selection, wherever it is made with true taste and feeling, will of itself form a distinction far greater than would at first be imagined, and will entirely separate the composition from the vulgarity and meanness of ordinary life; and, if metre be superadded thereto, I believe that a dissimilitude will be produced altogether sufficient for the gratification of a rational mind. What

---

[1] I here use the word "Poetry" (though against my own judgment) as opposed to the word Prose, and synonymous with metrical composition. But much confusion has been introduced into criticism by this contradistinction of Poetry and Prose, instead of the more philosophical one of Poetry and Matter of Fact, or Science. The only strict antithesis to Prose is Metre: nor is this, in truth, a *strict* antithesis; because lines and passages of metre so naturally occur in writing prose, that it would be scarcely possible to avoid them, even were it desirable.

other distinction would we have? Whence is it to come? And where is it to exist? Not, surely, where the Poet speaks through the mouths of his characters: it cannot be necessary here, either for elevation of style, or any of its supposed ornaments: for, if the Poet's subject be judiciously chosen, it will naturally, and upon fit occasion, lead him to passions the language of which, if selected truly and judiciously, must necessarily be dignified and variegated, and alive with metaphors and figures. I forbear to speak of an incongruity which would shock the intelligent Reader, should the Poet interweave any foreign splendour of his own with that which the passion naturally suggests: it is sufficient to say that such addition is unnecessary. And, surely, it is more probable that those passages, which with propriety abound with metaphors and figures, will have their due effect, if, upon other occasions where the passions are of a milder character, the style also be subdued and temperate.

But, as the pleasure which I hope to give by the Poems I now present to the Reader must depend entirely on just notions upon this subject, and, as it is in itself of the highest importance to our taste and moral feelings, I cannot content myself with these detached remarks. And if, in what I am about to say, it shall appear to some that my labour is unnecessary, and that I am like a man fighting a battle without enemies, I would remind such persons, that, whatever may be the language outwardly holden by men, a practical faith in the opinions which I am wishing to establish is almost unknown. If my conclusions are admitted, and carried as far as they must be carried if admitted at all, our judgments concerning the works of the greatest Poets both ancient and modern will be far different from what they are at present, both when we praise, and when we censure: and our moral feelings influencing and influenced by these judgments will, I believe, be corrected and purified.

Taking up the subject, then, upon general grounds, I ask what is meant by the word Poet? What is a Poet? To whom does he address himself? And what language is to be expected from him? He is a man speaking to men: a man, it is true, endued with more lively sensibility, more enthusiasm and tenderness, who has a greater knowledge of human nature, and a more comprehensive soul, than are supposed to be common among mankind; a man pleased with his own passions and volitions, and who rejoices more than other men in the spirit of life that is in him; delighting to contemplate similar volitions and passions as manifested in the goings-on of the Universe, and habitually impelled to create them where he does not find them. To these qualities he has added, a disposition to be affected more than other men by absent things as if they were present; an ability of conjuring up in himself passions, which are indeed far from being the same as those produced by real events, yet (especially in those parts of the general sympathy which are pleasing and delightful) do more nearly resemble the passions produced by real events, than any thing which, from the motions of their own minds merely, other men are accustomed to feel in themselves; whence, and from practice, he has acquired a greater readiness and power in expressing what he thinks and feels, and especially those thoughts and feelings which, by his own choice, or from the structure of his own mind, arise in him without immediate external excitement.

But, whatever portion of this faculty we may suppose even the greatest Poet to possess, there cannot be a doubt but that the language which it will suggest to him, must, in liveliness and truth, fall far short of that which is uttered by men in real life, under the actual pressure of those passions, certain shadows of which the Poet thus produces, or feels to be produced, in himself.

However exalted a notion we would wish to cherish of the character of a Poet, it is obvious, that, while he describes and imitates passions, his situation is altogether slavish and mechanical, compared with the freedom and power of real and substantial action and suffering. So that it will be the wish of the Poet to bring his feelings near to those of the persons whose feelings he describes, nay, for short spaces of time, perhaps, to let himself slip into an entire delusion, and even confound and identify his own feelings with theirs; modifying only the language which is thus suggested to him by a consideration that he describes for a particular purpose, that of giving pleasure. Here, then, he will apply the principle on which I have so much insisted, namely, that of selection; on this he will depend for removing what would otherwise be painful or disgusting in the passion; he will feel that there is no necessity to trick out or to elevate nature: and, the more industriously he applies this principle, the deeper will be his faith that no words, which *his* fancy or imagination can suggest, will be to be compared with those which are the emanations of reality and truth.

But it may be said by those who do not object to the general spirit of these remarks, that, as it is impossible for the poet to produce upon all occasions language as exquisitely fitted for the passion as that which the real passion itself suggests, it is proper that he should consider himself as in the situation of a translator, who deems himself justified when he substitutes excellencies of another kind for those which are unattainable by him; and endeavours occasionally to surpass his original, in order to make some amends for the general inferiority to which he feels that he must submit. But this would be to encourage idleness and unmanly despair. Further, it is the language of men who speak of what they do not understand; who talk of Poetry as of a matter of amusement and idle pleasure; who will converse with us as gravely about a *taste* for Poetry, as they express it, as if it were a thing as indifferent as a taste for Rope-dancing, or Frontiniac or Sherry. Aristotle, I have been told, hath said, that Poetry is the most philosophic of all writing: it is so: its object is truth, not individual and local, but general, and operative; not standing upon external testimony, but carried alive into the heart by passion; truth which is its own testimony, which gives strength and divinity to the tribunal to which it appeals, and receives them from the same tribunal. Poetry is the image of man and nature. The obstacles which stand in the way of the fidelity of the Biographer and Historian, and of their consequent utility, are incalculably greater than those which are to be encountered by the Poet who has an adequate notion of the dignity of his art. The Poet writes under one restriction only, namely, that of the necessity of giving immediate pleasure to a human Being possessed of that information which may be expected from him, not as a lawyer, a physician, a mariner, an astronomer, or a natural philosopher, but as a Man. Except this one restriction, there is no object standing between the Poet and the image of things; between this, and the Biographer and Historian there are a thousand.

Nor let this necessity of producing immediate pleasure be considered as a degradation of the Poet's art. It is far otherwise. It is an acknowledgment of the beauty of the universe, an acknowledgment the more sincere, because it is not formal, but indirect; it is a task light and easy to him who looks at the world in the spirit of love: further, it is a homage paid to the native and naked dignity of man, to the grand elementary principle of pleasure, by which he knows, and feels, and lives, and moves. We have no sympathy but what is propagated by pleasure: I would not be misunderstood; but wherever we sympathize with pain, it will be found that the sympathy is produced and carried on by subtle combinations with pleasure. We have no knowledge, that is, no general principles drawn from the contemplation of particular facts, but what has been built up by pleasure, and exists in us by pleasure alone. The Man of Science, the Chemist and Mathematician, whatever difficulties and disgusts they may have had to struggle with, know and feel this. However painful may be the objects with which the Anatomist's knowledge is connected, he feels that his knowledge is pleasure; and where he has no pleasure he has no knowledge. What then does the Poet? He considers man and the objects that surround him as acting and re-acting upon each other, so as to produce an infinite complexity of pain and pleasure; he considers man in his own nature and in his ordinary life as contemplating this with a certain quantity of immediate knowledge, with certain convictions, intuitions, and deductions, which by habit become of the nature of intuitions; he considers him as looking upon this complex scene of ideas and sensations, and finding every where objects that immediately excite in him sympathies which, from the necessities of his nature, are accompanied by an overbalance of enjoyment.

To this knowledge which all men carry about with them, and to these sympathies in which, without any other discipline than that of our daily life, we are fitted to take delight, the Poet principally directs his attention. He considers man and nature as essentially adapted to each other, and the mind of man as naturally the mirror of the fairest and most interesting qualities of nature. And thus the Poet, prompted by this feeling of pleasure which accompanies him through the whole course of his studies, converses with general nature with affections akin to those, which, through labour and length of time, the Man of Science has raised up in himself, by conversing with those particular parts of nature which are the objects of his studies. The knowledge both of the Poet and the Man of Science is pleasure; but the knowledge of the one cleaves to us as a necessary part of our existence, our natural and unalienable inheritance; the other is a personal and individual acquisition, slow to come to us, and by no habitual and direct sympathy connecting us with our fellow-beings. The Man of Science seeks truth as a remote and unknown benefactor; he cherishes and loves it in his solitude: the Poet, singing a song in which all human beings join with him, rejoices in the presence of truth as our visible friend and hourly companion. Poetry is the breath and finer spirit of all knowledge; it is the impassioned expression which is in the countenance of all Science. Emphatically may it be said of the Poet, as Shakspeare hath said of man, " that he looks before and after." He is the rock of defence of human nature; an upholder and preserver, carrying every where with him relationship and love. In spite of difference of soil and climate, of language and manners, of laws and customs, in spite of things silently gone out of mind, and things violently destroyed, the Poet binds together by passion and knowledge the vast empire of human society, as it is spread over the whole earth, and over all time. The objects of the Poet's thoughts are every where; though the eyes and senses of man are, it is true, his favourite guides, yet he will follow wheresoever he can find an atmosphere of sensation in which to move his wings. Poetry is the first and last of all knowledge—it is as immortal as the heart of man. If the labours of Men of Science should ever create any material revolution, direct or indirect, in our condition, and in the impressions which we habitually receive, the Poet will sleep then no more than at present, but he will be ready to follow the steps of the Man of Science, not only in those general indirect effects, but he will be at his side, carrying sensation into the midst of the objects of the Science itself. The remotest discoveries of the Chemist, the Botanist, or Mineralogist, will be as proper objects of the Poet's art as any upon which it can be employed, if the time should ever come when these things shall be familiar to us, and the relations under which they are contemplated by the followers of these respective Sciences shall be manifestly and palpably material to us as enjoying and suffering beings. If the time should ever come when what is now called Science, thus familiarized to men, shall be ready to put on, as it were, a form of flesh and blood, the Poet will lend his divine spirit to aid the transfiguration, and will welcome the Being thus produced, as a dear and genuine inmate of the household of man.—It is not, then, to be supposed that any one, who holds that sublime notion of Poetry which I have attempted to convey, will break in upon the sanctity and truth of his pictures by transitory and accidental ornaments, and endeavour to excite admiration of himself by arts, the necessity of which must manifestly depend upon the assumed meanness of his subject.

What I have thus far said applies to Poetry in general; but especially to those parts of composition where the Poet speaks through the mouths of his characters; and upon this point it appears to have such weight, that I will conclude, there are few persons of good sense, who would not allow that the dramatic parts of composition are defective, in proportion as they deviate from the real language of nature, and are coloured by a diction of the Poet's own, either peculiar to him as an individual Poet or belonging simply to Poets in general, to a body of men who, from the circumstance of their compositions being in metre, it is expected will employ a particular language.

It is not, then, in the dramatic parts of composition that we look for this distinction of language; but still it may be proper and necessary where the Poet speaks to us in his own person and character. To this I answer by referring my Reader to the description which I have before given of a Poet. Among the qualities which I have enumerated as principally conducing to form a Poet, is implied nothing differing in kind from other men, but only in degree. The sum of what I have there said is, that the Poet is chiefly distinguished from other men by a greater promptness to think and feel without immediate external excitement, and a greater power in expressing such thoughts and feelings as are produced in him in that manner. But these passions and thoughts and feelings are the general passions and thoughts and feelings of men. And with what are they connected? Undoubtedly with our moral sentiments and animal sensations, and with the causes which excite these; with the operations of the elements, and the appearances of the visible universe; with storm and sunshine, with the revolutions of the seasons, with cold and heat, with loss of friends and kindred, with injuries and resentments, gratitude and hope, with fear and sorrow. These, and the like, are the sensations and objects which the Poet describes, as they are the sensations of other men, and the objects which interest them. The Poet thinks and feels in the spirit of the passions of men. How, then, can his language differ in any material degree from that of all other men who feel vividly and see clearly? It might be *proved* that it is impossible. But supposing that this were not the case, the Poet might then be allowed to use a peculiar language when expressing his feelings for his own gratification, or that of men like himself. But Poets do not write for Poets alone, but for men. Unless therefore we are advocates for that admiration which depends upon ignorance, and that pleasure which arises from hearing what we do not understand, the Poet must descend from this supposed height, and, in order to excite rational sympathy, he must express himself as other men express themselves. To this it may be added, that while he is only selecting from the real language of men, or, which amounts to the same thing, composing accurately in the spirit of such selection, he is treading upon safe ground, and we know what we are to expect from him. Our feelings are the same with respect to metre; for, as it may be proper to remind the Reader, the distinction of metre is regular and uniform, and not, like that which is produced by what is usually called poetic diction,[1] arbitrary, and subject to infinite caprices upon which no calculation whatever can be made. In the one case, the Reader is utterly at the mercy of the Poet respecting what imagery or diction he may chuse to connect with the passion, whereas, in the other, the metre obeys certain laws, to which the Poet and Reader both willingly submit because they are certain, and because no interference is made by them with the passion but such as the concurring testimony of ages has shown to heighten and improve the pleasure which co-exists with it.

It will now be proper to answer an obvious question, namely, Why, professing these opinions, have I written in verse? To this, in addition to such answer as is included in what I have already said, I reply, in the first place, Because, however I may have restricted myself, there is still left open to me what confessedly

[1] See *Appendix*, page 193.

constitutes the most valuable object of all writing, whether in prose or verse, the great and universal passions of men, the most general and interesting of their occupations, and the entire world of nature, from which I am at liberty to supply myself with endless combinations of forms and imagery. Now, supposing for a moment that whatever is interesting in these objects may be as vividly described in prose, why am I to be condemned, if to such description I have endeavoured to superadd the charm which, by the consent of all nations, is acknowledged to exist in metrical language? To this, by such as are unconvinced by what I have already said, it may be answered that a very small part of the pleasure given by Poetry depends upon the metre, and that it is injudicious to write in metre, unless it be accompanied with the other artificial distinctions of style with which metre is usually accompanied, and that, by such deviation, more will be lost from the shock which will thereby be given to the Reader's associations than will be counterbalanced by any pleasure which he can derive from the general power of numbers. In answer to those who still contend for the necessity of accompanying metre with certain appropriate colours of style in order to the accomplishment of its appropriate end, and who also, in my opinion, greatly underrate the power of metre in itself, it might, perhaps, as far as relates to these Poems, have been almost sufficient to observe, that Poems are extant, written upon more humble subjects, and in a more naked and simple style than I have aimed at, which poems have continued to give pleasure from generation to generation. Now, if nakedness and simplicity be a defect, the fact here mentioned affords a strong presumption that poems somewhat less naked and simple are capable of affording pleasure at the present day; and, what I wished *chiefly* to attempt, at present, was to justify myself for having written under the impression of this belief.

But I might point out various causes why, when the style is manly, and the subject of some importance, words metrically arranged will long continue to impart such a pleasure to mankind as he who is sensible of the extent of that pleasure will be desirous to impart. The end of Poetry is to produce excitement in coexistence with an overbalance of pleasure. Now, by the supposition, excitement is an unusual and irregular state of the mind; ideas and feelings do not, in that state, succeed each other in accustomed order. But, if the words by which this excitement is produced are in themselves powerful, or the images and feelings have an undue proportion of pain connected with them, there is some danger that the excitement may be carried beyond its proper bounds. Now the co-presence of something regular, something to which the mind has been accustomed in various moods and in a less excited state, cannot but have great efficacy in tempering and restraining the passion by an intertexture of ordinary feeling, and of feeling not strictly and necessarily connected with the passion. This is unquestionably true, and hence, though the opinion will at first appear paradoxical, from the tendency of metre to divest language, in a certain degree, of its reality, and thus to throw a sort of half consciousness of unsubstantial existence over the whole composition, there can be little doubt, but that more pathetic situations and sentiments, that is, those which have a greater proportion of pain connected with them, may be endured in metrical composition, especially in rhyme, than in prose. The metre of the old ballads is very artless; yet they contain many passages which would illustrate this opinion, and, I hope, if the Poems referred to be attentively perused, similar instances will be found in them. This opinion may be further illustrated by appealing to the Reader's own experience of the reluctance with which he comes to the re-perusal of the distressful parts of *Clarissa Harlowe*, or *The Gamester*. While Shakspeare's writings, in the most pathetic scenes, never act upon us, as pathetic, beyond the bounds of pleasure—an effect which, in a much greater degree than might at first be imagined, is to be ascribed to small, but continual and regular impulses of pleasurable surprise from the metrical arrangement.—On the other hand, (what it must be allowed will much more frequently happen,) if the Poet's words should be incommensurate with the passion, and inadequate to raise the Reader to a height of desirable excitement, then, (unless the Poet's choice of his metre has been grossly injudicious,) in the feelings of pleasure which the Reader has been accustomed to connect with metre in general, and in the feeling, whether cheerful or melancholy, which he has been accustomed to connect with that particular movement of metre, there will be found something which will greatly contribute to impart passion to the words, and to effect the complex end which the Poet proposes to himself.

If I had undertaken a systematic defence of the theory upon which these poems are written, it would have been my duty to develope the various causes upon which the pleasure received from metrical language depends. Among the chief of these causes is to be reckoned a principle which must be well known to those who have made any of the Arts the object of accurate reflection; I mean the pleasure which the mind derives from the perception of similitude in dissimilitude. This principle is the great spring of the activity of our minds, and their chief feeder. From this principle the direction of the sexual appetite, and all the passions connected with it, take their origin: it is the life of our ordinary conversation; and upon the accuracy with which similitude in dissimilitude, and dissimilitude in similitude are perceived, depend our taste and our moral feelings. It would not have been a useless employment to have applied this principle to the consideration of metre, and to have shown that metre is hence enabled to afford much pleasure, and to have pointed out in what manner that pleasure is produced. But my limits will not permit me to enter upon this subject, and I must content myself with a general summary.

I have said that poetry is the spontaneous overflow of powerful feelings: it takes its origin from emotion recollected in tranquility: the emotion is contemplated till, by a species of re-action, the tranquillity gradually disappears, and an emotion, kindred to that which was before the subject of contemplation, is gradually produced and does itself actually exist in the mind. In this mood successful composition generally begins, and in a mood similar to this it is carried on; but the emotion of whatever kind, and in whatever degree, from various causes, is qualified by various pleasures, so that in describing any passions whatsoever, which are voluntarily described, the mind will, upon the whole, be in a state of enjoyment. Now if Nature be thus cautious in preserving in a state of enjoyment a being thus employed, the Poet ought to profit by the lesson thus held forth to him, and ought especially to take care, that, whatever passions he communicates to his Reader, those passions, if his Reader's mind be sound and vigorous, should always be accompanied with an overbalance of pleasure. Now the music of harmonious metrical language, the sense of difficulty overcome, and the blind association of pleasure which has been previously received from the works of rhyme or metre of the same or similar construction, and indistinct perception perpetually renewed of language closely resembling that of real life, and yet, in the circumstance of metre, differing from it so widely—all these imperceptibly make up a complex feeling of delight, which is of the most important use in tempering the painful feeling which will always be found intermingled with powerful descriptions of the deeper passions. This effect is always produced in pathetic and impassioned poetry; while, in lighter compositions, the ease and gracefulness with which the Poet manages his numbers are themselves confessedly a principal source of the gratification of the Reader. I might, perhaps, include all which it is *necessary* to say upon this subject, by affirming what few persons will deny, that, of two descriptions either of passions, manners, or characters, each of them equally well executed, the one in prose and the other in verse, the verse will be read a hundred times where the prose is read once. We see that Pope, by the power of verse alone, has contrived to render the plainest common sense interesting, and even frequently to invest it with the appearance of passion. In consequence of these convictions I related in metre the Tale of *Goody Blake and Harry Gill*, which is one of the rudest of this collection. I wished to draw attention to the truth, that the power of the human imagination is sufficient to produce such changes even in our physical nature as might almost appear miraculous. The truth is an important one; the fact (for it is a *fact*) is a valuable illustration of it: and I have the satisfaction of knowing that it has been communicated to many hundreds of people who would never have heard of it, had it not been narrated as a Ballad, and in a more impressive metre than is usual in Ballads.

Having thus explained a few of the reasons why I have written in verse, and why I have chosen subjects from common life, and endeavoured to bring my language near to the real language of men, if I have been too minute in pleading my own cause, I have at the same time been treating a subject of general interest; and it is for this reason that I request the Reader's permission to add a few words with reference solely to these particular poems, and to some defects which will probably be found in them. I am sensible that my associations must have sometimes been particular instead of general, and that, consequently, giving to things a false importance, sometimes from diseased impulses, I may have written upon unworthy subjects; but I am less apprehensive on this account, than that my language may frequently have suffered from those arbitrary connections of feelings and ideas with particular words and phrases, from which no man can altogether protect himself. Hence I have no doubt, that, in some instances, feelings, even of the ludicrous, may be given to my Readers by expressions which appeared to me tender and pathetic. Such faulty expressions, were I convinced they were faulty at present, and that they must necessarily continue to be so, I would willingly take all reasonable pains to correct. But it is dangerous to make these alterations on the simple authority of a few individuals, or even of certain classes of men; for where the understanding of an Author is not convinced, or his feelings altered, this cannot be done without great injury to himself: for his own feelings are his stay and support; and, if he sets them aside in one instance, he may be induced to repeat this act till his mind loses all confidence in itself, and becomes utterly debilitated. To this it may be added, that the Reader ought never to forget that he is himself exposed to the same errors as the Poet, and, perhaps, in a much greater degree: for there can be no presumption in saying, that it is not probable he will be so well acquainted with the various stages of meaning through which words have passed, or with the fickleness or stability of the relations of particular ideas to each other; and, above all, since he is so much less interested in the subject, he may decide lightly and carelessly.

Long as I have detained my Reader, I hope he will permit me to caution him against a mode of false criticism which has been applied to Poetry, in which the language closely resembles that of life and nature. Such verses have been triumphed over in parodies of which Dr. Johnson's stanza is a fair specimen.

> I put my hat upon my head
> And walked into the Strand,
> And there I met another man
> Whose hat was in his hand.

Immediately under these lines I will place one of the most justly-admired stanzas of the *Babes in the Wood*.

> These pretty babes with hand in hand
> Went wandering up and down;
> But never more they saw the Man
> Approaching from the Town.

In both these stanzas the words, and the order of the words, in no respect differ from the most unimpassioned conversation. There are words in both, for examale, 'the Strand," and " the Town," connected with none but the most familiar ideas; yet the one stanza we admit as admirable, and the other as a fair example of the superlatively contemptible. Whence arises this difference? Not from the metre, not from the language, not from the order of the words; but the *matter* expressed in Dr. Johnson's stanza is contemptible. The proper method of treating trivial and simple verses, to which Dr. Johnson's stanza would be a fair parallelism, is not to say, This is a bad kind of poetry, or, This is not poetry; but This wants sense; it is neither interesting in itself, nor can *lead* to any thing interesting; the images neither originate in that sane state of feeling which arises out of thought, nor can excite thought or feeling in the Reader. This is the only sensible manner of dealing with such verses. Why trouble yourself about the species till you have previously decided upon the genus? Why take pains to prove that an ape is not a Newton, when it is self-evident that he is not a man?

I have one request to make to my Reader, which is, that in judging these Poems he would decide by his own feelings genuinely, and not by reflection upon what will probably be the judgment of others. How common is it to hear a person say, "I myself do not object to this style of composition, or this or that expression, but, to such and such classes of people, it will appear mean or ludicrous!" This mode of criticism, so destructive of all sound unadulterated judgment, is almost universal: I have therefore to request, that the Reader would abide independently by his own feelings, and that, if he finds himself affected, he would not suffer such conjectures to interfere with his pleasure.

If an Author, by any single composition, has impressed us with respect for his talents, it is useful to consider this as affording a presumption, that on other occasions where we have been displeased, he, nevertheless, may not have written ill or absurdly; and, further, to give him so much credit for this one composition as may induce us to review what has displeased us, with more care than we should otherwise have bestowed upon it. This is not only an act of justice, but, in our decisions upon poetry especially, may conduce, in a high degreee, to the improvement of our own taste: for an *accurate* taste in poetry, and in all the other arts, as Sir Joshua Reynolds has observed, is an *acquired* talent, which can only be produced by thought and a long-continued intercourse with the best models of composition. This is mentioned, not with so ridiculous a purpose as to prevent the most inexperienced Reader from judging for himself (I have already said that I wish him to judge for himself), but merely to temper the rashness of decision, and to suggest, that, if Poetry be a subject on which much time has not been bestowed, the judgment may be erroneous; and that, in many cases, it necessarily will be so.

I know that nothing would have so effectually contributed to further the end which I have in view, as to have shown of what kind the pleasure is, and how that pleasure is produced, which is confessedly produced by metrical composition essentially different from that which I have here endeavoured to recommend: for the Reader will say that he has been pleased by such composition; and what can I do more for him? The power of any art is limited; and he will suspect, that, if I propose to furnish him with new friends, it is only upon condition of his abandoning his old friends. Besides, as I have said, the Reader is himself conscious of the pleasure which he has received from such composition, composition to which he has peculiarly attached the endearing name of Poetry; and all men feel an habitual gratitude, and something of an honourable bigotry for the objects which have long continued to please them; we not only wish to be pleased, but to be pleased in that particular way in which we have been accustomed to be pleased. There is a host of arguments in these feelings; and I should be the less able to combat them successfully, as I am willing to allow, that, in order entirely to enjoy the Poetry which I am recommending, it would be necessary to give up much of what is ordinarily enjoyed. But, would my limits have permitted me to point out how this pleasure is produced, I might have removed many obstacles, and assisted my Reader in perceiving that the powers of language are not so limited as he may suppose; and that it is possible for poetry to give other enjoyments, of a purer, more lasting, and more exquisite nature. This part of my subject I have not altogether neglected; but it has been less my present aim to prove, that the interest excited by some other kinds of poetry is less vivid, and less worthy of the nobler powers of the mind, than to offer reasons for presuming, that, if the object which I have proposed to myself were adequately attained, a species of poetry would be produced, which is genuine poetry; in its nature well adapted to interest mankind permanently, and likewise important in the multiplicity and quality of its moral relations.

From what has been said, and from a perusal of the Poems, the Reader will be able clearly to perceive the object which I have proposed to myself: he will determine how far I have attained this object; and, what is a much more important question, whether it be worth attaining; and upon the decision of these two questions will rest my claim to the approbation of the Public.

APPENDIX.

ON POETIC DICTION.

As, perhaps, I have no right to expect from a Reader of Observations on a volume of Poems that attentive perusal without which it is impossible, imperfectly as I have been compelled to express my meaning, that what is there said should, throughout, be fully understood, I am the more anxious to give an exact notion of the sense in which I use the phrase *poetic diction;* and for this purpose I will here add a few words concerning the origin of the phraseology which I have condemned under that name.—The earliest poets of all nations generally wrote from passion excited by real events; they wrote naturally, and as men: feeling powerfully as they did, their language was daring, and figurative. In succeeding times, Poets, and Men ambitious of the fame of Poets, perceiving the influence of such language, and desirous of producing the same effect without having the same animating passion, set themselves to a mechanical adoption of these figures of speech, and made use of them, sometimes with propriety, but much more frequently applied them to feelings and ideas with which they had no natural connexion whatsoever. A language was thus insensibly produced, differing materially from the real language of men in *any situation*. The Reader or Hearer of this distorted language found himself in a perturbed and unusual state of mind; when affected by the genuine language of passion he had been in a perturbed and unusual state of mind also: in both cases he was willing that his common judgment and understanding should be laid asleep, and he had no instinctive and infallible perception of the true to make him reject the false; the one served as a passport for the other. The agitation and confusion of mind were in both cases delightful, and no wonder if he confounded the one with the other, and believed them both to be produced by the same, or similar causes. Besides, the Poet spake to him in the character of a man to be looked up to, a man of genius and authority. Thus, and from a variety of other causes, this distorted language was received with admiration; and Poets, it is probable, who had before contented themselves for the most part with misapplying only expressions which at first had been dictated by real passion, carried the abuse still further, and introduced phrases composed apparently in the spirit of the original figurative language of passion, yet altogether of their own invention, and distinguished by various degrees of wanton deviation from good sense and nature.

It is indeed true that the language of the earliest Poets was felt to differ materially from ordinary language, because it was the language of extraordinary occasions; but it was really spoken by men, language which the Poet himself had uttered when he had been affected by the events which he described, or which he had heard uttered by those around him. To this language it is probable that metre of some sort or other was early superadded. This separated the genuine language of Poetry still further from common life, so that whoever read or heard the poems of these earliest Poets felt himself moved in a way in which he had not been accustomed to be moved in real life, and by causes manifestly different from those which acted upon him in real life. This was the great temptation to all the corruptions which have followed : under the protection of this feeling succeeding Poets constructed a phraseology which had one thing, it is true, in common with the genuine language of poetry, namely, that it was not heard in ordinary conversation ; that it was unusual. But the first Poets, as I have said, spake a language which, though unusual, was still the language of men. This circumstance, however, was disregarded by their successors ; they found that they could please by easier means : they became proud of a language which they themselves had invented, and which was uttered only by themselves ; and, with the spirit of fraternity, they arrogated it to themselves as their own. In process of time metre became a symbol or promise of this unusual language, and whoever took upon him to write in metre, according as he possessed more or less of true poetic genius, introduced less or more of this adulterated phraseology into his compositions, and the true and the false became so inseparably interwoven that the taste of men was gradually perverted ; and this language was received as a natural language : and at length, by the influence of books upon men, did to a certain degree really become so. Abuses of this kind were imported from one nation to another, and with the progress of refinement this diction became daily more and more corrupt, thrusting out of sight the plain humanities of nature by a motley masquerade of tricks, quaintnesses, hieroglyphics, and enigmas.

It would be highly interesting to point out the causes of the pleasure given by this extravagant and absurd language : but this is not the place ; it depends upon a great variety of causes, but upon none perhaps more than its influence in impressing a notion of the peculiarity and exaltation of the Poet's character, and in flattering the Reader's self-love by bringing him nearer to a sympathy with that character ; an effect which is accomplished by unsettling ordinary habits of thinking, and thus assisting the Reader to approach to that perturbed and dizzy state of mind in which if he does not find himself, he imagines that he is *balked* of a peculiar enjoyment which poetry can and ought to bestow.

The sonnet which I have quoted from Gray, in the Preface, except the lines printed in Italics, consists of little else but this diction, though not of the worst kind ; and indeed, if I may be permitted to say so, it is far too common in the best writers, both ancient and modern. Perhaps I can in no way, by positive example, more easily give my Reader a notion of what I mean by the phrase *poetic diction*, than by referring him to a comparison between the metrical paraphrase which we have of passages in the Old and New Testament, and those passages as they exist in our common Translation. See Pope's *Messiah* throughout : Prior's " Did sweeter sounds adorn my flowing tongue," etc., etc. " Though I speak with the tongues of men and of angels," etc., etc. See 1st Corinthians, chapter xiiith. By way of immediate example, take the following of Dr. Johnson :

> Turn on the prudent Ant thy heedless eyes,
> Observe her labours, Sluggard, and be wise ;
> No stern command, no monitory voice,
> Prescribes her duties, or directs her choice ;
> Yet, timely provident, she hastes away
> To snatch the blessings of a plenteous day ;
> When fruitful Summer loads the teeming plain,
> She crops the harvest and she stores the grain.
> How long shall sloth usurp thy useless hours,
> Unnerve thy vigour, and enchain thy powers ?
> While artful shades thy downy couch enclose,
> And soft solicitation courts repose,

> Amidst the drowsy charms of dull delight,
> Year chases year with unremitted flight,
> Till Want now following, fraudulent and slow,
> Shall spring to seize thee, like an ambushed foe.

From this hubbub of words pass to the original. "Go to the Ant, thou Sluggard, consider her ways, and be wise: which having no guide, overseer, or ruler, provideth her meat in the summer, and gathereth her food in the harvest. How long wilt thou sleep, O Sluggard? When wilt thou arise out of thy sleep? Yet a little sleep, a little slumber, a little folding of the hands to sleep. So shall thy poverty come as one that travaileth, and thy want as an armed man." Proverbs, chap. vi.

One more quotation, and I have done. It is from Cowper's verses, supposed to be written by Alexander Selkirk:

> Religion! what treasure untold
> Resides in that heavenly word!
> More precious than silver and gold,
> Or all that this earth can afford.
>
> But the sound of the church-going bell
> These valleys and rocks never heard,
> Ne'er sighed at the sound of a knell,
> Or smiled when a sabbath appeared.
>
> Ye winds, that have made me your sport,
> Convey to this desolate shore
> Some cordial endearing report
> Of a land I must visit no more.
>
> My Friends, do they now and then send
> A wish or a thought after me?
> O tell me I yet have a friend,
> Though a friend I am never to see.

I have quoted this passage as an instance of three different styles of composition. The first four lines are poorly expressed; some Critics would call the language prosaic; the fact is, it would be bad prose, so bad, that it is scarcely worse in metre. The epithet "church-going" applied to a bell, and that by so chaste a writer as Cowper, is an instance of the strange abuses which Poets have introduced into their language till they and their Readers take them as matters of course, if they do not single them out expressly as objects of admiration. The two lines, "Ne'er sigh'd at the sound," etc., are, in my opinion, an instance of the language of passion wrested from its proper use, and, from the mere circumstance of the composition being in metre, applied upon an occasion that does not justify such violent expressions; and I should condemn the passage, though perhaps few Readers will agree with me, as vicious poetic diction. The last stanza is throughout admirably expressed: it would be equally good whether in prose or verse, except that the Reader has an exquisite pleasure in seeing such natural language so naturally connected with metre. The beauty of this stanza tempts me to conclude with a principle which ought never to be lost sight of,—namely, that in works of imagination and sentiment, in proportion as ideas and feelings are valuable, whether the composition be in prose or in verse, they require and exact one and the same language. Metre is but adventitious to composition, and the phraseology for which that passport is necessary, even where it is graceful at all, will be little valued by the judicious.

SAMUEL TAYLOR COLERIDGE

(1772–1833)

Wordsworth and the Art of Poetry.

Certain Passages upon Poetry from the "Biographia Literaria."

> *The "Biographia Literaria" was published in 1817. The following passages comprise chapter xiv., which, besides dealing generally with poetic principles and the poetic art, forms the opening of Coleridge's reply to Wordsworth's preceding Essay. We need not add that the "Biographia" needs to be studied as a whole, for Coleridge's theory of poetry to be fully understood. But so much may fairly serve to represent him here.*

During the first year that Mr. Wordsworth and I were neighbours, our conversations turned frequently on the two cardinal points of poetry, the power of exciting the sympathy of the reader by a faithful adherence to the truth of nature, and the power of giving the interest of novelty by the modifying colours of imagination. The sudden charm, which accidents of light and shade, which moonlight or sunset, diffused over a known and familiar landscape, appeared to represent the practicability of combining both. These are the poetry of nature. The thought suggested itself (to which of us I do not recollect) that a series of poems might be composed of two sorts. In the one, the incidents and agents were to be, in part at least, supernatural; and the excellence aimed at was to consist in the interesting of the affections by the dramatic truth of such emotions, as would naturally accompany such situations, supposing them real. And real in this sense they have been to every human being who, from whatever source of delusion, has at any time believed himself under supernatural agency. For the second class, subjects were to be chosen from ordinary life; the characters and incidents were to be such as will be found in every village and its vicinity where there is a meditative and feeling mind to seek after them, or to notice them when they present themselves.

In this idea originated the plan of the *Lyrical Ballads;* in which it was agreed that my endeavours should be directed to persons and characters supernatural, or at least romantic; yet so as to transfer from our inward nature a human interest and a semblance of truth sufficient to procure for these shadows of imagination that willing suspension of disbelief for the moment, which constitutes poetic faith. Mr. Wordsworth, on the other hand, was to propose to himself as his object, to give the charm of novelty to things of every day, and to excite a feeling analogous to the supernatural, by awakening the mind's attention from the lethargy of custom, and directing it to the loveliness and the wonders of the world before us; an inexhaustible treasure, but for which, in consequence of the film of familiarity and selfish solicitude, we have eyes, yet see not, ears that hear not, and hearts that neither feel nor understand.

With this view I wrote the *Ancient Mariner,* and was preparing, among other poems, the *Dark Ladie,* and the *Christabel,* in which I should have more nearly realized my ideal than I had done in my first attempt. But Mr. Wordsworth's industry had proved so much more successful, and the number of his poems so much greater, that my compositions, instead of forming a balance, appeared rather an interpolation of heterogeneous matter. Mr. Wordsworth added two or three poems written in his own character, in the impassioned, lofty, and sustained diction which is characteristic of his genius. In this form the *Lyrical Ballads* were published; and were presented by him, as an experiment, whether subjects, which from their nature rejected the usual ornaments and extra-colloquial style of poems in general, might not be so managed in the language of ordinary life as to produce the pleasurable interest which it is the peculiar business of poetry to impart. To the second edition he added a preface of considerable length;

in which, notwithstanding some passages of apparently a contrary import, he was understood to contend for the extension of this style to poetry of all kinds, and to reject as vicious and indefensible all phrases and forms of style that were not included in what he (unfortunately, I think, adopting an equivocal expression) called the language of real life. From this preface, prefixed to poems in which it was impossible to deny the presence of original genius, however mistaken its direction might be deemed, arose the whole long-continued controversy. For from the conjunction of perceived power with supposed heresy I explain the inveteracy, and in some instances, I grieve to say, the acrimonious passions, with which the controversy has been conducted by the assailants.

Had Mr. Wordsworth's poems been the silly, the childish things which they were for a long time described as being; had they been really distinguished from the compositions of other poets merely by meanness of language and inanity of thought; had they indeed contained nothing more than what is found in the parodies and pretended imitations of them; they must have sunk at once, a dead weight, into the slough of oblivion, and have dragged the preface along with them. But year after year increased the number of Mr. Wordsworth's admirers. They were found, too, not in the lower classes of the reading public, but chiefly among young men of strong sensibility and meditative minds; and their admiration (inflamed perhaps in some degree by opposition) was distinguished by its intensity, I might almost say, by its religious fervour. These facts, and the intellectual energy of the author, which was more or less consciously felt, where it was outwardly and even boisterously denied, meeting with sentiments of aversion to his opinions, and of alarm at their consequences, produced an eddy of criticism, which would of itself have borne up the poems by the violence with which it whirled them round and round. With many parts of this preface, in the sense attributed to them, and which the words undoubtedly seem to authorize, I never concurred; but, on the contrary, objected to them as erroneous in principle, and as contradictory (in appearance at least) both to other parts of the same preface and to the author's own practice in the greater number of the poems themselves. Mr. Wordsworth, in his recent collection, has, I find, degraded this prefatory disquisition to the end of his second volume, to be read or not at the reader's choice. But he has not, as far as I can discover, announced any change in his poetic creed. At all events, considering it as the source of a controversy, in which I have been honoured more than I deserve by the frequent conjunction of my name with his, I think it expedient to declare, once for all, in what points I coincide with his opinions, and in what points I altogether differ. But in order to render myself intelligible, I must previously, in as few words as possible, explain my ideas, first, of a poem; and secondly, of poetry itself, in kind and in essence.

The office of philosophical disquisition consists in just distinction; while it is the privilege of the philosopher to preserve himself constantly aware that distinction is not division. In order to obtain adequate notions of any truth, we must intellectually separate its distinguishable parts; and this is the technical process of philosophy. But having so done, we must then restore them in our conceptions to the unity in which they actually co-exist; and this is the result of philosophy. A poem contains the same elements as a prose composition; the difference, therefore, must consist in a different combination of them, in consequence of a different object proposed. According to the difference of the object will be the difference of the combination. It is possible that the object may be merely to facilitate the recollection of any given facts or observations by artificial arrangement; and the composition will be a poem, merely because it is distinguished from prose by metre, or by rhyme, or by both conjointly. In this, the lowest sense, a man might attribute the name of a poem to the well-known enumeration of the days in the several months:

> Thirty days hath September,
> April, June, and November, etc.

and others of the same class and purpose. And as a particular pleasure is found in anticipating the recurrence of sound and quantities, all compositions that have this charm superadded, whatever be their contents, *may* be entitled poems.

So much for the superficial form. A difference of object and contents supplies an additional ground of distinction. The immediate purpose may be the communication of truths; either of truth absolute and demonstrable, as in works of science; or of facts experienced and recorded, as in history. Pleasure, and that of the highest and most permanent kind, may result from the attainment of the end; but it is not itself the immediate end. In other works the communication of pleasure may be the immediate purpose; and though truth, either moral or intellectual, ought to be the ultimate end, yet this will distinguish the character of the author, not the class to which the work belongs. Blest indeed is that state of society, in which the immediate purpose would be baffled by the perversion of the proper ultimate end; in which no charm of diction or imagery could exempt the Bathyllus even of an Anacreon, or the Alexis of Virgil, from disgust and aversion!

But the communication of pleasure may be the immediate object of a work not metrically composed; and that object may have been in a high degree attained, as in novels and romances. Would then the mere superaddition of metre, with or without rhyme, entitle these to the name of poems? The answer is, that nothing can permanently please, which does not contain in itself the reason why it is so, and not otherwise. If metre be superadded, all other parts must be made consonant with it. They must be such as to justify the perpetual and distinct attention to each part, which an exact correspondent recurrence of accent and sound are calculated to excite. The final definition then, so deduced, may be thus worded. A poem is that species of composition, which is opposed to works of science, by proposing for its immediate object pleasure, not truth; and from all other species (having this object in common with it) it is discriminated by proposing to itself such delight from the whole, as is compatible with a distinct gratification from each component part.

Controversy is not seldom excited in consequence of the disputants attaching each a different meaning to the same word; and in few instances has this been more striking than in disputes concerning the present subject. If a man chooses to call every composition a poem, which is rhyme, or measure, or both, I must leave his opinion uncontroverted. The distinction is at least competent to characterize the writer's intention. If it were subjoined, that the whole is likewise entertaining or affecting as a tale, or as a series of interesting reflections, I of course admit this as another fit ingredient of a poem, and an additional merit. But if the definition sought for be that of a legitimate poem, I answer, it must be one the parts of which mutually support and explain each other; all in their proportion harmonizing with, and supporting the purpose and known influences of metrical arrangement. The philosophic critics of all ages coincide with the ultimate judgment of all countries, in equally denying the praises of a just poem, on the one hand to a series of striking lines or distichs, each of which absorbing the whole attention of the reader to itself, disjoins it from its context, and makes it a separate whole, instead of a harmonizing part; and on the other hand, to an unsustained composition, from which the reader collects rapidly the general result unattracted by the component parts. The reader should be carried forward, not merely or chiefly by the mechanical impulse of curiosity, or by a restless desire to arrive at the final solution; but by the pleasurable activity of mind excited by the attractions of the journey itself. Like the motion of a serpent, which the Egyptians made the emblem of intellectual power; or like the path of sound through the air, at every step he pauses and half recedes, and from the retrogressive movement collects the force which again carries him onward. *Præcipitandus est liber spiritus*, says Petronius Arbiter most happily. The epithet, *liber*, here balances the preceding verb: and it is not easy to conceive more meaning condensed in fewer words.

But if this should be admitted as a satisfactory character of a poem, we have still to seek for a definition of poetry. The writings of Plato, and Bishop Taylor, and the *Theoria Sacra* of Burnet, furnish undeniable proofs that poetry of the highest kind may exist without metre, and even without the contradistinguishing objects of a poem. The first chapter of Isaiah (indeed a very large proportion of the whole book) is poetry in the most emphatic sense; yet it would be not less irrational than strange to assert, that pleasure, and not truth, was the immediate object of the prophet. In short, whatever specific import we attach to the word poetry, there will be found involved in it, as a necessary consequence, that a poem of any length neither can be, nor ought to be, all poetry. Yet if a harmonious whole is to be produced, the remaining parts must be preserved in keeping with the poetry; and this can be no otherwise effected than by such a studied selection and artificial arrangement as will partake of one, though not a peculiar, property of poetry. And this again can be no other than the property of exciting a more continuous and equal attention than the language of prose aims at, whether colloquial or written.

My own conclusions on the nature of poetry, in the strictest use of the word, have been in part anticipated in the preceding disquisition on the fancy and imagination. What is poetry? is so nearly the same question with, what is a poet? that the answer to the one is involved in the solution of the other. For it is a distinction resulting from the poetic genius itself, which sustains and modifies the images, thoughts, and emotions of the poet's own mind. The poet, described in ideal perfection, brings the whole soul of man into activity, with the subordination of its faculties to each other, according to their relative worth and dignity. He diffuses a tone and spirit of unity, that blends and, (as it were) fuses, each into each, by that synthetic and magical power, to which we have exclusively appropriated the name of imagination. This power, first put in action by the will and understanding, and retained under their irremissive, though gentle and unnoticed, control (*laxis effertur habenis*) reveals itself in the balance of reconciliation of opposite or discordant qualities : of sameness, with difference ; of the general, with the concrete ; the idea, with the image ; the individual, with the representative ; the sense of novelty and freshness, with old and familiar objects ; a more than usual state of emotion, with more than usual order ; judgment ever awake and steady self-possession, with enthusiasm and feeling profound or vehement ; and while it blends and harmonizes the natural and the artificial, still subordinates art to nature ; the manner to the matter ; and our admiration of the poet to our sympathy with the poetry. " Doubtless," as Sir John Davies observes of the soul (and his words may with slight alteration be applied, and even more appropriately, to the poetic imagination),—

> Doubtless this could not be, but that she turns
> Bodies to spirit by sublimation strange,
> As fire converts to fire, the things it burns,
> As we our food into our nature change.
>
> From their gross matter she abstracts their forms,
> And draws a kind of quintessence from things ;
> Which to her proper nature she transforms
> To bear them light on her celestial wings.
>
> Thus does she, when from individual states
> She doth abstract the universal kinds ;
> Which then re-clothed in divers names and fates
> Steal access through our senses to our minds.

Finally, good sense is the body of poetic genius, fancy its drapery, motion its life, and imagination the soul that is everywhere, and in each ; and forms all into one graceful and intelligent whole.

PERCY BYSSHE SHELLEY

(1792–1822)

A Defence of Poetry.

The " Defence " was written at Pisa in 1821, in reply to an article by Peacock in Ollier's " Literary Miscellany." It was intended to extend to three parts, only the first of which was completed. It was first published by Lady Shelley in the " Essays and Letters " in 1824.

ACCORDING to one mode of regarding those two classes of mental action, which are called reason and imagination, the former may be considered as mind contemplating the relations borne by one thought to another, however produced, and the latter, as mind acting upon those thoughts so as to colour them with its own light, and composing from them, as from elements, other thoughts, each containing within itself the principle of its own integrity. The one is the τὸ ποιειν, or the principle of synthesis, and has for its objects those forms which are common to universal nature and existence itself; the other is the τὸ λογιζειν, or principle of analysis, and its action regards the relations of things simply as relations; considering thoughts, not in their integral unity, but as the algebraical representations which conduct to certain general results. Reason is the enumeration of qualities already known; imagination is the perception of the value of those quantities, both separately and as a whole. Reason respects the differences, and imagination the similitudes of things. Reason is to imagination as the instrument to the agent, as the body to the spirit, as the shadow to the substance.

Poetry, in a general sense, may be defined to be " the expression of the imagination "; and poetry is connate with the origin of man. Man is an instrument over which a series of external and internal impressions are driven, like the alternations of an ever-changing wind over an Æolian lyre, which move it by their motion to ever-changing melody. But there is a principle within the human being, and perhaps within all sentient beings, which acts otherwise than in the lyre, and produces not melody alone, but harmony, by an internal adjustment of the sounds or motions thus excited to the impressions which excite them. It is as if the lyre could accommodate its chords to the motions of that which strikes them, in a determined proportion of sound; even as the musician can accommodate his voice to the sound of the lyre. A child at play by itself will express its delight by its voice and motions: and every inflexion of tone and every gesture will bear exact relation to a corresponding antitype in the pleasurable impressions which awakened it; it will be the reflected image of that impression; and as the lyre trembles and sounds after the wind has died away, so the child seeks, by prolonging in its voice and motions the duration of the effect, to prolong also a consciousness of the cause. In relation to the objects which delight a child, these expressions are, what poetry is to higher objects. The savage (for the savage is to ages what the child is to years) expresses the emotions produced in him by surrounding objects in a similar manner; and language and gesture, together with plastic or pictorial imitation, become the image of the combined effect of those objects, and of his apprehension of them. Man in society, with all his passions and his pleasures, next becomes the object of the passions and pleasures of man; an additional class of emotions produces an augmented treasure of expressions; and language, gesture, and the imitative arts, become at once the representation and the medium, the pencil and the picture, the chisel and the statue, the chord and the harmony. The social sympathies, or those laws from which, as from its elements, society results, begin to develop themselves from the moment that two human beings co-exist; the future is contained within the present, as the plant within the seed; and equality, diversity, unity, contrast, mutual dependence, become the principles alone capable of affording the motives according to which the will of a social being is determined to action, inasmuch as he is social; and constitute pleasure in sensation, virtue in sentiment, beauty in art, truth in reasoning, and love in the intercourse of kind. Hence men, even in the infancy of society, observe a certain order in their words and actions, distinct from that of the objects and the impressions represented by them, all expression being subject to the laws of that from which it proceeds. But let us dismiss those more general considerations which might involve an inquiry into the principles of society itself, and restrict our view to the manner in which the imagination is expressed upon its forms.

In the youth of the world, men dance and sing and imitate natural objects, observing in these actions, as in all others, a certain rhythm or order. And, although all men observe a similar, they observe not the same order, in the motions of the dance, in the melody of the song, in the combinations of language, in the series of their imitations of natural objects. For there is a certain order or rhythm belonging to each of these classes of mimetic representation, from which the hearer and the spectator receive an intenser and purer pleasure than from any other: the sense of an approximation to this order has been called taste by modern writers. Every man in the infancy of art, observes an order which approximates more or less closely to that from which this highest delight results: but the diversity is not sufficiently marked, as that its gradations should be sensible, except in those instances where the predominance of this faculty of approximation to the beautiful (for so we may be permitted to name the relation between this highest pleasure and its cause) is very great. Those in whom it exists in excess are poets, in the most universal sense of the word; and the pleasure resulting from the manner in which they express the influence of society or nature upon their own minds, communicates itself to others, and gathers a sort of reduplication from that community. Their language is vitally metaphorical; that is, it marks the before unapprehended relations of things and perpetuates their apprehension, until the words which represent them, become, through time, signs for portions or classes of thoughts instead of pictures of integral thoughts; and then if no new poets should arise to create afresh the associations which have been thus disorganized, language will be dead to all the nobler purposes of human intercourse. These similitudes or relations are finely said by Lord Bacon to be "the same footsteps of nature impressed upon the various subjects of the world"[1]—and he considers the faculty which perceives them as the storehouse of axioms common to all knowledge. In the infancy of society every author is necessarily a poet, because language itself is poetry; and to be a poet is to apprehend the true and the beautiful, in a word, the good which exists in the relation, subsisting, first between existence and perception, and secondly between perception and expression. Every original language near to its source is in itself the chaos of a cyclic poem: the copiousness of lexicography and the distinctions of grammar are the works of a later age, and are merely the catalogue and the form of the creations of poetry.

But poets, or those who imagine and express this indestructible order, are not only the authors of language and of music, of the dance, and architecture, and statuary, and painting: they are the institutors of laws, and the founders of civil society, and the inventors of the arts of life, and the teachers, who draw into a certain propinquity with the beautiful and the true, that partial apprehension of the agencies of the invisible world which is called religion. Hence all original religions are allegorical, or susceptible of allegory, and, like Janus, have a double face of false and true. Poets, according to the circumstances of the age and nation in which they appeared, were called, in the earlier epochs of the world, legislators, or prophets: a poet essentially comprises and unites both these characters. For he not only beholds intensely the present as it is, and discovers those laws according to which present things ought to be ordered, but he beholds the future in the present, and his thoughts are the germs of the flower and the fruit of latest time. Not that I assert

[1] *De Augment. Scient.*, cap. 1, lib. iii.

poets to be prophets in the gross sense of the word, or that they can foretell the form as surely as they foreknow the spirit of events : such is the pretence of superstition, which would make poetry an attribute of prophecy, rather than prophecy an attribute to poetry. A poet participates in the eternal, the infinite, and the one ; as far as relates to his conceptions, time and place and number are not. The grammatical forms which express the moods of time, and the difference of persons, and the distinction of place, are convertible with respect to the highest poetry without injuring it as poetry; and the choruses of Æschylus, and the Book of Job, and Dante's Paradise, would afford, more than any other writings, examples of this fact, if the limits of this essay did not forbid citation. The creations of sculpture, painting, and music are illustrations still more decisive.

Language, colour, form, and religious and civil habits of action, are all the instruments and materials of poetry ; they may be called poetry by that figure of speech which considers the effect as a synonyme of the cause. But poetry in a more restricted sense expresses those arrangements of language, and especially metrical language, which are created by that imperial faculty, whose throne is curtained within the invisible nature of man. And this springs from the nature itself of language, which is a more direct representation of the actions and passions of our internal being, and is susceptible of more various and delicate combinations, than colour, form, or motion, and is more plastic and obedient to the control of that faculty of which it is the creation. For language is arbitrarily produced by the imagination, and has relation to thoughts alone ; but all other materials, instruments, and conditions of art have relations among each other, which limit and interpose between conception and expression. The former is as a mirror which reflects, the latter as a cloud which enfeebles, the light of which both are mediums of communication. Hence the fame of sculptors, painters, and musicians, although the intrinsic powers of the great masters of these arts may yield in no degree to that of those who have employed language as the hieroglyphic of their thoughts, has never equalled that of poets in the restricted sense of the term; as two performers of equal skill will produce unequal effects from a guitar and a harp. The fame of legislators and founders of religions, so long as their institutions last, alone seems to exceed that of poets in the restricted sense; but it can scarcely be a question, whether, if we deduct the celebrity which their flattery of the gross opinions of the vulgar usually conciliates, together with that which belonged to them in their higher character of poets, any excess will remain.

We have thus circumscribed the word poetry within the limits of that art which is the most familiar and the most perfect expression of the faculty itself. It is necessary, however, to make the circle still narrower, and to determine the distinction between measured and unmeasured language; for the popular division into prose and verse is inadmissible in accurate philosophy.

Sounds as well as thoughts have relation both between each other and towards that which they represent, and a perception of the order of those relations has always been found connected with a perception of the order of the relations of thoughts. Hence the language of poets has ever affected a certain uniform and harmonious recurrence of sound, without which it were not poetry, and which is scarcely less indispensable to the communication of its influence, than the words themselves, without reference to that peculiar order. Hence the vanity of translation; it were as wise to cast a violet into a crucible that you might discover the formal principle of its colour and odour, as seek to transfuse from one language into another the creations of a poet. The plant must spring again from its seed, or it will bear no flower—and this is the burthen of the curse of Babel.

An observation of the regular mode of the recurrence of harmony in the language of poetical minds, together with its relation to music, produced metre, or a certain system of traditional forms of harmony and language. Yet it is by no means essential that a poet should accommodate his language to this traditional form, so that the harmony, which is its spirit, be observed. The practice is indeed convenient and popular, and to be preferred, especially in such composition as includes much action: but every great poet must inevitably innovate upon the example of his predecessors in the exact structure of his peculiar versification. The distinction between poets and prose writers is a vulgar error. The distinction between philosophers and poets has been anticipated. Plato was essentially a poet—the truth and splendour of his imagery, and the melody of his language, are the most intense that it is possible to conceive. He rejected the measure of the epic, dramatic, and lyrical forms, because he sought to kindle a harmony in thoughts divested of shape and action, and he forebore to invent any regular plan of rhythm which would include, under determinate forms, the varied pauses of his style. Cicero sought to imitate the cadence of his periods, but with little success. Lord Bacon was a poet.[1] His language has a sweet and majestic rhythm, which satisfies the sense, no less than the almost superhuman wisdom of his philosophy satisfies the intellect; it is a strain which distends, and then bursts the circumference of the reader's mind, and pours itself forth together with it into the universal element with which it has perpetual sympathy. All the authors of revolutions in opinion are not only necessarily poets as they are inventors, nor even as their words unveil the permanent analogy of things by images which participate in the life of truth; but as their periods are harmonious and rhythmical, and contain in themselves the elements of verse; being the echo of the eternal music. Nor are those supreme poets, who have employed traditional forms of rhythm on account of the form and action of their subjects, less capable of perceiving and teaching the truth of things, than those who have omitted that form. Shakspeare, Dante, and Milton (to confine ourselves to modern writers) are philosophers of the very loftiest power.

A poem is the very image of life expressed in its

[1] See the *Filum Labyrinthi*, and the *Essay on Death* particularly.

eternal truth. There is this difference between a story and a poem, that a story is a catalogue of detached facts, which have no other connection than time, place, circumstance, cause and effect; the other is the creation of actions according to the unchangeable forms of human nature, as existing in the mind of the Creator, which is itself the image of all other minds. The one is partial, and applies only to a definite period of time, and a certain combination of events which can never again recur; the other is universal, and contains within itself the germ of a relation to whatever motives or actions have place in the possible varieties of human nature. Time, which destroys the beauty and the use of the story of particular facts, stripped of the poetry which should invest them, augments that of poetry, and for ever develops new and wonderful applications of the eternal truth which it contains. Hence epitomes have been called the moths of just history; they eat out the poetry of it. A story of particular facts is as a mirror which obscures and distorts that which should be beautiful: poetry is a mirror which makes beautiful that which is distorted.

The parts of a composition may be poetical, without the composition as a whole being a poem. A single sentence may be considered as a whole, though it may be found in the midst of a series of unassimilated portions; a single word even may be a spark of inextinguishable thought. And thus all the great historians, Herodotus, Plutarch, Livy, were poets; and although the plan of these writers, especially that of Livy, restrained them from developing this faculty in its highest degree, they made copious and ample amends for their subjection, by filling all the interstices of their subjects with living images.

Having determined what is poetry, and who are poets, let us proceed to estimate its effects upon society.

Poetry is ever accompanied with pleasure: all spirits on which it falls open themselves to receive the wisdom which is mingled with its delight. In the infancy of the world, neither poets themselves nor their auditors are fully aware of the excellence of poetry: for it acts in a divine and unapprehended manner, beyond and above consciousness; and it is reserved for future generations to contemplate and measure the mighty cause and effect in all the strength and splendour of their union. Even in modern times, no living poet ever arrived at the fullness of his fame; the jury which sits in judgment upon a poet, belonging as he does to all time, must be composed of his peers: it must be impanelled by Time from the selectest of the wise of many generations. A poet is a nightingale, who sits in darkness and sings to cheer its own solitude with sweet sounds; his auditors are as men entranced by the melody of an unseen musician, who feel that they are moved and softened, yet know not whence or why. The poems of Homer and his contemporaries were the delight of infant Greece; they were the elements of that social system which is the column upon which all succeeding civilization has reposed. Homer embodied the ideal perfection of his age in human character; nor can we doubt that those who read his verses were awakened to an ambition of becoming like to Achilles, Hector, and Ulysses: the truth and beauty of friendship, patriotism, and persevering devotion to an object, were unveiled to the depths in these immortal creations: the sentiments of the auditors must have been refined and enlarged by a sympathy with such great and lovely impersonations, until from admiring they imitated, and from imitation they identified themselves with the objects of their admiration. Nor let it be objected, that these characters are remote from moral perfection, and that they can by no means be considered as edifying patterns for general imitation. Every epoch, under names more or less specious, has defied its peculiar errors; Revenge is the naked idol of the worship of a semi-barbarous age; and Self-deceit is the veiled image of unknown evil, before which luxury and satiety lie prostrate. But a poet considers the vices of his contemporaries the temporary dress in which his creations must be arrayed, and which cover without concealing the eternal proportions of their beauty. An epic or dramatic personage is understood to wear them around his soul, as he may the ancient armour or the modern uniform around his body; whilst it is easy to conceive a dress more graceful than either. The beauty of the internal nature cannot be so far concealed by its accidental vesture, but that the spirit of its form shall communicate itself to the very disguise, and indicate the shape it hides from the manner in which it is worn. A majestic form and graceful motions will express themselves through the most barbarous and tasteless costume. Few poets of the highest class have chosen to exhibit the beauty of their conceptions in its naked truth and splendour; and it is doubtful whether the alloy of costume, habit, etc., be not necessary to temper this planetary music for mortal ears.

The whole objection, however, of the immorality of poetry rests upon a misconception of the manner in which poetry acts to produce the moral improvement of man. Ethical science arranges the elements which poetry has created, and propounds schemes and proposes examples of civil and domestic life: nor is it for want of admirable doctrines that men hate, and despise, and censure, and deceive, and subjugate one another. But poetry acts in another and diviner manner. It awakens and enlarges the mind itself by rendering it the receptacle of a thousand unapprehended combinations of thought. Poetry lifts the veil from the hidden beauty of the world, and makes familiar objects be as if they were not familiar; it reproduces all that it represents, and the impersonations clothed in its Elysian light stand thenceforward in the minds of those who have once contemplated them, as memorials of that gentle and exalted content which extends itself over all thoughts and actions with which it co-exists. The great secret of morals is love; or a going out of our nature, and an identification of ourselves with the beautiful which exists in thought, action, or person, not our own. A man, to be greatly good, must imagine intensely and comprehensively; he must put himself in the place of another and of many others; the pains and pleasures of his species must become his own. The great instrument of moral good is the imagination;

and poetry administers to the effect by acting upon the cause. Poetry enlarges the circumference of the imagination by replenishing it with thoughts of ever new delight, which have the power of attracting and assimilating to their own nature all other thoughts, and which form new intervals and interstices whose void for ever craves fresh food. Poetry strengthens the faculty which is the organ of the moral nature of man, in the same manner as exercise strengthens a limb. A poet therefore would do ill to embody his own conceptions of right and wrong, which are usually those of his place and time, in his poetical creations, which participate in neither. By this assumption of the inferior office of interpreting the effect, in which perhaps after all he might acquit himself but imperfectly, he would resign a glory in a participation in the cause. There was little danger that Homer, or any of the eternal poets, should have so far misunderstood themselves as to have abdicated this throne of their widest dominion. Those in whom the poetical faculty, though great, is less intense, as Euripides, Lucan, Tasso, Spenser, have frequently affected a moral aim, and the effect of their poetry is diminished in exact proportion to the degree in which they compel us to advert to this purpose.

Homer and the cyclic poets were followed at a certain interval by the dramatic and lyrical poets of Athens, who flourished contemporaneously with all that is most perfect in the kindred expressions of the poetical faculty; architecture, painting, music, the dance, sculpture, philosophy, and we may add, the forms of civil life. For although the scheme of Athenian society was deformed by many imperfections which the poetry existing in chivalry and Christianity has erased from the habits and institutions of modern Europe; yet never at any other period has so much energy, beauty, and virtue been developed; never was blind strength and stubborn form so disciplined and rendered subject to the will of man, or that will less repugnant to the dictates of the beautiful and the true, as during the century which preceded the death of Socrates. Of no other epoch in the history of our species have we records and fragments stamped so visibly with the image of the divinity in man. But it is poetry alone, in form, in action, or in language, which has rendered this epoch memorable above all others, and the storehouse of examples to everlasting time. For written poetry existed at that epoch simultaneously with the other arts, and it is an idle inquiry to demand which gave and which received the light, which all, as from a common focus, have scattered over the darkest periods of succeeding time. We know no more of cause and effect than a constant conjunction of events: poetry is ever found to co-exist with whatever other arts contribute to the happiness and perfection of man. I appeal to what has already been established to distinguish between the cause and the effect.

It was at the period here adverted to, that the drama had its birth; and however a succeeding writer may have equalled or surpassed those few great specimens of the Athenian drama which have been preserved to us, it is indisputable that the art itself never was understood or practised according to the true philosophy of it, as at Athens. For the Athenians employed language, action, music, painting, the dance, and religious institutions, to produce a common effect in the representation of the highest idealisms of passion and of power; each division in the art was made perfect in its kind by artists of the most consummate skill, and was disciplined into a beautiful proportion and unity one towards the other. On the modern stage a few only of the elements capable of expressing the image of the poet's conception are employed at once. We have tragedy without music and dancing; and music and dancing without the highest impersonations of which they are the fit accompaniment, and both without religion and solemnity. Religious institution has indeed been usually banished from the stage. Our system of divesting the actor's face of a mask, on which the many expressions appropriated to his dramatic character might be moulded into one permanent and unchanging expression, is favourable only to a partial and inharmonious effect; it is fit for nothing but a monologue, where all the attention may be directed to some great master of ideal mimicry. The modern practice of blending comedy with tragedy, though liable to great abuse in point of practice, is undoubtedly an extension of the dramatic circle; but the comedy should be as in *King Lear*, universal, ideal, and sublime. It is perhaps the intervention of this principle which determines the balance in favour of *King Lear* against the *Œdipus Tyrannus* or the *Agamemnon*, or, if you will, the trilogies with which they are connected; unless the intense power of the choral poetry, especially that of the latter, should be considered as restoring the equilibrium. *King Lear*, if it can sustain this comparison, may be judged to be the most perfect specimen of the dramatic art existing in the world; in spite of the narrow conditions to which the poet was subjected by the ignorance of the philosophy of the drama which has prevailed in modern Europe. Calderon, in his religious *Autos*, has attempted to fulfil some of the high conditions of dramatic representation neglected by Shakespeare; such as the establishing a relation between the drama and religion, and the accommodating them to music and dancing; but he omits the observation of conditions still more important, and more is lost than gained by the substitution of the rigidly-defined and ever-repeated idealisms of a distorted superstition for the living impersonations of the truth of human passion.

But I digress.—The connection of scenic exhibitions with the improvement or corruption of the manners of men, has been universally recognized; in other words, the presence or absence of poetry in its most perfect and universal form has been found to be connected with good and evil in conduct or habit. The corruption which has been imputed to the drama as an effect, begins, when the poetry employed in its constitution ends: I appeal to the history of manners whether the periods of the growth of the one and the decline of the other have not corresponded with an exactness equal to any example of moral cause and effect.

The drama at Athens, or wheresoever else it may have approached to its perfection, ever co-existed with the moral and intellectual greatness of the age. The tragedies of the Athenian poets are as mirrors in which the spectator beholds himself, under a thin disguise of circumstance, stript of all but that ideal perfection and energy which every one feels to be the internal type of all that he loves, admires, and would become. The imagination is enlarged by a sympathy with pains and passions so mighty, that they distend in their conception the capacity of that by which they are conceived; the good affections are strengthened by pity, indignation, terror and sorrow; and an exalted calm is prolonged from the satiety of this high exercise of them into the tumult of familiar life: even crime is disarmed of half its horror and all its contagion by being represented as the fatal consequence of the unfathomable agencies of nature; error is thus divested of its wilfulness; men can no longer cherish it as the creation of their choice. In a drama of the highest order there is little food for censure or hatred; it teaches rather self-knowledge and self-respect. Neither the eye nor the mind can see itself, unless reflected upon that which it resembles. The drama, so long as it continues to express poetry, is as a prismatic and many-sided mirror, which collects the brightest rays of human nature and divides and reproduces them from the simplicity of these elementary forms, and touches them with majesty and beauty, and multiplies all that it reflects, and endows it with the power of propagating its like wherever it may fall.

But in periods of the decay of social life, the drama sympathizes with that decay. Tragedy becomes a cold imitation of the form of the great masterpieces of antiquity, divested of all harmonious accompaniment of the kindred arts, and often the very form misunderstood, or a weak attempt to teach certain doctrines, which the writer considers as moral truth; and which are usually no more than specious flatteries of some gross vice or weakness, with which the author, in common with his auditors, are infected. Hence what has been called the classical and domestic drama. Addison's *Cato* is a specimen of the one; and would it were not superfluous to cite examples of the other! To such purposes poetry cannot be made subservient. Poetry is a sword of lightning, ever unsheathed, which consumes the scabbard that would contain it. And thus we observe that all dramatic writings of this nature are unimaginative in a singular degree; they affect sentiment and passion, which, divested of imagination, are other names for caprice and appetite. The period in our own history of the grossest degradation of the drama is the reign of Charles II, when all forms in which poetry had been accustomed to be expressed became hymns to the triumph of kingly power over liberty and virtue. Milton stood alone illuminating an age unworthy of him. At such periods the calculating principle pervades all the forms of dramatic exhibition, and poetry ceases to be expressed upon them. Comedy loses its ideal universality: wit succeeds to humour; we laugh from self-complacency and triumph, instead of pleasure; malignity, sarcasm, and contempt succeed to sympathetic merriment; we hardly laugh, but we smile. Obscenity, which is ever blasphemy against the divine beauty in life, becomes, from the very veil which it assumes, more active if less disgusting: it is a monster for which the corruption of society for ever brings forth new food, which it devours in secret.

The drama being that form under which a greater number of modes of expression of poetry are susceptible of being combined than any other, the connexion of poetry and social good is more observable in the drama than in whatever other form. And it is indisputable that the highest perfection of human society has ever corresponded with the highest dramatic excellence; and that the corruption or extinction of the drama in a nation where it has once flourished, is a mark of a corruption of manners, and an extinction of the energies which sustain the soul of social life. But, as Machiavelli says of political institutions, that life may be preserved and renewed, if men should arise capable of bringing back the drama to it principles. And this is true with respect to poetry in its most extended sense: all language, institution and form, require not only to be produced but to be sustained: the office and character of a poet participates in the divine nature as regards providence, no less than as regards creation.

Civil war, the spoils of Asia, and the fatal predominance first of the Macedonian, and then of the Roman arms, were so many symbols of the extinction or suspension of the creative faculty in Greece. The bucolic writers, who found patronage under the lettered tyrants of Sicily and Egypt, were the latest representatives of its most glorious reign. Their poetry is intensely melodious; like the odour of the tuberose, it overcomes and sickens the spirit with excess of sweetness; while the poetry of the preceding age was as a meadow-gale of June, which mingles the fragrance of all the flowers of the field, and adds a quickening and harmonizing spirit of its own which endows the sense with a power of sustaining its extreme delight. The bucolic and erotic delicacy in written poetry is correlative with that softness in statuary, music, and the kindred arts, and even in manners and institutions, which distinguish the epoch to which I now refer. Nor is it the poetic faculty itself, or any mis-application of it, to which this want of harmony is to be imputed. An equal sensibility to the influence of the senses and the affections is to be found in the writings of Homer and Sophocles: the former, especially, has clothed sensual and pathetic images with irresistible attractions. Their superiority over these succeeding writers consists in the presence of those thoughts which belong to the inner faculties of our nature, not in the absence of those which are connected with the external: their incomparable perfection consists in a harmony of the union of all. It is not what the erotic poets have, but what they have not, in which their imperfection consists. It is not inasmuch as they were poets, but inasmuch as they were not poets, that they can be considered with any plausibility as connected with the corruption of their age. Had that corruption availed so as to extinguish in them the sensibility to pleasure, passion, and natural scenery, which is imputed to them as an imperfection, the last triumph of evil would have been achieved. For the end of social corruption is to destroy all sensibility to pleasure; and, therefore, it is corruption. It begins at the imagination and the intellect as at the core, and distributes itself thence as a paralysing venom, through the affections into the very appetites, until all become a torpid mass in which hardly sense survives. At the approach of such a period, poetry ever addresses itself to those faculties which are the last to be destroyed, and its voice is heard, like the footsteps of Astræa departing from the world. Poetry ever communicates all the pleasure which men are capable of receiving: it is ever still the light of life; the source of whatever of beautiful or generous or true can have place in an evil time. It will readily be confessed that those among the luxurious citizens of Syracuse and Alexandria, who were delighted with the poems of Theocritus, were less cold, cruel, and sensual than the remnant of their tribe. But corruption must utterly have destroyed the fabric of human society before poetry can ever cease. The sacred links of that chain have never been entirely disjoined, which descending through the minds of many men is attached to those great minds, whence as from a magnet the invisible effluence is sent forth, which at once connects, animates, and sustains the life of all. It is the faculty which contains within itself the seeds at once of its own and of social renovation. And let us not circumscribe the effects of the bucolic and erotic poetry within the limits of the sensibility of those to whom it was addressed. They may have perceived the beauty of those immortal compositions, simply as fragments and isolated portions: those who are more finely organized, or, born in a happier age, may recognize them as episodes to that great poem, which all poets, like the co-operating thoughts of one great mind, have built up since the beginning of the world.

The same revolutions within a narrower sphere had place in ancient Rome; but the actions and forms of its social life never seem to have been perfectly saturated with the poetical element. The Romans appear to have considered the Greeks as the selectest treasuries of the selectest forms of manners and of nature, and to have abstained from creating in measured language, sculpture, music, or architecture, anything which might bear a particular relation to their own condition, whilst it should bear a general one to the universal constitution of the world. But we judge from partial evidence, and we judge perhaps partially. Ennius, Varro, Pacuvius, and Accius, all great poets, have been lost. Lucretius is in the highest, and Virgil in a very high sense, a creator. The chosen delicacy of expressions of the latter, are as a mist of light which conceal from us the intense and exceeding truth of his conceptions of nature. Livy is instinct with poetry. Yet Horace, Catullus, Ovid, and generally the other great writers of the Virgilian age, saw man and nature in the mirror of Greece. The institutions also, and the religion of Rome, were less poetical that those of Greece, as the shadow is less vivid than the substance. Hence poetry in Rome seemed to follow, rather than accompany, the perfection of political and domestic society. The true poetry of Rome lived in its institutions; for whatever of beautiful, true, and majestic, they contained, could have sprung only from the faculty which creates the order in which they consist. The life of Camillus, the death of Regulus; the expectation of the senators, in their godlike state, of the victorious Gauls; the refusal of the republic to make peace with Hannibal, after the battle of Cannæ, were not the consequences of a refined calculation of the probable personal advantage to result from such a rhythm and order in the shows of life, to those who were at once the poets and the actors of these immortal dramas. The imagination beholding the beauty of this order, created it out of itself according to its own idea; the consequence was empire, and the reward ever-living fame. These things are not the less poetry, *quia carent vate sacro*. They are the episodes of that cyclic poem written by Time upon the memories of men. The Past, like an inspired rhapsodist, fills the theatre of everlasting generations with their harmony.

At length the ancient system of religion and manners

had fulfilled the circle of its revolutions. And the world would have fallen into utter anarchy and darkness, but that there were found poets among the authors of the Christian and chivalric systems of manners and religion, who created forms of opinion and action never before conceived ; which, copied into the imaginations of men, became as generals to the bewildered armies of their thoughts. It is foreign to the present purpose to touch upon the evil produced by these systems : except that we protest, on the ground of the principles already established, that no portion of it can be attributed to the poetry they contain.

It is probable that the poetry of Moses, Job, David, Solomon, and Isaiah had produced a great effect upon the mind of Jesus and his disciples. The scattered fragments preserved to us by the biographers of this extraordinary person, are all instinct with the most vivid poetry. But his doctrines seem to have been quickly distorted. At a certain period after the prevalence of a system of opinions founded upon those promulgated by him, the three forms into which Plato had distributed the faculties of mind underwent a sort of apotheosis, and became the object of the worship of the civilized world. Here it is to be confessed that " Light seems to thicken," and

> The crow makes wing to the rooky wood,
> Good things of day begin to droop and drowse,
> And night's black agents to their preys do rouse.

But mark how beautiful an order has sprung from the dust and blood of this fierce chaos ! how the world, as from a resurrection, balancing itself on the golden wings of knowledge and of hope, has reassumed its yet unwearied flight into the heaven of time. Listen to the music, unheard by outward ears, which is as a ceaseless and invisible wind, nourishing its everlasting course with strength and swiftness.

The poetry in the doctrines of Jesus Christ, and the mythology and institutions of the Celtic conquerors of the Roman empire, outlived the darkness and the convulsions connected with their growth and victory,

and blended themselves in a new fabric of manners
and opinion. It is an error to impute the ignorance
of the dark ages to the Christian doctrines or the predominance of the Celtic nations. Whatever of evil
their agencies may have contained sprang from the
extinction of the poetical principle, connected with
the progress of despotism and superstition. Men,
from causes too intricate to be here discussed, had
become insensible and selfish: their own will had become feeble, and yet they were its slaves, and thence
the slaves of the will of others: lust, fear, avarice,
cruelty, and fraud, characterized a race amongst whom
no one was to be found capable of *creating* in form,
language, or institution. The moral anomalies of such
a state of society are not justly to be charged upon any
class of events immediately connected with them, and
those events are most entitled to our approbation which
could dissolve it most expeditiously. It is unfortunate
for those who cannot distinguish words from thoughts,
that many of these anomalies have been incorporated
into our popular religion.

It was not until the eleventh century that the effects
of the poetry of the Christian and chivalric systems
began to manifest themselves. The principle of equality
had been discovered and applied by Plato in his
Republic, as the theoretical rule of the mode in which
the materials of pleasure and of power produced by
the common skill and labour of human beings ought
to be distributed among them. The limitations of
this rule were asserted by him to be determined only
by the sensibility of each, or the utility to result to all.
Plato, following the doctrines of Timæus and Pythagoras, taught also a moral and intellectual system of
doctrine, comprehending at once the past, the present,
and the future condition of man. Jesus Christ
divulged the sacred and eternal truths contained in
these views to mankind, and Christianity, in its abstract
purity, became the exoteric expression of the esoteric
doctrines of the poetry and wisdom of antiquity.
The incorporation of the Celtic nations with the
exhausted population of the south, impressed upon it

the figure of the poetry existing in their mythology and institutions. The result was a sum of the action and reaction of all the causes included in it; for it may be assumed as a maxim that no nation or religion can supersede any other without incorporating into itself a portion of that which it supersedes. The abolition of personal and domestic slavery, and the emancipation of women from a great part of the degrading restraints of antiquity, were among the consequences of these events.

The abolition of personal slavery is the basis of the highest political hope that it can enter into the mind of man to conceive. The freedom of women produced the poetry of sexual love. Love became a religion, the idols of whose worship were ever present. It was as if the statues of Apollo and the Muses had been endowed with life and motion, and had walked forth among their worshippers; so that earth became peopled by the inhabitants of a diviner world. The familiar appearance and proceedings of life became wonderful and heavenly, and a paradise was created as out of the wrecks of Eden. And as this creation itself is poetry, so its creators were poets; and language was the instrument of their art: " Galeotto fù il libro, e chi lo scrisse." The Provençal Trouveurs, or inventors, preceded Petrarch, whose verses are as spells, which unseal the inmost enchanted fountains of the delight which is in the grief of love. It is impossible to feel them without becoming a portion of that beauty which we contemplate: it were superfluous to explain how the gentleness and the elevation of mind connected with these sacred emotions can render men more amiable, more generous and wise, and lift them out of the dull vapours of the little world of self. Dante understood the secret things of love even more than Petrarch. His *Vita Nuova* is an inexhaustible fountain of purity of sentiment and language: it is the idealized history of that period, and those intervals of his life which were dedicated to love. His apotheosis of Beatrice in Paradise, and the gradations of his own love and her loveliness, by which as by steps he feigns himself to have ascended to the throne of the Supreme Cause, is the most glorious imagination of modern poetry. The acutest critics have justly reversed the judgment of the vulgar, and the order of the great acts of the *Divine Drama*, in the measure of the admiration which they accord to the Hell, Purgatory, and Paradise. The latter is a perpetual hymn of everlasting love. Love, which found a worthy poet in Plato alone of all the ancients, has been celebrated by a chorus of the greatest writers of the renovated world; and the music has penetrated the caverns of society, and its echoes still drown the dissonance of arms and superstition. At successive intervals, Ariosto, Tasso, Shakespeare, Spenser, Calderon, Rousseau, and the great writers of our own age, have celebrated the dominion of love, planting as it were trophies in the human mind of that sublimest victory over sensuality and force. The true relation borne to each other by the sexes into which human kind is distributed has become less misunderstood; and if the error which confounded diversity with inequality of the powers of the two sexes has been partially recognized in the opinions and institutious of modern Europe, we owe this great benefit to the worship of which chivalry was the law, and poets the prophets.

The poetry of Dante may be considered as the bridge thrown over the stream of time, which unites the modern and ancient world. The distorted notions of invisible things which Dante and his rival Milton have idealized, are merely the mask and the mantle in which these great poets walk through eternity enveloped and disguised. It is a difficult question to determine how far they were conscious of the distinction which must have subsisted in their minds between their own creeds and that of the people. Dante at least appears to wish to mark the full extent of it by placing Riphæus, whom Virgil calls *justissimus unus*, in Paradise, and observing a most heretical caprice in his distribution of rewards and punishments. And Milton's poem contains within itself a philosophical refutation of that system, of which, by a strange and natural antithesis, it has been a chief popular support. Nothing can exceed the energy and magnificence of the character of Satan as expressed in *Paradise Lost*. It is a mistake to suppose that he could ever have been intended for the popular personification of evil. Implacable hate, patient cunning, and a sleepless refinement of device to inflict the extremest anguish on an enemy, these things are evil; and, although venial in a slave, are not to be forgiven in a tyrant; although redeemed by much that ennobles his defeat in one subdued, are marked by all that dishonours his conquest in the victor. Milton's Devil as a moral being is as far superior to his God, as one who perseveres in some purpose which he has conceived to be excellent in spite of adversity and torture, is to one who in the cold security of undoubted triumph inflicts the most horrible revenge upon his enemy, not from any mistaken notion of inducing him to repent of a perseverance in enmity, but with the alleged design of exasperating him to deserve new torments. Milton has so far violated the popular creed (if this shall be judged to be a violation) as to have alleged no superiority of moral virtue to his God over his Devil. And this bold neglect of a direct moral purpose is the most decisive proof of the supremacy of Milton's genius. He mingled as it were the elements of human nature as colours upon a single pallet, and arranged them in the composition of his great picture according to the laws of epic truth; that is, according to the laws of that principle by which a series of actions of the external universe and of intelligent and ethical beings is calculated to excite the sympathy of succeeding generations of mankind. The *Divine Commedia* and *Paradise Lost* have conferred upon modern mythology a systematic form; and when change and time shall have added one more superstition to the mass of those which have arisen and decayed upon the earth, commentators will be learnedly employed in elucidating the religion of ancestral Europe, only not utterly forgotten because it will have been stamped with the eternity of genius.

Homer was the first and Dante the second epic poet: that is, the second poet, the series of whose creations bore a defined and intelligible relation to the knowledge and sentiment and religion of the age in which he lived, and of the ages which followed it, developing itself in correspondence with their development. For Lucretius had limed the wings of his swift spirit in the dregs of the sensible world; and Virgil, with a modesty that ill became his genius, had affected the fame of an imitator, even whilst he created anew all that he copied; and none among the flock of mock-birds, though their notes were sweet, Apollonius Rhodius, Quintus Calaber, Nonnus, Lucan, Statius, or Claudian, have sought even to fulfil a single condition of epic truth. Milton was the third epic poet. For if the title of epic in its highest sense be refused to the *Æneid*, still less can it be conceded to the *Orlando Furioso*, the *Gerusalemme Liberata*, the *Lusiad*, or the *Fairy Queen*.

Dante and Milton were both deeply penetrated with the ancient religion of the civilized world; and its spirit exists in their poetry probably in the same proportion as its forms survived in the unreformed worship of modern Europe. The one preceded and the other followed the Reformation at almost equal intervals. Dante was the first religious reformer, and Luther surpassed him rather in the rudeness and acrimony, than in the boldness of his censures of papal usurpation. Dante was the first awakener of entranced Europe; he created a language, in itself music and persuasion, out of a chaos of inharmonious barbarisms. He was the congregator of those great spirits who presided over the resurrection of learning; the Lucifer of that starry flock which in the thirteenth century shone forth from republican Italy, as from a heaven, into the darkness of the benighted world. His very words are instinct with spirit; each is as a spark, a burning atom of inextinguishable thought; and many yet lie covered in the ashes of their birth, and pregnant with the lightning which has yet found no conductor. All high poetry is infinite; it is as the first acorn, which contained all oaks potentially. Veil after veil may be undrawn, and the inmost naked beauty of the meaning never exposed. A great poem is a fountain for ever overflowing with the waters of wisdom and delight; and after one person and one age has exhausted all its divine effluence which their peculiar relations enable them to share, another and yet another succeeds, and new relations are ever developed, the source of an unforeseen and an unconceived delight.

The age immediately succeeding to that of Dante, Petrarch, and Boccaccio, was characterized by a revival of painting, sculpture, and architecture. Chaucer caught the sacred inspiration, and the superstructure of English literature is based upon the materials of Italian invention.

But let us not be betrayed from a defence into a critical history of poetry and its influence on society. Be it enough to have pointed out the effects of poets, in the large and true sense of the word, upon their own and all succeeding times.

But poets have been challenged to resign the civic crown to reasoners and mechanists on another plea. It is admitted that the exercise of the imagination is most delightful, but it is alleged that that of reason is more useful. Let us examine as the grounds of this distinction what is here meant by utility. Pleasure or good, in a general sense, is that which the consciousness of a sensitive and intelligent being seeks, and in which, when found, it acquiesces. There are two kinds of pleasure, one durable, universal, and permanent; the other transitory and particular. Utility may either express the means of producing the former or the latter. In the former sense, whatever strengthens and purifies the affections, enlarges the imagination, and adds spirit to sense, is useful. But a narrower meaning may be assigned to the word utility, confining it to express that which banishes the importunity of the wants of our animal nature, the surrounding men with security of life, the dispersing the grosser delusions of superstition, and the conciliating such a degree of mutual forbearance among men as may consist with the motives of personal advantage.

Undoubtedly the promoters of utility, in this limited sense, have their appointed office in society. They follow the footsteps of poets, and copy the sketches of their creations into the book of common life. They make space, and give time. Their exertions are of the highest value, so long as they confine their administration of the concerns of the inferior powers of our nature within the limits due to the superior ones. But whilst the sceptic destroys gross superstitions, let him spare to deface, as some of the French writers have defaced, the eternal truths charactered upon the imaginations of men. Whilst the mechanist abridges, and the political economist combines labour, let them beware that their speculations, for want of correspondence with those first principles which belong to the imagination, do not tend, as they have in modern England, to exasperate at once the extremes of luxury and want. They have exemplified the saying, "To him that hath, more shall be given; and from him that hath not, the little that he hath shall be taken away." The rich have become richer, and the poor have become poorer; and the vessel of the state is driven between the Scylla and Charybdis of anarchy and despotism. Such are the effects which must ever flow from an unmitigated exercise of the calculating faculty.

It is difficult to define pleasure in its highest sense; the definition involving a number of apparent paradoxes. For, from an inexplicable defect of harmony in the constitution of human nature, the pain of the inferior is frequently connected with the pleasures of the superior portions of our being. Sorrow, terror, anguish, despair itself, are often the chosen expressions of an approximation to the highest good. Our sympathy in tragic fiction depends on this principle; tragedy delights by affording a shadow of the pleasure which exists in pain. This is the source also of the melancholy which is inseparable from the sweetest melody. The pleasure that is in sorrow is sweeter than the pleasure of pleasure itself. And hence the saying, "It is better to go to the house of mourning, than to the house of mirth." Not that this highest species of pleasure is necessarily linked with pain. The delight of love and friendship, the ecstasy of the admiration of nature, the joy of the perception and still more of the creation of poetry, is often wholly unalloyed.

The production and assurance of pleasure in this highest sense is true utility. Those who produce and preserve this pleasure are poets or poetical philosophers.

The exertions of Locke, Hume, Gibbon, Voltaire, Rousseau,[1] and their disciples, in favour of oppressed and deluded humanity, are entitled to the gratitude of mankind. Yet it is easy to calculate the degree of moral and intellectual improvement which the world would have exhibited, had they never lived. A little more nonsense would have been talked for a century or two; and perhaps a few more men, women, and children burnt as heretics. We might not at this moment have been congratulating each other on the abolition of the Inquisition in Spain. But it exceeds all imagination to conceive what would have been the moral condition of the world if neither Dante, Petrarch, Boccaccio, Chaucer, Shakespeare, Calderon, Lord Bacon, nor Milton, had ever existed; if Raphael and Michael Angelo had never been born; if the Hebrew poetry had never been translated; if a revival of the study of Greek literature had never taken place; if no monuments of ancient sculpture had been handed down to us: and if the poetry of the religion of the ancient world had been extinguished together with its belief. The human mind could never, except by the intervention of these excitements, have been awakened to the invention of the grosser sciences, and that application of analytical reasoning to the aberrations of society, which it is now attempted to exalt over the direct expression of the inventive and creative faculty itself.

[1] Although Rousseau has been thus classed, he was essentially a poet. The others, even Voltaire, were mere reasoners.

We have more moral, political, and historical wisdom than we know how to reduce into practice; we have more scientific and economical knowledge than can be accommodated to the just distribution of the produce which it multiplies. The poetry in these systems of thought is concealed by the accumulation of facts and calculating processes. There is no want of knowledge respecting what is wisest and best in morals, government, and political economy, or at least, what is wiser and better than what men now practise and endure. But we let "*I dare not* wait upon *I would*, like the poor cat in the adage." We want the creative faculty to imagine that which we know; we want the generous impulse to act that which we imagine; we want the poetry of life: our calculations have outrun conception; we have eaten more than we can digest. The cultivation of those sciences which have enlarged the limits of the empire of men over the external world, has, for want of the poetical faculty, proportionally circumscribed those of the internal world; and man, having enslaved the elements, remains himself a slave. To what but a cultivation of the mechanical arts in a degree disproportioned to the presence of the creative faculty, which is the basis of all knowledge, is to be attributed the abuse of all invention for abridging and combining labour, to the exasperation of the inequality of mankind? From what other cause has it arisen that the discoveries which should have lightened, have added a weight to the curse imposed on Adam? Poetry, and the principle of Self, of which money is the visible incarnation, are the God and Mammon of the world.

The functions of the Poetical faculty are two-fold; by one it creates new materials of knowledge, and power, and pleasure; by the other it engenders in the mind a desire to reproduce and arrange them according to a certain rhythm and order which may be called the beautiful and the good. The cultivation of poetry is never more to be desired than at periods when, from an excess of the selfish and calculating principle, the accumulation of the materials of external life exceed the quantity of the power of assimilating them to the internal laws of human nature. The body has then become too unwieldy for that which animates it.

Poetry is indeed something divine. It is at once the centre and circumference of knowledge; it is that which comprehends all science, and that to which all science must be referred. It is at the same time the root and blossom of all other systems of thought; it is that from which all spring, and that which adorns all; and that which, if blighted, denies the fruit and the seed, and withholds from the barren world the nourishment and the succession of the scions of the tree of life. It is the perfect and consummate surface and bloom of all things; it is as the odour and the colour of the rose to the texture of the elements which compose it, as the form and splendour of unfaded beauty to the secrets of anatomy and corruption. What were virtue, love, patriotism, friendship—what were the scenery of this beautiful universe which we inhabit; what were our consolations on this side of the grave—and what were our aspirations beyond it, if poetry did not ascend to bring light and fire from those eternal regions where the owl-winged faculty of calculation dare not ever soar? Poetry is not like reasoning, a power to be exerted according to the determination of the will. A man cannot say, "I will compose poetry." The greatest poet even cannot say it; for the mind in creation is as a fading coal, which some invisible influence, like an inconstant wind, awakens to transitory brightness; this power arises from within, like the colour of a flower which fades and changes as it is developed, and the con.cious portions of our natures are unprophetic either of its approach or its departure. Could this influence be durable in its original purity and force, it is impossible to predict the greatness of the results; but when composition begins, inspiration is already on the decline, and the most glorious poetry that has ever been communicated to the world is probably a feeble shadow of the original conceptions of the poet. I appeal to the greatest poets of the present day, whether it is not an error to assert that the finest passages of poetry are produced by labour and study. The toil and the delay recommended by critics can be justly interpreted to mean no more than a careful observation of the inspired moments, and an artificial connexion of the spaces between their suggestions by the intertexture of conventional expressions; a necessity only imposed by the limitedness of the poetical faculty itself: for Milton conceived the *Paradise Lost* as a whole before he executed it in portions. We have his own authority also for the muse having " dictated " to him the " unpremeditated song." And let this be an answer to those who would allege the fifty-six various readings of the first line of the *Orlando Furioso*. Compositions so produced are to poetry what mosaic is to painting. This instinct and intuition of the poetical faculty is still more observable in the plastic and pictorial arts: a great statue or picture grows under the power of the artist as a child in the mother's womb; and the very mind which directs the hands in formation is incapable of accounting to itself for the origin, the gradations, or the media of the process.

Poetry is the record of the best and happiest moments of the happiest and best minds. We are aware of evanescent visitations of thought and feeling sometimes associated with place or person, sometimes regarding our own mind alone, and always arising unforeseen and departing unbidden, but elevating and delightful beyond all expression: so that even in the desire and the regret they leave, there cannot but be pleasure, participating as it does in the nature of its object. It is as it were the interpenetration of a diviner nature through our own; but its footsteps are like those of a wind over the sea, which the coming calm erases, and whose traces remain only as on the wrinkled sands which pave it. These and corresponding conditions of being are experienced principally by those of the most delicate sensibility and the most enlarged imagination; and the state of mind produced by them is at war with every base desire. The enthusiasm of virtue, love, patriotism, and friendship is essentially linked with such emotions; and whilst they last, self appears as what it is, an atom to a universe. Poets are not only subject to these experiences as spirits of the most refined organization, but they can colour all that they combine with the evanescent hues of this ethereal world; a word, a trait in the representation of a scene or a passion will touch the enchanted chord, and reanimate, in those who have ever experienced these emotions, the sleeping, the cold, the buried image of the past. Poetry thus makes immortal all that is best and most beautiful in the world; it arrests the vanishing apparitions which haunt the interlunations of life, and veiling them, or in language or in form, sends them forth among mankind, bearing sweet news of kindred joy to those with whom their sisters abide— abide, because there is no portal of expression from the caverns of the spirit which they inhabit into the universe of things. Poetry redeems from decay the visitations of the divinity in man.

Poetry turns all things to loveliness; it exalts the beauty of that which is most beautiful, and it adds beauty to that which is most deformed; it marries exultation and horror, grief and pleasure, eternity and change; it subdues to union under its light yoke all irreconcilable things. It transmutes all that it touches, and every form moving within the radiance of its presence is changed by wondrous sympathy to an incarnation of the spirit which it breathes: its secret alchemy turns to portable gold the poisonous waters which flow from death through life; it strips the veil of familiarity from the world, and lays bare the naked and sleeping beauty, which is the spirit of its forms.

All things exist as they are perceived: at least in relation to the percipient. "The mind is its own place, and of itself can make a heaven of hell, a hell of heaven." But poetry defeats the curse which binds us to be subjected to the accident of surrounding impressions. And whether it spreads its own figured curtain, or withdraws life's dark veil from before the scene of things, it equally creates for us a being within our being. It makes us the inhabitants of a world to which the familiar world is a chaos. It reproduces the common universe of which we are portions and percipients, and it purges from our inward sight the film of familiarity which obscures from us the wonder of our being. It compels us to feel that which we perceive, and to imagine that which we know. It creates anew the universe, after it has been annihilated in our minds by the recurrence of impressions blunted by reiteration. It justifies the bold and true words of Tasso—*Non merita nome di creatore, se non Iddio ed il Poeta*.

A poet, as he is the author to others of the highest wisdom, pleasure, virtue, and glory, so he ought personally to be the happiest, the best, the wisest, and the most illustrious of men. As to his glory, let time be challenged to declare whether the frame of any other institutor of human life be comparable to that of a poet. That he is the wisest, the happiest, and the best, inasmuch as he is a poet, is equally incontrovertible: the greatest poets have been men of the most spotless virtue, of the most consummate prudence, and, if we would look into the interior of their lives, the most fortunate of men: and the exceptions, as they regard those who possessed the poetic faculty in a high yet inferior degree, will be found on consideration to confine rather than destroy the rule. Let us for a moment stoop to the arbitration of popular breath, and usurping and uniting in our own persons the incompatible characters of accuser, witness, judge, and executioner, let us decide without trial, testimony, or form, that certain motives of those who are "there sitting where we dare not soar," are reprehensible. Let us assume that Homer was a drunkard, that Virgil was a flatterer, that Horace was a coward, that Tasso was a madman, that Lord Bacon was a peculator, that Raphael was a libertine, that Spenser was a poet laureate. It is inconsistent with this division of our subject to cite living poets, but posterity has done ample justice to the great names now referred to. Their errors have been weighed and found to have been dust in the balance; if their sins "were as scarlet, they are now white as snow"; they have been washed in the blood of the mediator and redeemer, Time. Observe in what a ludicrous chaos the imputations of real or fictitious crime have been confused in the contemporary calumnies against poetry and poets; consider how little is, as it appears—or appears, as it is; look to your own motives, and judge not, lest ye be judged.

Poetry, as has been said, differs in this respect from logic, that it is not subject to the control of the active powers of the mind, and that its birth and recurrence have no necessary connection with the consciousness or will. It is presumptuous to determine that these are the necessary conditions of all mental causation, when mental effects are experienced unsusceptible of being referred to them. The frequent recurrence of the poetical power, it is obvious to suppose, may produce in the mind a habit of order and harmony correlative with its own nature and with its effects upon other minds. But in the intervals of inspiration, and they may be frequent without being durable, a poet becomes a man, and is abandoned to the sudden reflux of the influences under which others habitually live. But as he is more delicately organized than other men, and sensible to pain and pleasure, both his own and that of others, in a degree unknown to them, he will avoid the one and pursue the other with an ardour proportioned to this difference. And he renders himself obnoxious to calumny, when he neglects to observe the circumstances under which these objects of universal pursuit and flight have disguised themselves in one another's garments.

But there is nothing necessarily evil in this error, and thus cruelty, envy, revenge, avarice, and the passions purely evil, have never formed any portion of the popular imputations on the lives of poets.

I have thought it most favourable to the cause of truth to set down these remarks according to the order in which they were suggested to my mind, by a consideration of the subject itself, instead of observing the formality of a polemical reply; but if the view which they contain be just, they will be found to involve a refutation of the arguers against poetry, so far at least as regards the first division of the subject. I can readily conjecture what should have moved the gall of some learned and intelligent writers who quarrel with certain versifiers; I confess myself, like them, unwilling to be stunned by the Theseids of the hoarse Codri of the day. Bavius and Mævius undoubtedly are, as they ever were, insufferable persons. But it belongs to a philosophical critic to distinguish rather than confound.

The first part of these remarks has related to poetry in its elements and principles; and it has been shown, as well as the narrow limits assigned them would permit, that what is called poetry, in a restricted sense, has a common source with all other forms of order and of beauty, according to which the materials of human life are susceptible of being arranged, and which is poetry in an universal sense.

The second part will have for its object an application of these principles to the present state of the cultivation of poetry, and a defence of the attempt to idealize the modern forms of manners and opinions, and compel them into a subordination to the imaginative and creative faculty. For the literature of England, an energetic development of which has ever preceded or accompanied a great and free development of the national will, has arisen as it were from a new birth. In spite of the low-thoughted envy which would undervalue contemporary merit, our own will be a memorable age in intellectual achievements, and we live among such philosophers and poets as surpass beyond comparison any who have appeared since the last national struggle for civil and religious liberty. The most unfailing herald, companion, and follower of the awakening of a great people to work a beneficial change in opinion or institution, is poetry. At such periods there is an accumulation of the power of communicating and receiving intense and impassioned conceptions respecting man and nature. The persons in whom this power resides, may often, as far as regards many portions of

A DEFENCE OF POETRY

their nature, have little apparent correspondence with that spirit of good of which they are the ministers. But even whilst they deny and abjure, they are yet compelled to serve, the power which is seated on the throne of their own soul. It is impossible to read the compositions of the most celebrated writers of the present day without being startled with the electric life which burns within their words. They measure the circumference and sound the depths of human nature with a comprehensive and all-penetrating spirit, and they are themselves perhaps the most sincerely astonished at its manifestations; for it is less their spirit than the spirit of the age. Poets are the hierophants of an unapprehended inspiration; the mirrors of the gigantic shadows which futurity casts upon the present; the words which express what they understand not; the trumpets which sing to battle, and feel not what they inspire; the influence which is moved not, but moves. Poets are the unacknowledged legislators of the world.

LORD BYRON

(1788–1824)

THE PRESENT STATE OF ENGLISH POETRY.

The Preface to "Don Juan," first published in 1822.

THAT this is the age of the decline of English poetry will be doubted by few who have calmly considered the subject. That there are men of genius among the present poets makes little against the fact, because it has been well said, that "next to him who forms the taste of his country, the greatest genius is he who corrupts it." No one has ever denied genius to Marino, who corrupted not merely the taste of Italy, but that of all Europe for nearly a century. The great cause of the present deplorable state of English poetry is to be attributed to that absurd and systematic depreciation of Pope, in which, for the last few years, there has been a kind of epidemical concurrence. Men of the most opposite opinions have united upon this topic. Warton and Churchill began it, having borrowed the hint probably from the heroes of the *Dunciad*, and their own internal conviction that their proper reputation can be as nothing till the most perfect and harmonious of poets—he who, having no fault, has had REASON made his reproach—was reduced to what they conceived to be his level; but even *they* dared not degrade him below Dryden. Goldsmith, and Rogers, and Campbell, his most successful disciples; and Hayley, who, however feeble, has left one poem "that will not be willingly let die" (the *Triumphs of Temper*), kept up the reputation of that pure and perfect style; and Crabbe, the first of living poets, has almost equalled the master. Then came Darwin, who was put down by a single poem in the *Antijacobin*;[1] and the Cruscans, from Merry to

[1] *The Loves of the Triangles*, the joint production of Messrs. Canning and Frere.

PRESENT STATE OF ENGLISH POETRY 243

Jerningham, who were annihilated (if *Nothing* can be said to be annihilated) by Gifford, the last of the wholesome satirists.

At the same time Mr. Southey was favouring the public with *Wat Tyler* and *Joan of Arc*, to the great glory of the drama and epos. I beg pardon: *Wat Tyler* with *Peter Bell*, was still in MS., and it was not till after Mr. Southey had received his Malmsey butt, and Mr. Wordsworth [1] became qualified to gauge it, that the great revolutionary tragedy came before the public and the Court of Chancery. Wordsworth was peddling his lyrical ballads, and brooding a preface, to be succeeded in due course by a postscript; both couched in such prose as must give peculiar delight to those who have read the prefaces of Pope and Dryden—scarcely less celebrated for the beauty of their prose, than for the charms of their verse. Wordsworth is the reverse of Molière's gentleman, who had been "talking prose all his life without knowing it"; for he thinks that he has been all his life writing both prose and verse, and neither of what he conceives to be such can be properly said to be either one or the other. Mr. Coleridge, the future *vates*, poet and seer of the *Morning Post* (an honour also claimed by Mr. Fitzgerald, of the *Rejected Addresses*, who ultimately prophesied the downfall of Bonaparte, to which he himself mainly contributed, by giving him the nickname of "*the Corsican*," was then employed in predicating the damnation of Mr. Pitt, and the desolation of England, in the two very best copies of verses he ever wrote: to wit, the infernal eclogue of *Fire, Famine, and Slaughter*, and the *Ode to the Departing Year*.

These three personages, Southey, Wordsworth, and

---

[1] Goldsmith has anticipated the definition of the Lake poetry, as far as such things can be defined. "Gentlemen, the present piece is not of your *common epic poems*, which come from the press like paper kites in summer; there are none of your Turnuses or Didos in it; *it is an historical description of nature*. I only beg you'll endeavour to make your souls in unison with mine, *and hear with the same enthusiasm with which I have written*." Would not this have made a proper proem to the *Excursion*, and the poet and his pedlar? It would have answered perfectly for that purpose, had it not unfortunately been written in good English.

Coleridge, had all of them a very natural antipathy to Pope; and I respect them for it, as the only original feeling or principle which they have contrived to preserve. But they have been joined in it by those who have joined them in nothing else: by the Edinburgh Reviewers, by the whole heterogeneous mass of living English poets, excepting Crabbe, Rogers, Gifford, and Campbell, who, both by precept and practice, have proved their adherence; and by me, who have shamefully deviated in practice, but have ever loved and honoured Pope's poetry with my whole soul, and hope to do so till my dying day. I would rather see all I have ever written lining the same trunk in which I actually read the eleventh book of a modern epic poem at Malta, in 1811 (I opened it to take out a change after the paroxysm of a tertian, in the absence of my servant, and found it lined with the name of the maker, Eyre, Cockspur Street, and with the epic poetry alluded to), than sacrifice what I firmly believe in as the Christianity of English poetry, the poetry of Pope.

But the Edinburgh Reviewers, and the Lakers, and Hunt and his school, and everybody else with their school, and even Moore without a school, and dilettanti lecturers at institutions, and elderly gentlemen who translate and imitate, and young ladies who listen and repeat, baronets who draw indifferent frontispieces for bad poets, and noblemen who let them dine with them in the country, the small body of the wits and the great body of the blues, have latterly united in a depreciation, of which their fathers would have been as much ashamed as their children will be. In the meantime, what have we got instead? The Lake school, which begun with an epic poem, " written in six weeks" (so *Joan of Arc* proclaimed herself), and finished with a ballad composed in twenty years, as *Peter Bell's* creator takes care to inform the few who will inquire. What have we got instead? A deluge of flimsy and unintelligible romances, imitated from Scott and myself, who have both made the best of our bad materials and erroneous system. What have we got instead? *Madoc*, which is neither an epic nor anything else; *Thalaba*,

Kehama, Gebir, and such gibberish, written in all metres and in no language. Hunt, who had powers to have made the *Story of Rimini* as perfect as a fable of Dryden, has thought fit to sacrifice his genius and his taste to some unintelligible notions of Wordsworth, which I defy him to explain. Moore has——But why continue?— All, with the exception of Crabbe, Rogers, and Campbell, who may be considered as having taken their station, will, by the blessing of God, survive their own reputation, without attaining any very extraordinary period of longevity. Of course there must be a still further exception in favour of those who, having never obtained any reputation at all, unless it be among provincial literati, and their own families, have none to lose; and of Moore, who, as the Burns of Ireland, possesses a fame which cannot be lost.

The greater part of the poets mentioned, however, have been able to gather together a few followers. A paper of the *Connoisseur* says, that "it is observed by the French, that a cat, a priest, and an old woman, are sufficient to constitute a religious sect in England." The same number of animals, with some difference in kind, will suffice for a poetical one. If we take Sir George Beaumont instead of the priest, and Mr. Wordsworth for the old woman, we shall nearly complete the quota required; but I fear that Mr. Southey will but indifferently represent the CAT, having shown himself but too distinctly to be of a species to which that noble creature is peculiarly hostile.

Nevertheless, I will not go so far as Wordsworth in his postscript, who pretends that *no* great poet ever had immediate fame; which, being interpreted, means that William Wordsworth is not quite so much read by his contemporaries as might be desirable. This assertion is as false as it is foolish. Homer's glory depended upon his present popularity: he recited,—and, without the strongest impression of the moment, who would have gotten the *Iliad* by heart, and given it to tradition? Ennius, Terence, Plautus, Lucretius, Horace, Virgil, Æschylus, Sophocles, Euripides, Sappho, Anacreon, Theocritus, all the great poets of antiquity, were the delight of their contemporaries. The very existence of a poet, previous to the invention of printing, depended upon his present popularity; and how often has it impaired his future fame? Hardly ever. History informs us, that the best have come down to us. The reason is evident; the most popular found the greatest number of transcribers for their MSS., and that the taste of their contemporaries was corrupt can hardly be avouched by the moderns, the mightiest of whom have but barely approached them. Dante, Petrarch, Ariosto, and Tasso, were all the darlings of the contemporary reader. Dante's poem was celebrated long before his death; and, not long after it, states negotiated for his ashes, and disputed for the sites of the composition of the *Divina Commedia*. Petrarch was crowned in the Capitol. Ariosto was permitted to pass free by the public robber who had read the *Orlando Furioso*. I would not recommend Mr. Wordsworth to try the same experiment with his *Smugglers*. Tasso, notwithstanding the criticisms of the Cruscanti, would have been crowned in the Capitol, but for his death.

It is easy to prove the immediate popularity of the chief poets of the only modern nation in Europe that has a poetical language, the Italian. In our own, Shakspeare, Spenser, Jonson, Waller, Dryden, Congreve, Pope, Young, Shenstone, Thomson, Johnson, Goldsmith, Gray, were all as popular in their lives as since. Gray's *Elegy* pleased instantly, and eternally. His *Odes* did not, nor yet do they, please like his *Elegy*. Milton's politics kept him down. But the Epigram of Dryden,[1] and the very sale of his work, in proportion to the less reading time of its publication, prove him to have been honoured by his contemporaries. I will venture to assert, that the sale of the *Paradise Lost* was greater in the first four years after its publication, than that of *The Excursion* in the same number, with the difference of nearly a century and a half between them of time, and of thousands in point of general readers. Notwithstanding Mr. Wordsworth's having pressed Milton into

---

[1] The well-known lines under Milton's picture,—

"Three poets, in three distant ages born," etc.

his service as one of those not presently popular, to favour his own purpose of proving that our grandchildren will read *him* (the said William Wordsworth), I would recommend him to begin first with our grandmothers. But he need not be alarmed; he may yet live to see all the envies pass away, as Darwin and Seward, and Hoole, and Hole,[1] and Hoyle,[2] have passed away; but their declension will not be his ascension: he is essentially a bad writer, and all the failures of others can never strengthen him. He may have a sect, but he will never have a public; and his " *audience* " will always be " *few*," without being " *fit*,"—except for Bedlam.

It may be asked, why, having this opinion of the present state of poetry in England, and having had it long, as my friends and others well know—possessing, or having possessed too, as a writer, the ear of the public for the time being—I have not adopted a different plan in my own compositions, and endeavoured to correct rather than encourage the taste of the day. To this I would answer, that it is easier to perceive the wrong than to pursue the right, and that I have never contemplated the prospect of " filling (with *Peter Bell*,[3] see its Preface) permanently a station in the literature of the country." Those who know me best know this; and that I have been considerably astonished at the temporary success of my works, having flattered no person and no party, and expressed opinions which are not those of the general reader. Could I have anticipated the degree of attention which has been accorded me, assuredly I would have studied more to deserve it. But I have lived in far countries abroad, or in the agitating world at home, which was not favourable to study or

---

[1] The Rev. Richard Hole. He published, in early life, a versification of *Fingal*, and, in 1789, *Arthur*, a Poetical Romance. He died in 1803.

[2] Charles Hoyle, of Trinity College, Cambridge, author of *Exodus*, an epic in thirteen books.

[3] " *Peter Bell* first saw the light in 1798. During this long interval, pains have been taken at different times to make the production less unworthy of a favourable reception; or rather, to fit it for filling *permanently* a station, however humble, in the literature of my country." *Wordsworth*, 1819.

reflection; so that almost all I have written has been mere passion—passion, it is true, of different kinds, but always passion: for in me (if it be not an Irishism to say so) my *indifference* was a kind of passion, the result of experience, and not the philosophy of nature. Writing grows a habit, like a woman's gallantry: there are women who have had no intrigue, but few who have had but one only; so there are millions of men who have never written a book, but few who have written only one. And thus, having written once, I wrote on; encouraged no doubt by the success of the moment, yet by no means anticipating its duration, and, I will venture to say, scarcely even wishing it. But then I did other things besides write, which by no means contributed either to improve my writings or my prosperity.

I have thus expressed publicly upon the poetry of the day the opinion I have long entertained and expressed of it to all who have asked it, and to some who would rather not have heard it: as I told Moore not very long ago, "we are all wrong except Rogers, Crabbe, and Campbell."[1] Without being old in years, I am old in days, and do not feel the adequate spirit within me to attempt a work which should show what I think right in poetry, and must content myself with having denounced what is wrong. There are, I trust, younger spirits rising up in England, who, escaping the contagion which has swept away poetry from our literature, will

[1] "I certainly ventured to differ from the judgment of my noble friend, no less in his attempts to depreciate that peculiar walk of the art in which he himself so grandly trod, than in the inconsistency of which I thought him guilty, in condemning all those who stood up for particular 'schools' of poetry, and yet, at the same time, maintaining so exclusive a theory of the art himself. How little, however, he attended to either the grounds or degrees of my dissent from him will appear by the following wholesale report of my opinion in *Detached Thoughts*:—'One of my notions different from those of my contemporaries is, that the present is not a high age of English poetry. There are *more* poets (soi-disant) than ever there were, and proportionally less poetry. This *thesis* I have maintained for some years, but, strange to say, it meeteth not with favour from my brethren of the shell. Even Moore shakes his head, and firmly believes that it is the grand age of British poesy." *Moore.*

recall it to their country, such as it once was and may still be.

In the meantime, the best sign of amendment will be repentance, and new and frequent editions of Pope and Dryden.

There will be found as comfortable metaphysics, and ten times more poetry in the *Essay on Man*, than in the *Excursion*. If you search for passion, where is it to be found stronger than in the *Epistle from Eloisa to Abelard*, or in *Palamon and Arcite*? Do you wish for invention, imagination, sublimity, character? Seek them in the *Rape of the Lock*, the *Fables of Dryden*, the *Ode for Saint Cecilia's Day*, and *Absolom and Achitophel*: you will discover, in these two poets only, *all* for which you must ransack innumerable metres, and God only knows how many *writers* of the day, without finding a tittle of the same qualities—with the addition, too, of wit, of which the latter have none. I have not, however, forgotten *Thomas Brown the Younger*, nor *The Fudge Family*,[1] nor *Whistlecraft;* but that is not wit—it is humour. I will say nothing of the harmony of Pope and Dryden in comparison, for there is not a living poet (except Rogers, Gifford, Campbell, and Crabbe), who can write an heroic couplet. The fact is, that the exquisite beauty of their versification has withdrawn the public attention from their other excellences, as the vulgar eye will rest more upon the splendour of the uniform than the quality of the troops. It is this very harmony, particularly in Pope, which has raised the vulgar and atrocious cant against him:—because his versification is perfect, it is assumed that it is his only perfection; because his truths are so clear, it is asserted that he has no invention; and because he is always intelligible, it is taken for granted that he has no genius. We are sneeringly told that he is the "Poet of Reason," as if this was a reason for his being a poet. Taking passage for passage, I will undertake to cite more lines teeming with *imagination* from Pope than from any *two* living poets, be they who they may. To take an instance at random from a species

---

[1] In 1812 Moore published *The Two-penny Postbag, by Thomas Brown the Younger;* and, in 1818, *The Fudge Family in Paris*.

of composition not very favourable to imagination—Satire: set down the character of Sporus, with all the wonderful play of fancy which is scattered over it, and place by its side an equal number of verses, from any two existing poets, of the same power and the same variety—where will you find them?

I merely mention one instance of many, in reply to the injustice done to the memory of him who harmonized our poetical language. The attorneys' clerks, and other self-educated genii, found it easier to distort themselves to the new models, than to toil after the symmetry of him who had enchanted their fathers. They were besides smitten by being told that the new school were to revive the language of Queen Elizabeth, the true English; as every body in the reign of Queen Anne wrote no better than French, by a species of literary treason.

Blank verse, which, unless in the drama, no one except Milton ever wrote who could rhyme, became the order of the day—or else such rhyme as looked still blanker than the verse without it. I am aware that Johnson has said, after some hesitation, that he could not "prevail upon himself to wish that Milton had been a rhymer." The opinions of that truly great man, whom it is also the present fashion to decry, will ever be received by me with that deference which time will restore to him from all; but, with all humility, I am not persuaded that the *Paradise Lost* would not have been more nobly conveyed to posterity, not perhaps in heroic couplets, although even *they* could sustain the subject if well balanced, but in the stanza of Spenser or of Tasso, or in the terza rima of Dante, which the powers of Milton could easily have grafted on our language. The *Seasons* of Thomson would have been better in rhyme, although still inferior to his *Castle of Indolence;* and Mr. Southey's *Joan of Arc* no worse, although it might have taken up six months instead of weeks in the composition. I recommend also to the lovers of lyrics the perusal of the present laureate's Odes by the side of Dryden's on *Saint Cecilia,* but let him be sure to read *first* those of Mr. Southey.

PRESENT STATE OF ENGLISH POETRY 251

To the heaven-born genii and inspired young scriveners of the day much of this will appear paradox: it will appear so even to the higher order of our critics; but it was a truism twenty years ago, and it will be a re-acknowledged truth in ten more.

JOHN KEATS

(1795–1821)

"The Genius of Poetry," and his own Art.

... Praise or blame has but a momentary effect on the man whose love of beauty in the abstract makes him a severe critic of his own works. My own domestic criticism has given me pain without comparison beyond what *Blackwood* or the *Quarterly* could inflict; and also, when I feel I am right, no external praise can give me such a glow as my own solitary reperception and ratification of what is fine. J. S. is perfectly right in regard to "the slipshod *Endymion*." That it is so is no fault of mine. No! though it may sound a little paradoxical, it is as good as I had power to make it by myself. Had I been nervous about its being a perfect piece, and with that view asked advice and trembled over every page, it would not have been written; for it is not in my nature to fumble. I will write independently. I have written independently *without judgment*. I may write independently and *with judgment*, hereafter. The Genius of Poetry must work out its own salvation in a man. It cannot be matured by law and precept, but by sensation and watchfulness in itself. That which is creative must create itself. In *Endymion* I leaped headlong into the sea, and thereby have become better acquainted with the soundings, the quicksands, and the rocks, than if I had stayed upon the green shore, and piped a silly pipe, and took tea and comfortable advice. I was never afraid of failure; for I would sooner fail than not be among the greatest. *Letters*.

A Few Axioms.

In poetry I have a few axioms, and you will see how far I am from their centre. First, I think poetry should surprise by a fine excess, and not by singularity; it should strike the reader as a wording of his own highest thoughts, and appear almost a remembrance. Second, its touches of beauty should never be half-way, thereby making the reader breathless instead of content. The rise, the progress, the setting, of imagery, should, like the sun, come natural to him, shine over him, and set soberly although in magnificence, leaving him in the luxury of twilight. But it is easier to think what poetry should be than to write it. And this leads me to another axiom: That, if poetry comes not as naturally as the leaves to a tree, it had better not come at all.

Letters.

The Poetical Character.

As to the poetical character itself (I mean that sort of which, if I am anything, I am a member—that sort distinguished from the Wordsworthian or egotistical sublime, which is a thing *per se*, and stands alone), it is not itself—it has no self. It is everything, and nothing—it has no character. It enjoys light, and shade. It lives in gusto, be it foul or fair, high or low, rich or poor, mean or elevated—it has as much delight in conceiving an Iago as an Imogen. What shocks the virtuous philosopher delights the chameleon poet. It does no harm from its relish of the dark side of things, any more than from its taste for the bright one, because they both end in speculation. A poet is the most unpoetical of anything in existence, because he has no identity: he is continually in for, and filling, some other body. The sun, the moon, the sea, and men and women who are creatures of impulse, are poetical, and have about them an unchangeable attribute; the poet has none, no identity. He is certainly the most unpoetical of all God's creatures. If then he has no self, and if I am a poet, where is the wonder that I should say I would write no more? Might I not at that very instant have been cogitating on the characters of Saturn and Ops? It is a wretched thing to confess, but it is a very fact, that not one word I ever utter can be taken for granted as an opinion growing out of my identical nature. How can it when I have *no* nature? When I am in a room with people,

if I ever am free from speculating on creations of my own brain, then not myself goes home to myself, but the identity of every one in the room begins to press upon me [so] that I am in a very little time annihilated. Not only among men; it would be the same in a nursery of children.
Letters.

Preface to "Endymion."

Knowing within myself the manner in which this poem has been produced, it is not without a feeling of regret that I make it public. What manner I mean will be quite clear to the reader, who must soon perceive great inexperience, immaturity, and every error denoting a feverish attempt rather than a deed accomplished. The two first books, and indeed the two last, I feel sensible, are not of such completion as to warrant their passing the press; nor should they, if I thought a year's castigation would do them any good. It will not: the foundations are too sandy. It is just that this youngster should die away—a sad thought for me, if I had not some hope that, while it is dwindling, I may be plotting, and fitting myself for verses fit to live in.

This may be speaking too presumptuously, and may deserve a punishment. But no feeling man will be forward to inflict it; he will leave me alone with the conviction that there is not a fiercer hell than the failure in a great object. This is not written with the least atom of purpose to forestall criticisms of course, but from the desire I have to conciliate men who are competent to look, and who do look, with a zealous eye to the honour of English literature.

The imagination of a boy is healthy, and the mature imagination of a man is healthy. But there is a space of life between in which the soul is in a ferment, the character undecided, the way of life uncertain, the ambition thick-sighted. Thence proceeds mawkishness, and all the thousand bitters which those men I speak of must necessarily taste in going over the following pages.

I hope I have not in too late a day touched the beautiful mythology of Greece, and dulled its brightness; for I wish to try once more before I bid it farewell.

WALTER SAVAGE LANDOR

(1775–1864)

Poetry without Body.

From the 'Imaginary Conversations." First published in 1824. Second Conversation between Southey and Porson: Porson loquitur.

I HATE both poetry and wine without body. Look at Shakespeare, Bacon, and Milton; were these your pure-imagination men? ... Did the two of them who wrote in verse build upon nothing? Did their predecessors? And, pray, whose daughter was the muse they invoked? Why, Memory's. They stood among substantial men, and sang upon recorded actions. The plain of Scamander, the promontory of Sigœum, the palaces of Tros and Dardanus, the citadel in which the Fates sang mournfully under the image of Minerva, seem fitter places for the Muses to alight on, than artificial rockwork, or than faery-rings.

ROBERT BROWNING

(1812–1889)

SHELLEY AND THE ART OF POETRY.

First published as an Introductory Essay to "Letters of Percy Bysshe Shelley" (1852). The Letters proved to be forgeries.

... WE accept gladly the biography of an objective poet, as the phrase now goes; one whose endeavour has been to reproduce things external (whether the phenomena of the scenic universe, or the manifested action of the human heart and brain) with an immediate reference, in every case, to the common eye and apprehension of his fellow-men, assumed capable of receiving and profiting by this reproduction. It has been obtained through the poet's double faculty of seeing external objects more clearly, widely, and deeply, than is possible to the average mind, at the same time that he is so acquainted and in sympathy with its narrower comprehension as to be careful to supply it with no other materials than it can combine into an intelligible whole. The auditory of such a poet will include, not only the intelligences which, save for such assistance, would have missed the deeper meaning and enjoyment of the original objects, but also the spirits of a like endowment with his own, who, by means of his abstract, can forthwith pass to the reality it was made from, and either corroborate their impressions of things known already, or supply themselves with new from whatever shows in the inexhaustible variety of existence may have hitherto escaped their knowledge. Such a poet is properly the ποιήτης, the fashioner; and the thing fashioned, his poetry, will of necessity be substantive, projected from himself and distinct. We are ignorant what the inventor of *Othello* conceived of that fact as he beheld it in completeness, how he accounted for it, under what known law he registered its nature, or to what unknown law he traced its coincidence. We learn only what he intended we should learn by that particular exercise of his power,—the fact itself,—which, with its infinite significances, each of us receives for the first time as a creation, and is hereafter left to deal with, as, in proportion to his own intelligence, he best may. We are ignorant, and would fain be otherwise.

Doubtless, with respect to such a poet, we covet his biography. We desire to look back upon the process of gathering together in a lifetime, the materials of the work we behold entire; of elaborating, perhaps under difficulty and with hindrance, all that is familiar to our admiration in the apparent facility of success. And the inner impulse of this effort and operation, what induced it? Did a soul's delight in its own extended sphere of vision set it, for the gratification of an insuppressible power, on labour, as other men are set on rest? Or did a sense of duty or of love lead it to communicate its own sensations to mankind? Did an irresistible sympathy with men compel it to bring down and suit its own provision of knowledge and beauty to their narrow scope? Did the personality of such an one stand like an open watch-tower in the midst of the territory it is erected to gaze on? and were the storms and calms, the stars and meteors, its watchman was wont to report of, the habitual variegation of his every-day life, as they glanced across its open roof or lay reflected on its four-square parapet? Or did some sunken and darkened chamber of imagery witness, in the artificial illumination of every storied compartment we are permitted to contemplate, how rare and precious were the outlooks through here and there an embrasure upon a world beyond, and how blankly would have pressed on the artificer the boundary of his daily life, except for the amorous diligence with which he had rendered permanent by art whatever came to diversify the gloom? Still, fraught with instruction and interest as such details undoubtedly are, we can, if needs be, dispense with them. The man passes, the work remains. The work speaks for itself, as we say: and the biography of the worker is no more necessary to an understanding or enjoyment of it, than is a model or anatomy of some tropical tree, to the right tasting of the fruit we are familiar with on the market-stall—or a geologist's map and stratification, to the prompt recognition of the hill-top, our land-mark of every day.

We turn with stronger needs to the genius of an opposite tendency—the subjective poet of modern classification. He, gifted like the objective poet with the fuller perception of nature and man, is impelled to embody the thing he perceives, not so much with reference to the many below as to the one above him, the supreme Intelligence which apprehends all things in their absolute truth,—an ultimate view ever aspired to, if but partially attained, by the poet's own soul. Not what man sees, but what God sees—the *Ideas* of Plato, seeds of creation lying burningly on the Divine Hand—it is toward these that he struggles. Not with the combination of humanity in action, but with the primal elements of humanity he has to do; and he digs where he stands—preferring to seek them in his own soul as the nearest reflex of that absolute Mind, according to the intuitions of which he desires to perceive and speak. Such a poet does not deal habitually with the picturesque groupings and tempestuous tossings of the forest-trees, but with their roots and fibres naked to the chalk and stone. He does not paint pictures and hang them on the walls, but rather carries them on the retina of his own eyes: we must look deep into his human eyes, to see those pictures on them. He is rather a seer, accordingly, than a fashioner, and what he produces will be less a work than an effluence. That effluence cannot be easily considered in abstraction from his personality,—being indeed the very radiance and aroma of his personality, projected from it but not separated. Therefore, in our approach to the poetry, we necessarily approach the personality of the poet; in apprehending it we apprehend him, and certainly we cannot love it without loving him. Both for love's and for understanding's sake we desire to know him, and as readers of his poetry must be readers of his biography also.

I shall observe, in passing, that it seems not so much from any essential distinction in the faculty of the two poets or in the nature of the objects contemplated by either, as in the more immediate adaptability of these objects to the distinct purpose of each, that the objective poet, in his appeal to the aggregate human mind, chooses to deal with the doings of men (the result of which dealing, in its pure form, when even description, as suggesting a describer, is dispensed with, is what we call dramatic poetry), while the subjective poet, whose study has been himself, appealing through himself to the absolute Divine mind, prefers to dwell upon those external scenic appearances which strike out most abundantly and uninterruptedly his inner light and power, selects that silence of the earth and sea in which he can best hear the beating of his individual heart, and leaves the noisy, complex, yet imperfect exhibitions of nature in the manifold experience of man around him, which serve only to distract and suppress the working of his brain. These opposite tendencies of genius will be more readily descried in their artistic effect than in their moral spring and cause. Pushed to an extreme and manifested as a deformity, they will be seen plainest of all in the fault of either artist, when subsidiarily to the human interest of his work his occasional illustrations from scenic nature are introduced as in the earlier works of the originative painters—men and women filling the foreground with consummate mastery, while mountain, grove and rivulet show like an anticipatory revenge on that succeeding race of landscape-painters whose "figures" disturb the perfection of their earth and sky. It would be idle to inquire, of these two kinds of poetic faculty in operation, which is the higher or even rarer endowment. If the subjective might seem to be the ultimate requirement of every age, the objective, in the strictest state, must still retain its original value. For it is with this world, as starting point and basis alike, that we shall always have to concern ourselves: the world is not to be learned and thrown aside, but reverted to and relearned. The spiritual comprehension may be infinitely subtilized, but the raw material it operates upon, must remain. There may be no end of the poets who communicate to us what they see in an object with reference to their own individuality; what it was before they saw it, in reference to the aggregate human mind, will be as desirable to know as ever. Nor is there any reason why these two modes of poetic faculty may not issue hereafter from the same poet in successive perfect works, examples of which, according to what are now considered the exigencies of art, we have hitherto possessed in distinct individuals only. A mere running in of the one faculty upon the other, is, of course, the ordinary circumstance. Far more rarely it happens that either is found so decidedly prominent and superior, as to be pronounced comparatively pure: while of the perfect shield, with the gold and the silver side set up for all comers to challenge, there has yet been no instance. Either faculty in its eminent state is doubtless conceded by Providence as a best gift to men, according to their especial want. There is a time when the general eye has, so to speak, absorbed its fill of the phenomena around it, whether spiritual or material, and desires rather to learn the exacter significance of what it possesses, than to receive any augmentation of what is possessed. Then is the opportunity for the poet of loftier vision, to lift his fellows, with their half-apprehensions, up to his own sphere, by intensifying the import of details and rounding the universal meaning. The influence of such an achievement will not soon die out. A tribe of successors (Homerides) working more or less in the same spirit, dwell on his discoveries and reinforce his doctrine; till, at unawares, the world is found to be subsisting wholly on the shadow of a reality, on sentiments diluted from passions, on the tradition of a fact, the convention of a moral, the straw of last year's harvest. Then is the imperative call for the appearance of another sort of poet, who shall at once replace this intellectual rumination of food swallowed long ago, by a supply of the fresh and living swathe; getting at new substance by breaking up the assumed wholes into parts of independent and unclassed value, careless of the unknown laws for recombining them (it will be the business of yet another poet to suggest those hereafter), prodigal of objects for men's outer and not inner sight, shaping for their uses a new and different creation from the last, which it displaces by the right of life over death,—to endure until, in the inevitable process, its very sufficiency to itself shall require, at length, an exposition of its affinity to something higher,—when the positive yet conflicting facts shall again precipitate themselves under an harmonizing law, and one more degree will be apparent for a poet to climb in that mighty ladder, of which, however cloud-involved and undefined may glimmer the topmost step, the world dares no longer doubt that its gradations ascend.

Such being the two kinds of artists, it is naturally, as I have shown, with the biography of the subjective poet that we have the deeper concern. Apart from his recorded life altogether, we might fail to determine with satisfactory precision to what class his productions belong, and what amount of praise is assignable to the producer. Certainly, in the face of any conspicuous achievement of genius, philosophy, no less than sympathetic instinct, warrants our belief in a great moral purpose having mainly inspired even where it does not visibly look out of the same. Greatness in a work suggests an adequate instrumentality; and none of the lower incitements, however they may avail to initiate or even effect many considerable displays of power, simulating the nobler inspiration to which they are mistakenly referred, have been found able, under the ordinary conditions of humanity, to task themselves to the end of so exacting a performance as a poet's complete work. As soon will the galvanism, that provokes to violent action the muscles of a corpse, induce it to cross the chamber steadily: sooner. The love of displaying power for the display's sake, the love of riches, of distinction, of notoriety,—the desire of a triumph over rivals, and the vanity in the applause of friends,—each and all of such whetted appetites grow intenser by exercise and increasingly sagacious as to the best and readiest means of self-appeasement,—while for any of their ends, whether the money or the pointed finger of the crowd, or the flattery and hate to heart's content, there are cheaper prices to pay, they will all find soon enough, than the bestowment of a life upon a labour, hard, slow, and not sure. Also, assuming the proper moral aim to have produced a work, there are many and various states of an aim : it may be more intense than clear-sighted, or too easily satisfied with a lower field of activity than a steadier aspiration would reach. All the bad poetry in the world (accounted poetry, that is, by its affinities) will be found to result from some one of the infinite degrees of discrepancy between the attributes of the poet's soul, occasioning a want of correspondency between his work and the verities of nature—issuing in poetry, false under whatever form, which shows a thing not as it is to mankind generally, nor as it is to the particular describer, but as it is supposed to be for some unreal neutral mood, midway between both and of value to neither, and living its brief minute simply through the indolence of whoever accepts it or his incapacity to denounce a cheat. Although of such depths of failure there can be no question here, we must in every case betake ourselves to the review of a poet's life ere we determine some of the nicer questions concerning his poetry—more especially if the performance we seek to estimate aright, has been obstructed and cut short of completion by circumstances,—a disastrous youth or a premature death. We may learn from the biography whether his spirit invariably saw and spoke from the last height to which it had attained. An absolute vision is not for this world, but we are permitted a continual approximation to it, every degree of which in the individual, provided it exceed the attainment of the masses, must procure him a clear advantage. Did the poet ever attain to a higher platform than where he rested and exhibited a result ? Did he know more than he spoke of ?

I concede, however, in respect to the subject of our study as well as some few other illustrious examples, that the unmistakable quality of the verse would be evidence enough, under usual circumstances, not only of the kind and degree of the intellectual but of the moral constitution of Shelley: the whole personality of the poet shining forward from the poems, without much need of going further to seek it. The *Remains*—produced within a period of ten years, and at a season of life when other men of at all comparable genius have hardly done more than prepare the eye for future sight and the tongue for speech—present us with the complete enginery of a poet, as signal in the excellence of its several adaptitudes as transcendent in the combination of effects—examples, in fact, of the whole poet's function of beholding with an understanding keenness the universe, nature and man, in their actual state of perfection in imperfection,—of the whole poet's virtue of being untempted by the manifold partial developments of beauty and good on every side, into leaving them the ultimates he found them,—induced by the facility of the gratification of his own sense of those qualities, or by the pleasure of acquiescence in the short-comings of his predecessors in art, and the pain of disturbing their conventionalisms,—the whole poet's virtue, I repeat, of looking higher than any manifestation yet made of both beauty and good, in order to suggest from the utmost actual realization of the one a corresponding capability in the other, and out of the calm, purity and energy of nature, to reconstitute and store up for the forthcoming stage of man's being, a gift in repayment of that former gift, in which man's own thought and passion had been lavished by the poet on the else-incompleted magnificence of the sunrise, the else-uninterpreted mystery of the lake,—so drawing out, lifting up, and assimilating this ideal of a future man, thus descried as possible, to the present reality of the poet's soul already arrived at the higher state of development, and still aspirant to elevate and extend itself in conformity with its still-improving perceptions of, no longer the eventual Human, but the actual Divine. In conjunction with which noble and rare powers, came the subordinate power of delivering these attained results to the world in an embodiment of verse more closely answering to and indicative of the process of the informing spirit, (failing as it occasionally does, in art, only to succeed in highest art,)—with a diction more adequate to the task in its natural and acquired richness, its material colour and spiritual transparency,—the whole being moved by and suffused with a music at once of the soul and the sense, expressive both of an external might of sincere passion and an internal fitness and consonancy,—than can be attributed to any other writer whose record is among us. Such was the spheric poetical faculty of Shelley, as its own self-sufficing central light, radiating equally through immaturity and accomplishment, through many fragments and occasional completion, reveals it to a competent judgment.

But the acceptance of this truth by the public, has been retarded by certain objections which cast us back on the evidence of biography, even with Shelley's poetry in our hands. Except for the particular character of these objections, indeed, the non-appreciation of his contemporaries would simply class, now that it is over, with a series of experiences which have necessarily happened and needlessly been wondered at, ever since the world began, and concerning which any present anger may well be moderated, no less in justice to our forerunners than in policy to ourselves. For the misapprehensiveness of his age is exactly what a poet is sent to remedy; and the interval between his operation and the generally perceptible effect of it, is no greater, less indeed, than in many other departments of the great human effort. The " E pur si muove " [" It "— the earth—" moves, nevertheless "] of the astronomer [Galileo Galilei], was as bitter a word as any uttered before or since by a poet over his rejected living work, in that depth of conviction which is so like despair.

But in this respect was the experience of Shelley peculiarly unfortunate—that the disbelief in him as a man, even preceded the disbelief in him as a writer; the misconstruction of his moral nature preparing the way for the misappreciation of his intellectual labours. There existed from the beginning,—simultaneous with, indeed anterior to his earliest noticeable works, and

SHELLEY AND THE ART OF POETRY

not brought forward to counteract any impression they had succeeded in making,—certain charges against his private character and life, which, if substantiated to their whole breadth, would materially disturb, I do not attempt to deny, our reception and enjoyment of his works, however wonderful the artistic qualities of these. For we are not sufficiently supplied with instances of genius of his order, to be able to pronounce certainly how many of its constituent parts have been tasked and strained to the production of a given lie, and how high and pure a mood of the creative mind may be dramatically simulated as the poet's habitual and exclusive one. The doubts, therefore, arising from such a question, required to be set at rest, as they were effectually, by those early authentic notices of Shelley's career and the corroborative accompaniment of his letters, in which not only the main tenor and principal result of his life, but the purity and beauty of many of the processes which had conduced to them, were made apparent enough for the general reader's purpose—whoever lightly condemned Shelley first, on the evidence of reviews and gossip, as lightly acquitting him now, on that of memoirs and correspondence. Still, it is advisable to lose no opportunity of strengthening and completing the chain of biographical testimony ; much more, of course, for the sake of the poet's original lovers, whose volunteered sacrifice of particular principle in favour of absorbing sympathy we might desire to dispense with, than for the sake of his foolish haters, who have long since diverted upon other objects their obtuseness or malignancy. A full life of Shelley should be written at once, while the materials for it continue in reach ; not to minister to the curiosity of the public, but to obliterate the last stain of that false life which was forced on the public's attention before it had any curiosity on the matter,—a biography, composed in harmony with the present general disposition to have faith in him, yet not shrinking from a candid statement of all ambiguous passages, through a reasonable confidence that the most doubtful of them will be found consistent with a belief in the eventual perfection of his character, according to the poor limits of our humanity. Nor will men persist in confounding, any more than God confounds, with genuine infidelity and an atheism of the heart, those passionate, impatient struggles of a boy towards distant truth and love, made in the dark, and ended by one sweep of the natural seas before the full moral sunrise could shine out on him. Crude convictions of boyhood, conveyed in imperfect and inapt forms of speech,—for such things all boys have been pardoned. There are growing-pains, accompanied by temporary distortion, of the soul also. And it would be hard indeed upon this young Titan of genius, murmuring in divine music his human ignorances, through his very thirst for knowledge, and his rebellion, in mere aspiration to law, if the melody itself substantiated the error, and the tragic cutting short of life perpetuated into sins, such faults as, under happier circumstances, would have been left behind by the consent of the most arrogant moralist, forgotten on the lowest steps of youth.

The responsibility of presenting to the public a biography of Shelley, does not, however, lie with me: I have only to make it a little easier by arranging these few supplementary letters, with a recognition of the value of the whole collection. This value I take to consist in a most truthful conformity of the Correspondence, in its limited degree, with the moral and intellectual character of the writer as displayed in the highest manifestations of his genius. Letters and poems are obviously an act of the same mind, produced by the same law, only differing in the application to the individual or collective understanding. Letters and poems may be used indifferently as the basement of our opinion upon the writer's character; the finished expression of a sentiment in the poems, giving light and significance to the rudiments of the same in the letters, and these, again, in their incipiency and unripeness, authenticating the exalted mood and reattaching it to the personality of the writer. The musician speaks on the note he sings with: there is no change in the scale, as he diminishes the volume into familiar intercourse. There is nothing of that jarring between the man and the author, which has been found so amusing or so melancholy; no dropping of the tragic mask, as the crowd melts away; no mean discovery of the real motives of a life's achievement, often, in other lives, laid bare as pitifully as when, at the close of a holiday, we catch sight of the internal lead-pipes and wood-valves, to which, and not to the ostensible conch and dominant Triton of the fountain, we have owed our admired waterwork. No breaking out, in household privacy, of hatred, anger and scorn, incongruous with the higher mood and suppressed artistically in the book: no brutal return to self-delighting, when the audience of philanthropic schemes is out of hearing: no indecent stripping off the grander feeling and rule of life as too costly and cumbrous for everyday wear. Whatever Shelley was, he was with an admirable sincerity. It was not always truth that he thought and spoke; but in the purity of truth he spoke and thought always. Everywhere is apparent his belief in the existence of Good, to which Evil is an accident; his faithful holding by what he assumed to be the former, going everywhere in company with the tenderest pity for those acting or suffering on the opposite hypothesis. For he was tender, though tenderness is not always the characteristic of very sincere natures; he was eminently both tender and sincere. And not only do the same affection and yearning after the well-being of his kind, appear in the letters as in the poems, but they express themselves by the same theories and plans, however crude and unsound. There is no reservation of a subtler, less costly, more serviceable remedy for his own ill, than he has proposed for the general one; nor does he ever contemplate an object on his own account, from a less elevation than he uses in exhibiting it to the world. How shall we help believing Shelley to have been, in his ultimate attainment, the splendid spirit of his own best poetry, when we find even his carnal speech to agree faithfully, at faintest as at strongest, with the tone and rhythm of his most oracular utterances?

For the rest, these new letters are not offered as presenting any new feature of the poet's character.

Regarded in themselves, and as the substantive productions of a man, their importance would be slight. But they possess interest beyond their limits, in confirming the evidence just dwelt on, of the poetical mood of Shelley being only the intensification of his habitual mood; the same tongue only speaking, for want of the special excitement to sing. The very first letter, as one instance for all, strikes the key-note of the predominating sentiment of Shelley throughout his whole life—his sympathy with the oppressed. And when we see him at so early an age, casting out, under the influence of such a sympathy, letters and pamphlets on every side, we accept it as the simple exemplification of the sincerity, with which, at the close of his life, he spoke of himself, as—

> One whose heart a stranger's tear might wear
> As water-drops the sandy fountain-stone;
> Who loved and pitied all things, and could moan
> For woes which others hear not, and could see
> The absent with the glance of phantasy,
> And with the poor and trampled sit and weep,
> Following the captive to his dungeon deep—
> [One who was] as a nerve o'er which do creep
> The else-unfelt oppressions of this earth.

Such sympathy with his kind was evidently developed in him to an extraordinary and even morbid degree, at a period when the general intellectual powers it was impatient to put in motion, were immature or deficient.

I conjecture, from a review of the various publications of Shelley's youth, that one of the causes of his failure at the outset, was the peculiar *practicalness* of his mind, which was not without a determinate effect on his progress in theorizing. An ordinary youth, who turns his attention to similar subjects, discovers falsities, incongruities, and various points for amendment, and, in the natural advance of the purely critical spirit unchecked by considerations of remedy, keeps up before his young eyes so many instances of the same error and wrong, that he finds himself unawares arrived at the startling conclusion, that all must be changed—or nothing: in the face of which plainly impossible achievement, he is apt (looking perhaps a little more serious by the time he touches at the decisive issue), to feel, either carelessly or considerately, that his own attempting a single piece of service would be worse than useless even, and to refer the whole task to another age and person— safe in proportion to his incapacity. Wanting words to speak, he has never made a fool of himself by speaking. But, in Shelley's case, the early fervour and power to *see*, was accompanied by as precocious a fertility to *contrive:* he endeavoured to realize as he went on idealizing; every wrong had simultaneously its remedy, and, out of the strength of his hatred for the former, he took the strength of his confidence in the latter—till suddenly he stood pledged to the defence of a set of miserable little expedients, just as if they represented great principles, and to an attack upon various great principles, really so, without leaving himself time to examine whether, because they were antagonistical to the remedy he had suggested, they must therefore be identical or even essentially connected with the wrong he sought to cure,—playing with blind passion into the hands of his enemies, and dashing at whatever red cloak was held forth to him, as the cause of the fireball he had last been stung with—mistaking Churchdom for Christianity, and for marriage, " the sale of love " and the law of sexual oppression.

Gradually, however, he was leaving behind him this low practical dexterity, unable to keep up with his widening intellectual perception; and, in exact proportion as he did so, his true power strengthened and proved itself. Gradually he was raised above the contemplation of spots and the attempt at effacing them, to the great Abstract Light, and, through the discrepancy of the creation, to the sufficiency of the First Cause. Gradually he was learning that the best way of removing abuses is to stand fast by truth. Truth is one, as they are manifold; and innumerable negative effects are produced by the upholding of one positive principle. I shall say what I think,—had Shelley lived he would have finally ranged himself with the Christians; his very instinct for helping the weaker side (if numbers make strength), his very "hate of hate," which at first mistranslated itself into delirious Queen Mab notes and the like, would have got clearer-sighted by exercise. The preliminary step to following Christ, is the leaving the dead to bury their dead—not clamouring on His doctrine for an especial solution of difficulties which are referable to the general problem of the universe. Already he had attained to a profession of "a worship to the Spirit of good within, which requires (before it sends that inspiration forth, which impresses its likeness upon all it creates) devoted and disinterested homage," *as Coleridge says*—and Paul likewise. And we find in one of his last exquisite fragments, avowedly a record of one of his own mornings and its experience, as it dawned on him at his soul and body's best in his boat on the Serchio—that as surely as

> The stars burnt out in the pale blue air,
> And the thin white moon lay withering there—
> Day had kindled the dewy woods,
> And the rocks above, and the stream below,
> And the vapours in their multitudes,
> And the Apennine's shroud of summer snow—
> Day had awakened all things that be;

just so surely, he tells us (stepping forward from this delicious dance-music, choragus-like, into the grander measure befitting the final enunciation),

> All rose to do the task He set to each,
> Who shaped us to His ends and not our own;
> The million rose to learn, and One to teach
> What none yet ever knew or can be known.

No more difference than this, from David's pregnant conclusion so long ago!

Meantime, as I call Shelley a moral man because he was true, simple-hearted, and brave, and because what he acted corresponded to what he knew, so I call him a man of religious mind, because every audacious negative cast up by him against the Divine, was interpenetrated with a mood of reverence and adoration,—and because I find him everywhere taking for granted some of the capital dogmas of Christianity, while most vehemently denying their historical basement. There is such a thing as an efficacious knowledge of and belief in the politics of Junius, or the poetry of Rowley, though a man should at the same time dispute the title of Chatterton to the one, and consider the author of the other, as Byron wittily did, " really, truly, nobody at all." [1] There is even such a thing, we come to learn wonderingly in these very letters, as a profound sensibility and adaptitude for art, while the science of the percipient is so little advanced as to admit of his stronger admiration for Guido (and Carlo Dolce !) than for Michael Angelo. A Divine Being has Himself said, that " a word against the Son of man shall be forgiven to a man," while " a word against the spirit of God " (implying a general deliberate preference of perceived evil to perceived good) " shall not be forgiven to a man." Also, in religion, one earnest and unextorted assertion of belief should outweigh, as a matter of testimony, many assertions of unbelief. The fact that there is a gold-region is established by the finding of one lump, though you miss the vein never so often.

He died before his youth ended. In taking the measure of him as a man, he must be considered on the whole and at his ultimate spiritual stature, and not be judged of at the immaturity and by the mistakes of ten years before : that, indeed, would be to judge of the author of *Julian and Maddalo* by *Zastrozzi*. Let the whole truth be told of his worst mistake. I believe for my own part, that if anything could now shame or grieve Shelley, it would be an attempt to vindicate him at the expense of another.

[1] Or, to take our illustrations from the writings of Shelley himself, there is such a thing as admirably appreciating a work by Andrea Verocchio,—and fancifully characterizing the Pisan Torre Guelfa by the Ponte a Mare, black against the sunsets,—and consummately painting the islet of San Clemente with its penitentiary for rebellious priests, to the west between Venice and the Lido—while you believe the first to be a fragment of an antique sarcophagus,—the second, Ugolino's Tower of Famine (the vestiges of which should be sought for in the Piazza de' Cavalieri)—and the third (as I convinced myself last summer at Venice), San Servolo with its madhouse—which, far from being " windowless," is as full of windows as a barrack.

In forming a judgment, I would, however, press on the reader the simple justice of considering tenderly his constitution of body as well as mind, and how unfavourable it was to the steady symmetries of conventional life ; the body, in the torture of incurable disease, refusing to give repose to the bewildered soul, tossing in its hot fever of the fancy,—and the laudanum-bottle making but a perilous and pitiful truce between these two. He was constantly subject to "that state of mind" (I quote his own note to *Hellas*) "in which ideas may be supposed to assume the force of sensation, through the confusion of thought with the objects of thought, and excess of passion animating the creations of the imagination" : in other words, he was liable to remarkable delusions and hallucinations. The nocturnal attack in Wales, for instance, was assuredly a delusion ; and I venture to express my own conviction, derived from a little attention to the circumstances of either story, that the idea of the enamoured lady following him to Naples, and of the "man in the cloak" who struck him at the Pisan post-office, were equally illusory,—the mere projection, in fact, from himself, of the image of his own love and hate.

> To thirst and find no fill—to wail and wander
> With short unsteady steps—to pause and ponder—
> To feel the blood run through the veins and tingle
> When busy thought and blind sensation mingle—
> To nurse the image of *unfelt caresses*
> Till dim imagination just possesses
> The half-created shadow—

of unfelt caresses—and of unfelt blows as well : to such conditions was his genius subject. It was not at Rome only (where he heard a mystic voice exclaiming, "Cenci, Cenci," in reference to the tragic theme which occupied him at the time),—it was not at Rome only that he mistook the cry of "old rags." The habit of somnambulism is said to have extended to the very last days of his life.

Let me conclude with a thought of Shelley as a poet. In the hierarchy of creative minds, it is the presence of the highest faculty that gives first rank, in virtue of its kind, not degree; no pretension of a lower nature, whatever the completeness of development or variety of effect, impeding the precedency of the rarer endowment though only in the germ. The contrary is sometimes maintained; it is attempted to make the lower gifts (which are potentially included in the higher faculty) of independent value, and equal to some exercise of the special function. For instance, should not a poet possess common sense? Then the possession of abundant common sense implies a step towards becoming a poet. Yes; such a step as the lapidary's, when, strong in the fact of carbon entering largely into the composition of the diamond, he heaps up a sack of charcoal in order to compete with the Koh-i-noor. I pass at once, therefore, from Shelley's minor excellences to his noblest and predominating characteristic.

This I call his simultaneous perception of Power and Love in the absolute, and of Beauty and Good in the concrete, while he throws, from his poet's station between both, swifter, subtler, and more numerous films for the connexion of each with each, than have been thrown by any modern artificer of whom I have knowledge; proving how, as he says,

> The spirit of the worm beneath the sod,
> In love and worship blends itself with God.

I would rather consider Shelley's poetry as a sublime fragmentary essay towards a presentment of the correspondency of the universe to Deity, of the natural to the spiritual, and of the actual to the ideal, than I would isolate and separately appraise the worth of many detachable portions which might be acknowledged as utterly perfect in a lower moral point of view, under the mere conditions of art. It would be easy to take my stand on successful instances of objectivity in Shelley: there is the unrivalled *Cenci;* there is the *Julian and Maddalo* too; there is the magnificent *Ode to Naples*: why not regard, it may be said, the less organized matter as the radiant elemental foam and solution, out of which would have been evolved, eventually, creations as perfect even as those? But I prefer to look for the highest attainment, not simply the high—and, seeing it, I hold by it. There is surely enough of the work "Shelley" to be known enduringly among men, and, I believe, to be accepted of God, as human work may; and round the imperfect proportions of such, the most elaborated productions of ordinary art must arrange themselves as inferior illustrations.

It is because I have long held these opinions in assurance and gratitude, that I catch at the opportunity offered to me of expressing them here; knowing that the alacrity to fulfil an humble office conveys more love than the acceptance of the honour of a higher one, and that better, therefore, than the signal service it was the dream of my boyhood to render to his fame and memory, may be the saying of a few inadequate words upon these scarcely more important supplementary letters of Shelley.

PARIS, *Dec.* 4, 1851.

MATTHEW ARNOLD

(1822–1888)

On Translating Homer.

These pages are from the essay evoked by Francis W. Newman's translation of the "Iliad" (1861).

Homer is rapid in his movement, Homer is plain in his words and style, Homer is simple in his ideas, Homer is noble in his manner. Cowper renders him ill because he is slow in his movement, and elaborate in his style; Pope renders him ill because he is artificial both in his style and in his words; Chapman renders him ill because he is fantastic in his ideas; Mr. Newman renders him ill because he is odd in his words and ignoble in his manner. All four translators diverge from their original at other points besides those named; but it is at the points thus named that their divergence is greatest. For instance, Cowper's diction is not as Homer's diction, nor his nobleness as Homer's nobleness; but it is in movement and grammatical style that he is most unlike Homer. Pope's rapidity is not of the same sort as Homer's rapidity, nor are his plainness of ideas and his nobleness as Homer's plainness of ideas and nobleness: but it is in the artificial character of his style and diction that he is most unlike Homer. Chapman's movement, words, style, and manner, are often far enough from resembling Homer's movement, words, style, and manner; but it is the fantasticality of his ideas which puts him farthest from resembling Homer. Mr. Newman's movement, grammatical style, and ideas, are a thousand times in strong contrast with Homer's; still it is by the oddness of his diction and the ignobleness of his manner that he contrasts with Homer the most violently.

Therefore the translator must not say to himself: "Cowper is noble, Pope is rapid, Chapman has a good diction, Mr. Newman has a good cast of sentence;

I will avoid Cowper's slowness, Pope's artificiality, Chapman's conceits, Mr. Newman's oddity; I will take Cowper's dignified manner, Pope's impetuous movement, Chapman's vocabulary, Mr. Newman's syntax, and so make a perfect translation of Homer." Undoubtedly, in certain points the versions of Chapman, Cowper, Pope, and Mr. Newman, all of them have merit; some of them very high merit, others a lower merit; but even in these points they have none of them precisely the same kind of merit as Homer, and therefore the new translator, even if he can imitate them in their good points, will still not satisfy his judge, the scholar, who asks him for Homer and Homer's kind of merit, or, at least, for as much of them as it is possible to give.

So the translator really has no good model before him for any part of his work, and has to invent everything for himself. He is to be rapid in movement, plain in speech, simple in thought, and noble; and *how* he is to be either rapid, or plain, or simple, or noble, no one yet has shown him. I shall try to-day to establish some practical suggestions which may help the translator of Homer's poetry to comply with the four grand requirements which we make of him.

His version is to be rapid; and of course, to make a man's poetry rapid, as to make it noble, nothing can serve him so much as to have, in his own nature, rapidity and nobleness. *It is the spirit that quickeneth;* and no one will so well render Homer's swift-flowing movement as he who has himself something of the swift-moving spirit of Homer. Yet even this is not quite enough. Pope certainly had a quick and darting spirit, as he had, also, real nobleness; yet Pope does not render the movement of Homer. To render this the translator must have, besides his natural qualifications, an appropriate metre.

I have sufficiently shown why I think all forms of our ballad-metre unsuited to Homer. It seems to me to be beyond question that, for epic poetry, only three metres can seriously claim to be accounted capable of the grand style. Two of these will at once occur to everyone,—the ten-syllable, or so-called *heroic*, couplet, and blank verse. I do not add to these the Spenserian stanza, although Dr. Maginn, whose metrical eccentricities I have already criticized, pronounces this stanza the one right measure for a translation of Homer. It is enough to observe that if Pope's couplet, with the simple system of correspondences that its rhymes introduce, changes the movement of Homer, in which no such correspondences are found, and is therefore a bad measure for a translator of Homer to employ, Spenser's stanza, with its far more intricate system of correspondences, must change Homer's movement far more profoundly, and must therefore be for the translator a far worse measure than the couplet of Pope. Yet I will say, at the same time, that the verse of Spenser is more fluid, slips more easily and quickly along, than the verse of almost any other English poet.

> By this the northern wagoner had set
> His seven-fold team behind the steadfast star
> That was in ocean waves yet never wet,
> But firm is fixt, and sendeth light from far
> To all that in the wide deep wandering are.[1]

One cannot but feel that English verse has not often moved with the fluidity and sweet ease of these lines. It is possible that it may have been this quality of Spenser's poetry which made Dr. Maginn think that the stanza of *The Faery Queen* must be a good measure for rendering Homer. This it is not: Spenser's verse is fluid and rapid, no doubt, but there are more ways than one of being fluid and rapid, and Homer is fluid and rapid in quite another way than Spenser. Spenser's manner is no more Homeric than is the manner of the one modern inheritor of Spenser's beautiful gift,—the poet, who evidently caught from Spenser his sweet and easy slipping movement, and who has exquisitely employed it; a Spenserian genius, nay, a genius by natural endowment richer probably than even Spenser; that light which shines so unexpectedly and without fellow in our century, an Elizabethan born too late, the early lost and admirably gifted Keats.

[1] *The Faery Queen*, canto ii. stanza 1.

I say then that there are really but three metres,—the ten-syllable couplet, blank verse, and a third metre which I will not yet name, but which is neither the Spenserian stanza nor any form of ballad-verse,—between which, as vehicles for Homer's poetry, the translator has to make his choice. Everyone will at once remember a thousand passages in which both the ten-syllable couplet and blank verse prove themselves to have nobleness. Undoubtedly the movement and manner of this,

> Still raise for good the supplicating voice,
> But leave to Heaven the measure and the choice,

are noble. Undoubtedly, the movement and manner of this:

> High on a throne of royal state, which far,
> Outshone the wealth of Ormus and of Ind,

are noble also. But the first is in a rhymed metre; and the unfitness of a rhymed metre for rendering Homer I have already shown. I will observe too, that the fine couplet which I have quoted comes out of a satire, a didactic poem; and that it is in didactic poetry that the ten-syllable couplet has most successfully essayed the grand style. In narrative poetry this metre has succeeded best when it essayed a sensibly lower style, the style of Chaucer, for instance; whose narrative manner, though a very good and sound manner, is certainly neither the grand manner nor the manner of Homer.

The rhymed ten-syllable couplet being thus excluded, blank verse offers itself for the translator's use. The first kind of blank verse which naturally occurs to us is the blank verse of Milton, which has been employed, with more or less modification, by Mr. Cary in translating Dante, by Cowper, and by Mr. Wright in translating Homer. How noble this metre is in Milton's hands, how completely it shows itself capable of the grand, nay, of the grandest, style, I need not say. To this metre, as used in the *Paradise Lost*, our country owes the glory of having produced one of the only two poetical works in the grand style which are to be found in the modern languages; the *Divine Comedy* of Dante is the other. England and Italy here stand alone; Spain, France, and Germany, have produced great poets, but neither Calderon, nor Corneille, nor Schiller, nor even Goethe, has produced a body of poetry in the true grand style in the sense in which the style of the body of Homer's poetry, or Pindar's, or Sophocles's, is grand. But Dante has, and so has Milton; and in this respect Milton possesses a distinction which even Shakspeare, undoubtedly the supreme poetical power in our literature, does not share with him. Not a tragedy of Shakspeare but contains passages in the worst of all styles, the affected style; and the grand style, although it may be harsh, or obscure, or cumbrous, or over-laboured, is never affected. In spite, therefore, of objections which may justly be urged against the plan and treatment of the *Paradise Lost*, in spite of its possessing, certainly, a far less enthralling force of interest to attract and to carry forward the reader than the *Iliad* or the *Divine Comedy*, it fully deserves, it can never lose, its immense reputation; for, like the *Iliad* and the *Divine Comedy*, nay, in some respects to a higher degree than either of them, it is in the grand style.

But the grandeur of Milton is one thing, and the grandeur of Homer is another. Homer's movement, I have said again and again, is a flowing, a rapid movement; Milton's, on the other hand, is a laboured, a self-retarding movement. In each case, the movement, the metrical cast, corresponds with the mode of evolution of the thought, with the syntactical cast, and is indeed determined by it. Milton charges himself so full with thought, imagination, knowledge, that his style will hardly contain them. He is too full-stored to show us in much detail one conception, one piece of knowledge; he just shows it to us in a pregnant allusive way, and then he presses on to another; and all this fullness, this pressure, this condensation, this self-constraint, enters into his movement, and makes it what it is,—noble, but difficult and austere. Homer is quite different; he says a thing, and says it to the end, and then begins another, while Milton is trying to press a thousand things into one. So that whereas, in reading Milton, you never lose the sense of laborious and condensed fullness, in reading Homer you never lose the sense of flowing and abounding ease. With Milton line runs into line, and all is straitly bound together: with Homer line runs off from line, and all hurries away onward. Homer begins, Μῆνιν ἄειδε, Θεά, —at the second word announcing the proposed action: Milton begins:

> Of man's first disobedience, and the fruit
> Of that forbidden tree, whose mortal taste
> Brought death into the world, and all our woe,
> With loss of Eden, till one greater Man
> Restore us, and regain the blissful seat,
> Sing, heavenly muse.

So chary of a sentence is he, so resolute not to let it escape him till he has crowded into it all he can, that it is not till the thirty-ninth word in the sentence that he will give us the key to it, the word of action, the verb. Milton says:

> O for that warning voice, which he, who saw
> The Apocalypse, heard cry in heaven aloud.

He is not satisfied, unless he can tell us, all in one sentence, and without permitting himself to actually mention the name, that the man who had the warning voice was the same man who saw the Apocalypse. Homer would have said, " O for that warning voice, which *John* heard "—and if it had suited him to say that John also saw the Apocalypse, he would have given us that in another sentence. The effect of this allusive and compressed manner of Milton is, I need not say, often very powerful; and it is an effect which other great poets have often sought to obtain much in the same way: Dante is full of it, Horace is full of it; but wherever it exists, it is always an un-Homeric effect. " The losses of the heavens," says Horace, " fresh moons speedily repair; we, when we have gone

EVERYMAN'S LIBRARY

A LIST OF THE 990 VOLUMES ARRANGED UNDER AUTHORS

Anonymous works are given under titles
Anthologies, *Composite Volumes, Dictionaries, etc., are arranged at the end of the list*

Abbott's Rollo at Work, etc., 275
Addison's Spectator, 164–7
Aeschylus' Lyrical Dramas, 62
Aesop's and Other Fables, 657
Aimard's The Indian Scout, 428
Ainsworth's Tower of London, 400
  ,, Old St. Paul's, 522
  ,, Windsor Castle, 709
  ,, The Admirable Crichton, 804
  ,, Rookwood, 870
A Kempis's Imitation of Christ, 484
Alcott's Little Women and Good Wives, 248
  ,, Little Men, 512
Alpine Club: Peaks, Passes, and Glaciers, 778
Andersen's Fairy Tales, 4
  ,, More Fairy Tales, 822
Anglo-Saxon Chronicle, 624
Anson's Voyages, 510
Aquinas's (Thomas), Selected Writings, 953
Aristophanes' Acharnians, etc., 344
  ,, Frogs, etc., 516
Aristotle's Ethics, 547
  ,, Politics, 605
  ,, Poetics, and Demetrius on Style, etc., 901
Arnold's (Matthew) Essays, 115
  ,, Poems, 334
  ,, Study of Celtic Literature, etc., 458
Aucassin and Nicolette, 497
Augustine's (St.) Confessions, 200
  ,, (St.) City of God, 982–3
Aurelius' (Marcus) Meditations, 9
Austen's (Jane) Sense and Sensibility, 21
  ,, Pride and Prejudice, 22
  ,, Mansfield Park, 23
  ,, Emma, 24
  ,, Northanger Abbey, and Persuasion, 25

Bacon's Essays, 10
  ,, Advancement of Learning, 719
Bagehot's Literary Studies, 520, 521
Baker's (Sir S. W.) Cast up by the Sea, 539
Ballantyne's Coral Island, 245
  ,, Martin Rattler, 246
  ,, Ungava, 276
Balzac's Wild Ass's Skin, 26
  ,, Eugénie Grandet, 169
  ,, Old Goriot, 170
  ,, Atheist's Mass, etc., 229
  ,, Christ in Flanders, etc., 284

Balzac's The Chouans, 285
  ,, Quest of the Absolute, 286
  ,, Cat and Racket, etc., 349
  ,, Catherine de Médici, 419
  ,, Cousin Pons, 463
  ,, The Country Doctor, 530
  ,, Rise and Fall of César Birotteau, 596
  ,, Lost Illusions, 656
  ,, The Country Parson, 686
  ,, Ursule Mirouët, 733
Barbusse's Under Fire, 798
Barca's (Mme C. de la) Life in Mexico, 664
Bates's Naturalist on the Amazons, 446
Baxter's (Richard) Autobiography, 868
Beaumont and Fletcher's Selected Plays, 506
Beaumont's (Mary) Joan Seaton, 597
Bede's Ecclesiastical History, 479
Belloc's Stories, Essays, and Poems, 948
Belt's Naturalist in Nicaragua, 561
Bennett's The Old Wives' Tale, 919
Berkeley's (Bishop) Principles of Human Knowledge, New Theory of Vision, etc., 483
Berlioz (Hector), Life of, 602
Binns's Life of Abraham Lincoln, 783
Björnson's Plays, 625, 696
Blackmore's Lorna Doone, 304
  ,, Springhaven, 350
Blackwell's Pioneer Work for Women, 667
Blake's Poems and Prophecies, 792
Bligh's A Book of the 'Bounty,' 950
Boccaccio's Decameron, 845, 846
Boehme's The Signature of All Things, etc., 569
Bonaventura's The Little Flowers, The Life of St. Francis, etc., 485
Borrow's Wild Wales, 49
  ,, Lavengro, 119
  ,, Romany Rye, 120
  ,, Bible in Spain, 151
  ,, Gypsies in Spain, 697
Boswell's Life of Johnson, 1, 2
  ,, Tour to the Hebrides, 387
Boult's Asgard and Norse Heroes, 680
Boyle's The Sceptical Chymist, 559
Bright's (John) Speeches, 252
Brontë's (A.) The Tenant of Wildfell Hall, and Agnes Grey, 685
Brontë's (C.) Jane Eyre, 287
  ,, Shirley, 288

July 1951.   *The Publishers regret that some of the volumes are out of print. A Selected List is available showing volumes in stock.*

Brontë's (C.) Villette, 351
" The Professor, 417
Brontë's (E.) Wuthering Heights, 243
Brown's (Dr. John) Rab and His Friends, etc., 116
Browne's (Frances) Granny's Wonderful Chair, 112
Browne's (Sir Thos.) Religio Medici, etc., 92
Browning's Poems, 1833-44, 41
" " 1844-64, 42
" " 1871-90, 964
" The Ring & the Book, 502
Buchanan's Life and Adventures of Audubon, 601
Bulfinch's The Age of Fable, 472
" Legends of Charlemagne, 556
Bunyan's Pilgrim's Progress, 204
" Grace Abounding, and Mr. Badman, 815
Burke's American Speeches and Letters, 340
" Reflections on the French Revolution, etc., 460
Burnet's History of His Own Times, 85
Burney's (Fanny) Evelina, 352
" Diary, A Selection, edited by Lewis Gibbs, 960
Burns's Poems and Songs, 94
Burton's East Africa, 500
Burton's (Robert) Anatomy of Melancholy, 886-8
Butler's Analogy of Religion, 90
Butler's (Samuel) Erewhon and Erewhon Revisited, 881
Butler's The Way of All Flesh, 895
Buxton's Memoirs, 773
Byron's Complete Poetical and Dramatic Works, 486-8
" Letters, 931

Caesar's Gallic War, etc., 702
Calderon's Plays, 819
Canton's Child's Book of Saints, 61
" Invisible Playmate, etc., 566
Carlyle's French Revolution, 31, 32
" Letters, etc., of Cromwell, 266-8
" Sartor Resartus, 278
" Past and Present, 608
" Essays, 703, 704
" Reminiscences, 875
Carroll's (Lewis) Alice in Wonderland, etc., 836
Castiglione's The Courtier, 807
Cellini's Autobiography, 51
Cervantes's Don Quixote, 385, 386
Chaucer's Canterbury Tales, 307
Chesterfield's Letters to his Son, 823
Chesterton's (Cecil) A History of the United States, 965
Chesterton's (G. K.) Stories, Essays, and Poems, 913
Chrétien de Troyes's Arthurian Romances, 698
Cibber's Apology for his Life, 668
Cicero's Select Letters and Orations, 345
Clarke's Tales from Chaucer, 537
Cobbett's Rural Rides, 638, 639
Coleridge's Biographia, 11

Coleridge's Golden Book of Poetry, 43
" Lectures on Shakespeare, 162
Collins's Woman in White, 464
" The Moonstone, 979
Collodi's Pinocchio, 538
Conrad's Lord Jim, 925
" Nigger of the 'Narcissus,' etc., 980
Converse's Long Will, 328
" House of Prayer, 923
Cook's (Captain) Voyages, 99
Cooper's The Deerslayer, 77
" The Pathfinder, 78
" Last of the Mohicans, 79
" The Pioneer, 171
" The Prairie, 172
Cowper's Letters, 774
" Poems, 872
Cox's Tales of Ancient Greece, 721
Craik's Manual of English Literature, 346
Craik (Mrs.). See Mulock
Creasy's Fifteen Decisive Battles, 300
Crèvecœur's Letters from an American Farmer, 640
Curtis's Prue and I, and Lotus, 418

Dana's Two Years before the Mast, 588
Dante's Divine Comedy, 308
Darwin's Origin of Species, 811
" Voyage of the Beagle, 104
Dasent's Story of Burnt Njal, 558
Daudet's Tartarin of Tarascon, 423
Defoe's Robinson Crusoe, 59
" Captain Singleton, 74
" Memoirs of a Cavalier, 283
" Journal of Plague, 289
" Tour through England and Wales, 820, 821
" Moll Flanders, 837
De Joinville's Memoirs of the Crusades, 333
de la Mare's Stories and Poems, 940
Demosthenes' Select Orations, 546
Dennis's Cities and Cemeteries of Etruria, 183, 184
De Quincey's Lake Poets, 163
" Opium-Eater, 223
" English Mail Coach, etc., 609
De Retz (Cardinal), Memoirs of, 735, 736
Descartes' Discourse on Method, 570
Dickens's Barnaby Rudge, 76
" Tale of Two Cities, 102
" Old Curiosity Shop, 173
" Oliver Twist, 233
" Great Expectations, 234
" Pickwick Papers, 235
" Bleak House, 236
" Sketches by Boz, 237
" Nicholas Nickleby, 238
" Christmas Books, 239
" Dombey and Son, 240
" Martin Chuzzlewit, 241
" David Copperfield, 242
" American Notes, 290
" Child's History of England, 291
, Hard Times, 292

Dickens's Little Dorrit, 293
" Our Mutual Friend, 294
" Christmas Stories, 414
" Uncommercial Traveller, 546
" Edwin Drood, 725
" Reprinted Pieces, 744
Disraeli's Coningsby, 535
Dodge's Hans Brinker, 620
Donne's Poems, 867
Dostoevsky's Crime and Punishment, 501
" The House of the Dead, 533
" Letters from the Underworld, etc., 654
" The Idiot, 682
" Poor Folk, and The Gambler, 711
" The Brothers Karamazov, 802, 803
.. The Possessed, 861, 862
Dowden's Life of R. Browning, 701
Dryden's Dramatic Essays, 568
" Poems, 910
Dufferin's Letters from High Latitudes, 499
Dumas's The Three Musketeers, 81
" The Black Tulip, 174
" Twenty Years After, 175
" Marguerite de Valois, 326
" The Count of Monte Cristo, 393, 394
" The Forty-Five, 420
" Chicot the Jester, 421
" Vicomte de Bragelonne, 593-5
" Le Chevalier de Maison Rouge, 614
Du Maurier's Trilby, 863
Duruy's History of France, 737, 738

Eddington's Nature of the Physical World, 922
Edgar's Cressy and Poictiers, 17
" Runnymede and Lincoln Fair, 320
" Heroes of England, 471
Edgeworth's Castle Rackrent, etc., 410
Eighteenth-Century Plays, 818
Eliot's Adam Bede, 27
" Silas Marner, 121
" Romola, 231
" Mill on the Floss, 325
" Felix Holt, 353
" Scenes of Clerical Life, 468
" Middlemarch, 854, 855
Ellis's (Havelock) Selected Essays, 930
Elyot's Gouernour, 227
Emerson's Essays, 12
" Representative Men, 279
" Nature, Conduct of Life, etc., 322
" Society and Solitude, etc., 567
" Poems, 715
Epictetus' Moral Discourses, 404
Erckmann-Chatrian's The Conscript and Waterloo, 354
" Story of a Peasant, 706, 707
Euclid's Elements, 891
Euripides' Plays, 63, 271

Evans's Holy Graal, 445
Evelyn's Diary, 220, 221
Everyman and other Interludes, 381
Ewing's (Mrs.) Mrs. Overtheway's Remembrances, etc., 730
" Jackanapes, Daddy Darwin's Dovecot, and The Story of a Short Life, 731

Fall of the Nibelungs, 312
Faraday's Experimental Researches in Electricity, 576
Ferrier's (Susan) Marriage, 816
Fielding's Tom Jones, 355, 356
" Amelia, 852, 853
" Joseph Andrews, 467
" Jonathan Wild, and the Journal of a Voyage to Lisbon, 877
Finlay's Byzantine Empire, 33
" Greece under the Romans, 185
Flaubert's Madame Bovary, 808
" Salammbô, 869
" Sentimental Education, 969
Fletcher's (Beaumont and) Selected Plays, 506
Ford's Gatherings from Spain, 152
Forster's Life of Dickens, 781, 782
Forster's (E. M.) A Passage to India, 972
Fox's (Charles James) Selected Speeches, 759
Fox's (George) Journal, 754
France's (Anatole) Sign of the Reine Pédauque & Revolt of the Angels, 967
Francis' (Saint) The Little Flowers, etc., 485
Franklin's Journey to the Polar Sea, 447
Franklin's (Benjamin) Autobiography, 316
Freeman's Old English History for Children, 540
French Medieval Romances, 557
Froissart's Chronicles, 57
Froude's Short Studies, 13, 705
" Henry VIII, 372-4
" Edward VI, 375
" Mary Tudor, 477
" History of Queen Elizabeth's Reign, 583-7
" Life of Benjamin Disraeli, Lord Beaconsfield, 666

Galsworthy's Country House, 917
Galt's Annals of the Parish, 427
Galton's Inquiries into Human Faculty, 263
Gaskell's Cranford, 83
" Life of Charlotte Brontë, 318
" Sylvia's Lovers, 524
" Mary Barton, 598
" Cousin Phillis, etc., 615
" North and South, 680
Gatty's Parables from Nature, 158
Geoffrey of Monmouth's Histories of the Kings of Britain, 577
George's Progress and Poverty, 560
Gibbon's Roman Empire, 431-6, 474-6

Gibbon's Autobiography, 511
Gilchrist's Life of Blake, 971
Gilfillan's Literary Portraits, 348
Giraldus Cambrensis, Wales, 272
Gleig's Life of Wellington, 341
„ The Subaltern, 708
Goethe's Faust, 335
„ Wilhelm Meister, 599, 600
„ Conversations with Eckermann, 851
Gogol's Dead Souls, 726
„ Taras Bulba, 740
Goldsmith's Vicar of Wakefield, 295
„ Poems and Plays, 740
„ Citizen of the World, etc., 902
Goncharov's Oblomov, 878
Gore's Philosophy of the Good Life, 924
Gorki's Through Russia, 741
Gotthelf's Ulric the Farm Servant, 228
Gray's Poems and Letters, 628
Green's Short History of the English People, 727, 728
Grettir Saga, 699
Grimms' Fairy Tales, 56
Grossmith's Diary of a Nobody, 963
Grote's History of Greece, 186–97
Gudrun, 880

Hahnemann's The Organon of the Rational Art of Healing, 663
Hakluyt's Voyages, 264, 265, 313, 314, 338, 339, 388, 389
Hallam's Constitutional History, 621–3
Hamilton's The Federalist, 519
Harte's Luck of Roaring Camp, 681
Harvey's Circulation of Blood, 262
Hawthorne's Wonder Book, 5
„ The Scarlet Letter, 122
„ House of Seven Gables, 176
„ The Marble Faun, 424
„ Twice Told Tales, 531
„ Blithedale Romance, 592
Hazlitt's Characters of Shakespeare's Plays, 65
„ Table Talk, 321
„ Lectures, 411
„ Spirit of the Age and Lectures on English Poets, 459
„ Plain Speaker, 814
Hebbel's Plays, 694
Heimskringla: The Olaf Sagas, 717
„ Sagas of the Norse Kings, 847
Heine's Prose and Poetry, 911
Helps's (Sir Arthur) Life of Columbus, 332
Herbert's Temple, 309
Herodotus, 405, 406
Herrick's Hesperides, 310
Hobbes's Leviathan, 691
Holinshed's Chronicle, 800
Holmes's Life of Mozart, 564
Holmes's (O. W.) Autocrat, 66
„ Professor, 67
„ Poet, 68
Homer's Iliad, 453
„ Odyssey, 454

Hooker's Ecclesiastical Polity, 201, 202
Horace's Complete Poetical Works, 515
Houghton's Life and Letters of Keats, 801
Howard's (E.) Rattlin the Reefer, 857
Howard's (John) State of the Prisons, 835
Hudson's (W. H.) A Shepherd's Life, 926
„ Far Away and Long Ago, 956
Hughes's (E. R.) Chinese Philosophy in Classical Times, 973
Hughes's (Thomas) Tom Brown's Schooldays, 58
Hugo's (Victor) Les Misérables, 363, 364
„ Notre Dame, 422
„ Toilers of the Sea, 509
Hume's Treatise of Human Nature, etc., 548, 549
Hunt's (Leigh) Selected Essays, 829
Hutchinson's (Col.) Memoirs, 317
Huxley's (Aldous) Stories, Essays, and Poems, 935
Huxley's (T. H.) Man's Place in Nature, 47
„ Select Lectures and Lay Sermons, 498

Ibsen's The Doll's House, etc., 494
„ Ghosts, etc., 552
„ Pretender, Pillars of Society, Rosmersholm, 659
„ Brand, 716
„ Lady Inger, etc., 729
„ Peer Gynt, 747
Ingelow's Mopsa the Fairy, 619
Irving's Sketch Book, 117
„ Conquest of Granada, 478
„ Life of Mahomet, 513
Italian Short Stories, 876

James's (G. P. R.) Richelieu, 357
James's (Henry) The Turn of the Screw, and The Aspern Papers, 912
„ The Ambassadors, 987
James (Wm.) Selections from, 739
Jefferies's (Richard) After London, and Amaryllis at the Fair, 951
„ Bevis, 850 [770–1
Johnson's (Dr.) Lives of the Poets,
Jones (Thomas) & Gwyn Jones, The Mabinogion, 97
Jonson's (Ben) Plays, 489, 490
Josephus's Wars of the Jews, 712

Kalidasa's Shakuntala, 629
Kant, Critique of Pure Reason, 909
Keats's Poems, 101
Keble's Christian Year, 690
King's Life of Mazzini, 562
Kinglake's Eothen, 337
Kingsley's (Chas.) Westward Ho!, 20
„ Heroes, 113
„ Hypatia, 230
„ Water Babies, and Glaucus, 277

Kingsley's (Chas.) Hereward the Wake, 296
" Alton Locke, 462
" Yeast, 611
" Madam How and Lady Why, 777
" Poems, 793
Kingsley's (Henry) Ravenshoe, 28
" Geoffrey Hamlyn, 417
Kingston's Peter the Whaler, 6
" Three Midshipmen, 7
Kirby's Kalevala, 259, 260
Koran, 380

Lamb's Tales from Shakespeare, 8
" Essays of Elia, 14
" Letters, 342, 343
Lander's Imaginary Conversations and Poems, 890
Lane's Modern Egyptians, 315
Langland's Piers Plowman, 571
Latimer's Sermons, 40
Law's Serious Call, 91
Lawrence's The White Peacock, 914
" Stories, Essays, and Poems, 958
Layamon's (Wace and) Arthurian Chronicles, 578
Lear (Edmund). *See under* Anthologies
Leibniz' Philosophical Writings, 905
Le Sage's Gil Blas, 437, 438
Leslie's Memoirs of John Constable, 563
Lessing's Laocoön, etc., 843
Lever's Harry Lorrequer, 177
Lewes's Life of Goethe, 269
Lincoln's Speeches, etc., 206
Livy's History of Rome, 603, 669, 670, 749, 755, 756
Locke's Civil Government, 751
" Essay on Human Understanding, 984
Lockhart's Life of Napoleon, 3
" Life of Scott, 55
" Life of Burns, 156
Longfellow's Poems, 382
Lönnrott's Kalevala, 259, 260
Loti's Iceland Fisherman, 920
Lover's Handy Andy, 178
Lowell's Among My Books, 607
Lucretius' On the Nature of Things, 750
Lützow's History of Bohemia, 432
Lyell's Antiquity of Man, 700
Lynd's Essays on Life and Literature, 990
Lytton's Harold, 15
" Last of the Barons, 18
" Last Days of Pompeii, 80
" Pilgrims of the Rhine, 390
" Rienzi, 532

Macaulay's England, 34–6
" Essays, 225, 226
" Speeches on Politics, etc., 399
" Miscellaneous Essays, 439
MacDonald's Sir Gibbie, 678
" Phantastes, 732
Machiavelli's Prince, 280
" Florentine History, 376
Maine's Ancient Law, 734

Malory's Le Morte D'Arthur, 45, 46
Malthus on the Principles of Population, 692, 693
Mandeville's Travels, 812
Mann's (Thomas) Stories & Episodes, 962
Manning's Sir Thomas More, 19
" Mary Powell, and Deborah's Diary, 324
Marlowe's Plays and Poems, 383
Marryat's Mr. Midshipman Easy, 82
" Little Savage, 159
" Masterman Ready, 160
" Peter Simple, 232
" Children of New Forest, 247
" Percival Keene, 358
" Settlers in Canada, 370
" King's Own, 580
" Jacob Faithful, 618
Martineau's Feats on the Fjords, 429
Martinengo-Cesaresco's Folk-Lore and other Essays, 673
Marx's Capital, 848, 849
Maugham's (Somerset) Cakes and Ale, 932
Maupassant's Short Stories, 907
Mazzini's Duties of Man, etc., 224
Melville's Moby Dick, 179
" Typee, 180
" Omoo, 297
Meredith's The Ordeal of Richard Feverel, 916
Mérimée's Carmen, etc., 834
Merivale's History of Rome, 433
Mickiewicz's Pan Tadeusz, 842
Mignet's French Revolution, 713
Mill's Utilitarianism, Liberty, Representative Government, 482
" Rights of Woman, 825
Miller's Old Red Sandstone, 103
Milman's History of the Jews, 377, 378
Milton's Poems, 384
" Areopagitica and other Prose Works, 795
Mitford's Our Village, 927
Molière's Comedies, 830, 831
Mommsen's History of Rome, 542–5
Montagu's (Lady) Letters, 69
Montaigne's Essays, 440–2
Moore's (George) Esther Waters, 933
More's Utopia, and Dialogue of Comfort against Tribulation, 461
Morier's Hajji Baba, 679
Morris's (Wm.) Early Romances, 261
" Life and Death of Jason, 575
Morte D'Arthur Romances, 634
Motley's Dutch Republic, 86–8
Mulock's John Halifax, 123

Neale's Fall of Constantinople, 655
Newcastle's (Margaret, Duchess of) Life of the First Duke of Newcastle, etc., 722
Newman's Apologia Pro Vita Sua, 636
" On the Scope and Nature of University Education, and a Paper on Christianity and Scientific Investigation, 723
Nietzsche's Thus Spake Zarathustra, 892

Oliphant's Salem Chapel, 244
Omar Khayyám, 819
Osborne (Dorothy), Letters of, 674
Ovid: Selected Works, 955
Owen's (Robert) A New View of Society, etc., 799

Paine's Rights of Man, 718
Palgrave's Golden Treasury, 96
Paltock's Peter Wilkins, 676
Park's (Mungo) Travels, 205
Parkman's Conspiracy of Pontiac, 302, 303
Pascal's Pensées, 874
Paston Letters, 752, 753
Pater's Marius the Epicurean, 903
Peacock's Headlong Hall, 327
Pearson's The Grammar of Science, 939
Penn's The Peace of Europe, Some Fruits of Solitude, etc., 724
Pepys's Diary, 53, 54
Percy's Reliques, 148, 149
Pinnow's (H.) History of Germany, 929
Pitt's Orations, 145
Plato's Republic, 64
,, Dialogues, 456, 457
Plutarch's Lives, 407–9
,, Moralia, 565
Poe's Tales of Mystery and Imagination, 336
,, Poems and Essays, 791
Polo's (Marco) Travels, 306
Pope's Complete Poetical Works, 760
Prescott's Conquest of Peru, 301
,, Conquest of Mexico, 397, 398
Prevost's Manon Lescaut, etc., 834
Priestley's Angel Pavement, 938
Procter's Legends and Lyrics, 150
Pushkin's The Captain's Daughter, etc., 898

Quiller-Couch's Hetty Wesley, 864
,, Cambridge Lectures, 974

Rabelais's Gargantua and Pantagruel, 826, 827
Radcliffe's (Mrs. Ann) The Mysteries of Udolpho, 865, 866
Ramayana and Mahabharata, 403
Reade's The Cloister and the Hearth, 29
,, Peg Woffington, 299
Reid's (Mayne) Boy Hunters of the Mississippi, 582
,, The Boy Slaves, 797
Renan's Life of Jesus, 805
Reynolds's Discourses, 118
Ricardo's Principles of Political Economy and Taxation, 590
Richardson's Pamela, 683, 684
,, Clarissa, 882–5
Roberts's (Morley) Western Avernus, 762
Robertson's Religion and Life, 37
,, Christian Doctrine, 38
,, Bible Subjects, 39
Robinson's (Wade) Sermons, 637
Roget's Thesaurus, 630, 631
Rossetti's (D. G.) Poems, 627

Rousseau's Emile, 518
,, Social Contract and other Essays, 660
,, Confessions, 859, 860
Ruskin's Seven Lamps of Architecture, 207
,, Modern Painters, 208–12
,, Stones of Venice, 213–15
,, Unto this Last, etc., 216
,, Elements of Drawing, etc., 217
,, Pre-Raphaelitism, etc., 218
,, Sesame and Lilies, 219
,, Ethics of the Dust, 282
,, Crown of Wild Olive, and Cestus of Aglaia, 323
,, Time and Tide, etc., 450
,, The Two Boyhoods, 688
Russell's Life of Gladstone, 661

Sand's (George) The Devil's Pool, and François the Waif, 534
Scheffel's Ekkehard, 529
Scott's (M.) Tom Cringle's Log, 710
Scott's (Sir W.) Ivanhoe, 16
,, Fortunes of Nigel, 71
,, Woodstock, 72
,, Waverley, 75
,, The Abbott, 124
,, Anne of Geierstein, 125
,, The Antiquary, 126
,, Highland Widow, and Betrothed, 127
,, Black Dwarf, Legend of Montrose 128
,, Bride of Lammermoor, 129
,, Castle Dangerous, Surgeon's Daughter, 130
,, Robert of Paris, 131
,, Fair Maid of Perth, 132
,, Guy Mannering, 133
,, Heart of Midlothian, 134
,, Kenilworth, 135
,, The Monastery, 136
,, Old Mortality, 137
,, Peveril of the Peak, 138
,, The Pirate, 139
,, Quentin Durward, 140
,, Redgauntlet, 141
,, Rob Roy, 142
,, St. Ronan's Well, 143
,, The Talisman, 144
,, Lives of the Novelists, 331
,, Poems and Plays, 550, 551
Seebohm's Oxford Reformers, 665
Seeley's Ecce Homo, 305
Sewell's (Anna) Black Beauty, 748
Shakespeare's Comedies, 153
,, Histories, etc., 154
,, Tragedies, 155 [908
Shchedrin's The Golovlyov Family,
Shelley's Poetical Works, 257, 258
Shelley's (Mrs.) Frankenstein, 616
Sheppard's Charles Auchester, 505
Sheridan's Plays, 95
Sienkiewicz's Tales, 871
,, Quo Vadis?, 970
Sismondi's Italian Republics, 250
Smeaton's Life of Shakespeare, 514
Smith's Wealth of Nations, 412, 413
Smith's (George) Life of Wm. Carey, 395
Smollett's Roderick Random, 790
,, Peregrine Pickle, 838, 839

Smollett's The Expedition of Humphry Clinker, 975
Somerville and Ross: Experiences of an Irish R.M., 978
Sophocles' Dramas, 114
Southey's Life of Nelson, 52
Spectator, 164-7
Speke's Source of the Nile, 50
Spencer's (Herbert) Essays on Education, 504
Spenser's Faerie Queene, 443, 444
" The Shepherd's Calendar, 879
Spinoza's Ethics, etc., 481
Spyri's Heidi, 431
Stanley's Memorials of Canterbury, Eastern Church, 251 [89
Steele's The Spectator, 164-7
Stendhal's Scarlet and Black, 945,
Sterne's Tristram Shandy, 617 [946
" Sentimental Journey, and Journal to Eliza, 796
Stevenson's Treasure Island, and Kidnapped, 763
" Master of Ballantrae, and The Black Arrow, 764
" Virginibus Puerisque, and Familiar Studies of Men and Books, 765
" An Inland Voyage, Travels with a Donkey, and Silverado Squatters, 766
" Dr. Jekyll and Mr. Hyde, The Merry Men, etc., 767
" Poems, 768
" In the South Seas, and Island Nights' Entertainments, 769
" St. Ives, 904
Stow's Survey of London, 589
Stowe's Uncle Tom's Cabin, 371
Strickland's Queen Elizabeth, 100
Surtees' Jorrocks's Jaunts, 817
Swedenborg's Heaven and Hell, 379
" Divine Love and Wisdom, 635
" Divine Providence, 658
" The True Christian Religion, 893
Swift's Gulliver's Travels, Unabridged Edition, 60
" Tale of a Tub, etc., 347
" Journal to Stella, 757
Swinburne's (A. C.), Poems and Prose, 961
Swinnerton's The Georgian Literary Scene, 943
Swiss Family Robinson, 430
Synge's Plays, Poems & Prose, 968

Tacitus' Annals, 273
" Agricola and Germania, 274
Taylor's Words and Places, 517
Tchekhov's Plays and Stories, 941
Tennyson's Poems, 44, 626
Thackeray's Esmond 73
" Vanity Fair, 298
" The Rose and the Ring, etc., 359
" Pendennis, 425, 426
" Newcomes, 465, 466
" The Virginians, 507, 508
" English Humorists, and The Four Georges, 610

Thackeray's Roundabout Papers, 687
Thierry's Norman Conquest, 198, 199
Thoreau's Walden, 281
Thucydides' Peloponnesian War, 455
Tolstoy's Master & Man, Other Parables & Tales, 469
" War and Peace, 525-7
" Childhood, Boyhood, and Youth, 591
" Anna Karenina, 612, 613
Trench's On the Study of Words and English Past and Present, 788
Trollope's Barchester Towers, 30
" Framley Parsonage, 181
" The Warden, 182
" Dr. Thorne, 360 [361
" Small House at Allington,
" Last Chronicles of Barset, 391, 392 [761
" Golden Lion of Granpère,
" Phineas Finn, 832, 833
Trotter's The Bayard of India, 396
" Hodson of Hodson's Horse,
" Warren Hastings, 452 [401
Turgenev's Virgin Soil, 528
" Liza, 677
" Fathers and Sons, 742
" Smoke, 988
Twain's (Mark) Tom Sawyer and Huckleberry Finn, 976
Tyndall's Glaciers of the Alps, 98
Tytler's Principles of Translation, 168

Vasari's Lives of the Painters, 784-7
Verne's (Jules) Twenty Thousand Leagues under the Sea, 319
" Dropped from the Clouds, 367
" Abandoned, 368
" The Secret of the Island, 369
" Five Weeks in a Balloon, and Around the World in Eighty Days, 779
Virgil's Æneid, 161
" Eclogues and Georgics, 222
Voltaire's Life of Charles XII, 270
" Age of Louis XIV, 780
" Candide and Other Tales, 936

Wace and Layamon's Arthurian Chronicles, 578
Wakefield's Letter from Sydney, etc., 828
Walpole's Letters, 775
Walpole's (Hugh) Mr. Perrin and Mr. Trail, 918
Walton's Compleat Angler, 70
Waterton's Wanderings in South America, 772 [899
Webster and Ford's Selected Plays,
Wells's The Time Machine, and The Wheels of Chance, 915
" Ann Veronica, 977
Wesley's Journal, 105-8
White's Selborne, 48
Whitman's Leaves of Grass, 573
Whyte-Melville's Gladiators, 523
Wilde's Plays, Prose Writings and Poems, 858
Wollstonecraft's Rights of Woman, 825
Wood's (Mrs. Henry) The Channings, 84

Woolf's To the Lighthouse, 949
Woolman's Journal, etc., 402
Wordsworth's Shorter Poems, 203
  ,,   Longer Poems, 311

Xenophon's Cyropaedia, 672

Yellow Book, 503
Yonge's The Dove in the Eagle's Nest, 329
  ,,   The Book of Golden Deeds, 330
  ,,   The Heir of Redclyffe, 362
  ,,   The Little Duke, 470
  ,,   The Lances of Lynwood, 579
Young's (Arthur) Travels in France and Italy, 720

Zola's Germinal 897

Anthologies, Composite Volumes, Dictionaries, etc.

A Book of British Ballads, 572
A Book of Heroic Verse, 574
A Book of Nonsense, by Edward Lear, and Others, 806
A Century of Essays, An Anthology, 653
A New Book of Sense and Nonsense, 813
American Short Stories of the Nineteenth Century, 840
An Anthology of English Prose: From Bede to Stevenson, 675
An Encyclopaedia of Gardening, by Walter P. Wright, 555
Ancient Hebrew Literature, 4 vols.
Anglo-Saxon Poetry, 794   [253–6
Annals of Fairyland, 365, 366, 541
Anthology of British Historical Speeches and Orations, 714
Atlas of Classical Geography, 451
Atlases, Literary and Historical: Europe, 496; America, 553; Asia, 633; Africa and Australasia, 662
Chinese Philosophy in Classical Times, 973
Dictionary, Biographical, of English Literature, 449
  ,,   Biographical, of Foreign Literature, 900
  ,,   of Dates, New Edition to end of 1939, 554
  ,,   Everyman's English, 776
  ,,   of Non-Classical Mythology, 632
  ,,   Smaller Classical, 495
English Galaxy of Shorter Poems, The, Chosen and Edited by Gerald Bullett, 959

English Religious Verse, Edited by G. Lacey May, 937
English Short Stories, An Anthology, 743
Fairy Gold, 157
Fairy Tales from the Arabian Nights, French Short Stories, 896   [249
Ghost Stories, Edited by John Hampden, 952
Golden Book of Modern English Poetry, 921   [746
Golden Treasury of Longer Poems,
Hindu Scriptures, Edited by Dr. Nicol Macnicol, 944
International Modern Plays, 989
Mabinogion, The, 97
Minor Elizabethan Drama, 491, 492
Minor Poets of the Eighteenth Century, 844
Minor Poets of the Seventeenth Century, 873
Modern Humour, Edited by Guy Pocock and M. M. Bozman, 957
Modern Plays, 942
Modern Short Stories, Edited by John Hadfield, 954
Mother Goose, 473
Muses' Pageant, The, 581, 606, 671
New Golden Treasury, 695
New Testament, The, 93
Plays for Boys and Girls, 966
Poems of Our Time, 981
Poetry Book for Boys and Girls, 894
Political Liberty, a Symposium, 745
Portuguese Voyages, 986
Prayer Books of King Edward VI, First and Second, 448
Prelude to Poetry, 789
Reader's Guide to Everyman's Library, revised edition, covering the first 950 vols., 889
Restoration Plays, 604
Russian Short Stories, 758
Selections from St. Thomas Aquinas, Edited by the Rev. Father M. C. D'Arcy, 953
Shorter Novels: Elizabethan, 824
  ,,   Jacobean and Restoration, 841
  ,,   Eighteenth Century, 856
Silver Poets of the Sixteenth Century, 985
Story Book for Boys and Girls, 934
Table Talk, 906
Tales of Detection, 928
Theology in the English Poets, 493
Thesaurus of English Words and Phrases, Roget's, 630, 631
Twenty One-Act Plays, Selected by John Hampden, 947

LONDON: J. M. DENT & SONS LTD.
NEW YORK: E. P. DUTTON & CO. INC.

down where the pious Æneas, where the rich Tullus and Ancus are,—*pulvis et umbra sumus.*"[1] He never actually says *where* we go to; he only indicates it by saying that it is that place where Æneas, Tullus, and Ancus are. But Homer, when he has to speak of going down to the grave, says definitely, ἐς Ἠλύσιον πεδίον —ἀθάνατοι πέμψουσιν[2]—"The immortals shall send thee *to the Elysian plain;*" and it is not till after he has definitely said this, that he adds, that it is there that the abode of departed worthies is placed: ὅθι ξανθὸς Ῥαδάμανθυς—"Where the yellow-haired Rhadamanthus is." Again; Horace, having to say that punishment sooner or later overtakes crime, says it thus:

> Raro antecedentem scelestum
> Deseruit pede Pœna claudo.[3]

The thought itself of these lines is familiar enough to Homer and Hesiod; but neither Homer nor Hesiod, in expressing it, could possibly have so complicated its expression as Horace complicates it, and purposely complicates it, by his use of the word *deseruit*. I say that this complicated evolution of the thought necessarily complicates the movement and rhythm of a poet; and that the Miltonic blank verse, of course the first model of blank verse which suggests itself to an English translator of Homer, bears the strongest marks of such complication, and is therefore entirely unfit to render Homer.

If blank verse is used in translating Homer, it must be a blank verse of which English poetry, naturally swayed much by Milton's treatment of this metre, offers at present hardly any examples. It must not be Cowper's blank verse, who has studied Milton's pregnant manner with such effect, that, having to say of Mr. Throckmorton that he spares his avenue, although it is the fashion with other people to cut down theirs, he says that Benevolus "reprieves The obsolete prolixity

[1] *Odes*, IV. vii. 13.
[2] *Odyssey*, iv. 563.
[3] *Odes*, III. ii. 31.

of shade." It must not be Mr. Tennyson's blank verse.

> For all experience is an arch, wherethrough
> Gleams that untravelled world, whose distance fades
> For ever and for ever, as we gaze.

It is no blame to the thought of those lines, which belongs to another order of ideas than Homer's, but it is true, that Homer would certainly have said of them, "It is to consider too curiously to consider so." It is no blame to their rhythm, which belongs to another order of movement than Homer's, but it is true that these three lines by themselves take up nearly as much time as a whole book of the *Iliad*. No; the blank verse used in rendering Homer must be a blank verse of which perhaps the best specimens are to be found in some of the most rapid passages of Shakspeare's plays,—a blank verse which does not dovetail its lines into one another, and which habitually ends its lines with monosyllables. Such a blank verse might no doubt be very rapid in its movement, and might perfectly adapt itself to a thought plainly and directly evolved; and it would be interesting to see it well applied to Homer. But the translator who determines to use it, must not conceal from himself that in order to pour Homer into the mould of this metre, he will have entirely to break him up and melt him down, with the hope of then successfully composing him afresh; and this is a process which is full of risks. It may, no doubt, be the real Homer that issues new from it. It is not certain beforehand that it cannot be the real Homer, as it is certain that from the mould of Pope's couplet or Cowper's Miltonic verse it cannot be the real Homer that will issue. Still, the chances of disappointment are great. The result of such an attempt to renovate the old poet may be an Æson; but it may also, and more probably will be a Pelias.

When I say this, I point to the metre which seems to me to give the translator the best chance of preserving the general effect of Homer,—that third metre which I have not yet expressly named, the hexameter.

I know all that is said against the use of hexameters in English poetry; but it comes only to this, that, among us, they have not yet been used on any considerable scale with success. *Solvitur ambulando*: this is an objection which can best be met by *producing* good English hexameters. And there is no reason in the nature of the English language why it should not adapt itself to hexameters as well as the German language does; nay, the English language, from its greater rapidity, is in itself better suited than the German for them. The hexameter, whether alone or with the pentameter, possesses a movement, an expression, which no metre hitherto in common use amongst us possesses, and which I am convinced English poetry, as our mental wants multiply, will not always be content to forego. Applied to Homer, this metre affords to the translator the immense support of keeping him more nearly than any other metre to Homer's movement; and, since a poet's movement makes so large a part of his general effect, and to reproduce this general effect is at once the translator's indispensable business and so difficult for him, it is a great thing to have this part of your model's general effect already given you in your metre, instead of having to get it entirely for yourself.

These are general considerations; but there are also one or two particular considerations which confirm me in the opinion that for translating Homer into English verse the hexameter should be used. The most successful attempt hitherto made at rendering Homer in English, the attempt in which Homer's general effect has been best retained, is an attempt made in the hexameter measure. It is a version of the famous lines in the third book of the *Iliad*, which end with that mention of Castor and Pollux from which Mr. Ruskin extracts the sentimental consolation already noticed by me. The author is the accomplished Provost of Eton, Dr. Hawtrey; and this performance of his must be my excuse for having taken the liberty to single him out for mention, as one of the natural judges of a translation of Homer, along with Professor Thompson and Professor Jowett, whose connection with Greek literature is official. The passage is short [1]; and Dr. Hawtrey's version of it is suffused with a pensive grace which is, perhaps, rather more Virgilian than Homeric; still it is the one version of any part of the *Iliad* which in some degree reproduces for me the original effect of Homer: it is the best, and it is in hexameters.

[1] So short, that I quote it entire:

> Clearly the rest I behold of the dark-eyed sons of Achaia;
> Known to me well are the faces of all; their names I remember;
> Two, two only remain, whom I see not among the commanders,
> Castor fleet in the car,—Polydeukes brave with the cestus,—
> Own dear brethren of mine,—one parent loved us as infants.
> Are they not here in the host, from the shores of loved Lacedæmon
> Or, though they came with the rest in ships that bound through the waters,
> Dare they not enter the fight or stand in the council of Heroes,
> All for fear of the shame and the taunts my crime has awakened?
>   So said she:—they long since in Earth's soft arms were reposing,
> There, in their own dear land, their Fatherland, Lacedæmon,
>
> *English Hexameter Translations*, London, 1847, p. 242.

I have changed Dr. Hawtrey's "Kastor," "Lakedaimon," back to the familiar "Castor," "Lacedæmon," in obedience to my own rule that everything *odd* is to be avoided in rendering Homer, the most natural and least odd of poets. I see Mr. Newman's critic in the *National Review* urges our generation to bear with the unnatural effect of these rewritten Greek names, in the hope that by this means the effect of them may have to the next generation become natural. For my part, I feel no disposition to pass all my own life in the wilderness of pedantry, in order that a posterity which I shall never see may one day enter an orthographical Canaan; and, after all, the real question is this: whether our living apprehension of the Greek world is more checked by meeting in an English book about the Greeks, names not spelt letter for letter as in the original Greek, or by meeting names which make us rub our eyes and call out, "How exceedingly odd!"

The Latin names of the Greek deities raise in most cases the idea of quite distinct personages from the personages whose idea is raised by the Greek names. Hera and Juno are actually, to every scholar's imagination, two different people. So in all these cases the Latin names must, at any inconvenience, be abandoned when we are dealing with the Greek world. But I think it can be in the sensitive imagination of Mr. Grote only, that "Thucydides" raises the idea of a different man from Θουκυδίδης.

ROBERT BRIDGES

(1844)

Poetry and Poetic Diction.

From an address to the Tredegar and District Co-operative Society on November 27, 1917, under the title of "The Necessity of Poetry," and published in 1918 by the Oxford University Press.

THE same impulse which prompts us to express our delight in the beauty of certain emotions, and of the images in which we clothe them, also prompts us to make the expression beautiful in sound. Even when there is no *conscious* art, the very sense of the beauty of the thought will tend to produce a sympathetic corresponding beauty in the language. And immediately that any consciousness of this arises, we find ourselves consciously inventing beautiful forms: and this is conscious ART. Man is by Nature an artist. The earliest relics of his draftsmanship date back to a time when he probably had but the first rudiments of speech; and, as his speech developed, he was bound to take an aesthetic view of it, that is, to be more pleased with some sounds than with others.

Among all the means of beautifying speech, Rhythm stands out apart: and the first question that an inquirer will ask about poetic form will be this: Why is poetry written in metres? Is metre natural to it, or is it a mere convention and dispensable?

Rhythm of words.

Rhythm is a difficult subject, and we must be content to let it pass. The basis of our feeling for rhythm is probably the comfortable satisfaction of easy and graceful muscular motion; and if you wish for an idea of rhythm you should train your feelings to follow the movements of a fine skater or a good dancer.

Speech-rhythm is infinite. Well-written prose is as rhythmical as verse, and in both prose and verse the rhythms should be congenial to the sense. The difference between the rhythms of prose and verse is this, that poetry selects certain rhythms and makes systems of them, and these repeat themselves: and this is metre. Whereas the rule for rhythm in well-constructed prose is to avoid appearance of artifice; so that the rhythms must not appear to repeat themselves; or if they are repeated for any emotional or logical effect, they should not appear to make verses. This condition may be most simply stated by saying that metrical verse is forbidden in prose. With this one exception the rhythms of prose are quite free: and this freedom from constraint causes the best prose to be, in its rhythmic quality, superior to a poorly constructed poem, where the repetition of the metre has often enough no relation to the meaning, and only serves to hamper the diction; as you can see by comparing the metrical version of a Psalm—even though Milton wrote it—with the prose in the Prayer-book.

There is a fine hymn by Isaac Watts, "O God our help in ages past," frequently sung in our churches, which in ears familiar with Coverdale's prose version of the original Psalm xc sounds futile and feeble, and almost insincere in its decadent artificiality.

When words are merely strung together so as to fit into a poetic metre, much more of the possible beauty of rhythmic speech is sacrificed than can be gained by the rhyme and prescribed cadences that please a common ear.

But the poets of the world, in their purpose of making speech beautiful, chose to set it out in metres: why then did they do so? why should poetry have *confined* itself to metres?

This very natural inquiry may be honestly satisfied by an appeal to the stupendous results attained by the great poetic metres. The examination of these being out of the question, I will read three examples of English blank verse.

First Shakespeare; this is how the somewhat footy little artist in the *Merchant of Venice* can talk:

> How sweet the moonlight sleeps upon this bank!
> Here will we sit, and let the sounds of music
> Creep in our ears: soft stillness and the night
> Become the touches of sweet harmony.
> Sit, Jessica: look, how the floor of heaven
> Is thick inlaid with patines of bright gold.
> There's not the smallest orb which thou beholdest
> But in his motion like an angel sings,
> Still quiring to the young-eyed cherubins.
> *Such harmony is in immortal souls:*
> *But whilst this muddy vesture of decay*
> *Doth grossly close it in, we cannot hear it.*

Now Milton; the Attendant Spirit in *Comus* introduces himself.

> Before the starry threshold of Jove's Court
> My mansion is, where those *immortal shapes*
> Of bright aëreal spirits live insphear'd
> In Regions mild of calm and serene Air,
> Above the smoke and stirr of this dim spot,
> Which men call Earth, and with low-thoughted care
> Confin'd, and pester'd in this pin-fold here,
> Strive to keep up a frail, and feverish being
> Unmindful of the crown that Vertue gives
> After this mortal change, to her true Servants
> Amongst the enthron'd Gods on Sainted seats.
>   Yet some there be that by due steps aspire
> To lay their just hands on that *Golden Key*
> *That opes the Palace of Eternity:*
> To such my errand is, and but for such,
> I would not soil these pure Ambrosial weeds,
> With the rank vapours of this Sin-worn mould.

Now Shelley, where the Spirit of the Earth talks with Prometheus.

>   Ere Babylon was dust,
> The Magus Zoroaster, my dead child,
> Met his own image walking in the garden.
> That apparition, sole of men, he saw.
> *For know there are two worlds of life and death:*
> *One, that which thou beholdest; but the other*
> Is underneath the grave, where do inhabit
> *The shadows of all forms that think and live*
> Till death unite them, and they part no more:
> *Dreams and the light imaginings of men*

> *And all that faith creates or love desires,*
> Terrible, strange, sublime and beauteous shapes.
> There thou art, and dost hang, a writhing shade,
> 'Mid whirlwind-peopled mountains: all the gods
> Are there, and all the powers of nameless worlds,
> Vast, sceptred phantoms: heroes, men and beasts;
> And Demogorgon, a tremendous gloom.

These passages are in the most *prosaic* of all our English metres, and though it has no rhyme to mark its periods, yet the metrical unit is so effective and convincing that one cannot imagine it to be wrong in principle.

The common explanation of the metrical charm is, I believe, the love of patterns, and it is true that metrical poems can all be well considered as word-patterns; there are certain stanza-forms in which the pattern is very obtrusive: yet I prefer to take a somewhat wider principle for basis.

First, all artistic beauty exhibits a mastery, a triumph of grace: and this implies a difficulty overcome,—for no mastery of grace can appear in the doing of whatever you suppose any man could do with equal ease if he chose. And since in a perfect work (music perhaps provides the best examples) all difficulty is so mastered that it entirely disappears, and would not be thence inferred,—it is necessary that for general appreciation there should be some recognition or consciousness of the formal conditions, in which the difficulty is implicit. And thus one of the uses of second-rate works of art is that they reveal and remind us of the material obstacles.

Now the limitation of metre is of a kind which particularly satisfies the conditions just described: because it offers a form which the hearers recognize and desire, and by its recurrence keeps it steadily in view. Its practical working may be seen in the unpopularity of poems that are written in unrecognized metres, and the favour shown to well-established forms by the average reader. His pleasure is in some proportion to his appreciation of the problem.

Secondly, a great deal of our pleasure in beauty, whether natural or artistic, depends on slight variations of a definite form. Fancy if all roses were as similar in shape as all equilateral triangles! The fundamental motive of this pleasure may be described as a balance between the expected and the unexpected—the expected being a sedative soothing lulling principle, and the unexpected a stimulating awakening principle. Too much of the type would be tedious, too much of the unexpected would worry. The unexpected stimulates the consciousness, but you must also be conscious of the type. Or this *balance* may be regarded as a *strife* between two things, the fixed type and the freedom of the variations: and metre gives the best possible opportunity for this kind of play, which is really comparable to Nature's, for no two lines of a poem are exactly alike: they differ much as do the leaves of a tree: and a pleasure arises from our knowledge of the normal rhythm (the type) beneath the varieties which the poet delights to extend and elaborate: his skill in this sort of embroidery being to push its disguises as far as he dare without breaking away from the type.

The ancient Greeks were as pre-eminent in scientific thought as they were in art, and since their early poetry still maintains its pre-eminence we are scarcely in a position to question the propriety of the metrical principles which we have inherited from them. If any man should ever invent a form superior to metre, the world would be much indebted to him; but we can hardly imagine it, and may therefore take metre as a necessity of the conditions and justified by results.

Diction.

I hope by such considerations to have demonstrated the propriety and almost the necessity of the metrical form of poetry. The other beauties of speech can be grouped under Diction.

However spontaneously the perfect poem may spring up in the poet's mind, like a melody in the mind of Mozart, the conditions to be fulfilled—over and above the elaboration of the metre—are

First, the right words: secondly, those words in the right order: thirdly, the agreeable sound of them in sequence.

And these three rightnesses are the factors of style, that supreme gift which immortalizes the utterance of such different minds as Blaise Pascal and Robert Burns: for the laws are very similar in prose and in poetry. I shall pass them over, because such a brief account of them as we should have time for would be dull.[1]

---

[1] If any one should be curious to see how dull, he may read to the end of this note, which I append for the sake of completeness.

First as to the choice of words: What words are the right words in poetic diction? Plainly their sound must be one ruling consideration—as may be proved by the ill effect of extreme dissonance: yet their chief power lies either in their absolute correctness, or in what is called their suggestiveness, and this, which is the greater poetic beauty, lurks commonly in the fringes of the concepts, as was explained when we spoke of words as ideas. When correctness and suggestiveness coincide their power can be so great that quality of sound is sometimes outclassed; and harshness is unheeded. This we willingly concede to the imperfection of language, which is not so constituted as to combine all excellences, whence the lesser must give way. Our English words especially have been shamefully and shabbily degraded, and are daily worsening, so as to be often very ill-adapted for poetic use. And the swarming homophones need special treatment.

As to the sound of words in sequence. Pure Euphony, i.e. the agreeable sound of a sequence of syllables, is as difficult a subject as rhythm: and it is like rhythm in this, that the ultimate judge is the expert ear, which depends on a natural gift: and again, as in rhythm, there are certain conditions which almost all men would agree to call pleasant, and others which they would deem unpleasant: but there is no universal principle that can be adduced to check the vagaries of taste or false fancy, since what theories have been proposed are themselves examples of false fancy: Either, for instance, that the vowels correspond respectively to the primary colours, and should be grouped as those colours should be: or that euphony is actually a musical melody made by the inherent pitch of the vowels, the sequences of which must be determined exactly as if we were composing a musical air of those inherent notes. The great indefinable complication is that this euphony, especially in poetry, is fused with the meaning: and this fusion of sound and sense is the magic of the greatest poetry. But even where the poet's success is most conspicuous and con-

On order of words.

But I think I may venture a short account of order. What is meant by a right ORDER *of words*? The principle is important and very simple, but in application so subtle that it is seldom recognized. You may easily come at it by imagining the talk of savages in a language that has no grammar. In such a language a speaker could not make himself understood except by putting his words in a certain order. If, for instance, he wished to tell you that he went from one place to another, from A to B, and had no prepositions like our *to* and *from*, he would have to put A first and B second; that is, he would have to set his nouns in the order in which he wished the idea of his movement to enter your mind. And this principle remains the primary law of order in good speech, whether prose or poetry: the words should be in the order of the ideas; and poetry differs from prose only in its more aesthetic and subtler conception of the proper sequence, and in the greater artifices that it is able to employ, and the greater difficulties that it has to overcome.

There are all manner of exceptions to this rule; but the most apparent inconsistencies are manifestly dependent on the primary value of the rule: for instance, an idea in an unexpected position in the sentence is often most effective: but the surprise is

vincing, we are often quite unable to determine on what it actually depends: it is known only by its effects.

In English we find, strangely enough, that the eye comes meddling in with the business of the ear, and causes delusion. Our words are so commonly spelt so differently from their pronunciation that few writers know what sounds they are dictating; the word is a visible thing, "pleasant to the eye and desirable to make one wise," it is perhaps of ancient and high descent, with a heroic history, it comes "trailing clouds of glory": but that it has been phonetically degraded into an unworthy or ugly sound is overlooked. . . .

Euphony must also include the purely musical effects of a metre, when this is in delicate agreement with the mood of the poem: it so enhances the emotional effect of a harmonious sequence of words as to overrule common proprieties of order, and the melody will require that the sonorous words shall respect its intention and fall into the positions that it prescribes.

due to its being either grammatically or conceptually out of order.

The commonest cause of ineffective expression in bad writers of verse is that they choose their grammar so as to set the words that they wish to use in the order most convenient to the metre. The born writer or speaker is the man whose ideas flow spontaneously in a simple grammar which preserves the right order of ideas. A fixed poetic metre must of course increase the difficulty of right order, and thus heighten the beauty and triumph and rarity of full success.

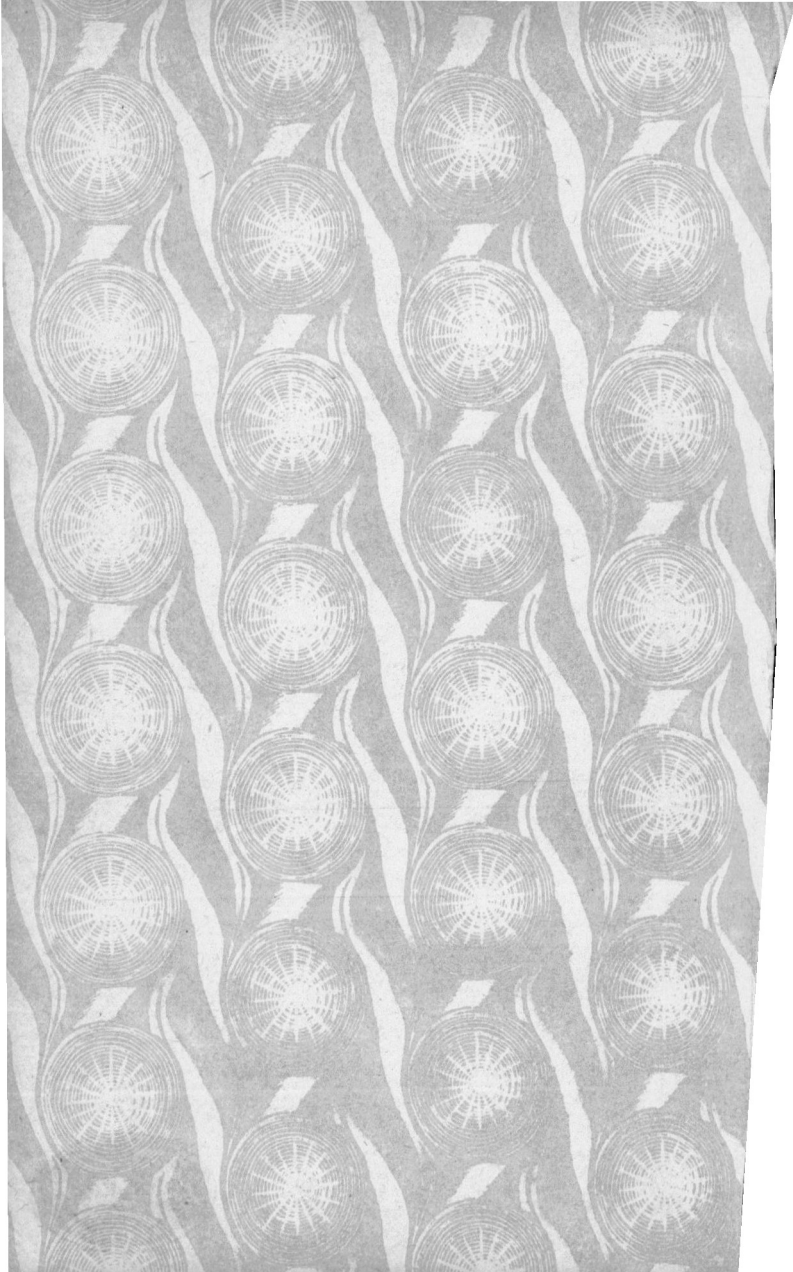

passage in which he expounds this desire is the more interesting, because it bears evidence, as do his own poems, that he had read his Shelley to some purpose: "It is the desire," he says, "of the moth for the star. It is no mere appreciation of the Beauty before us, but a wild effort to reach the Beauty above. Inspired by an ecstatic prescience of the glories beyond the grave, we struggle by multiform combinations among the things and thoughts of time to attain a portion of that Loveliness whose very elements perhaps appertain to eternity alone." Browning, in the remarkable essay which follows in the text[1] on Shelley's art, works out this idea with a difference in profound terms. It is enough to refer any reader who does not already know it to one of the most eloquent pleas of the past century on behalf of the poet's function.

IV.

After Browning's essay there are still many critical references to the practice of verse, the divisions, functions, subject matter and language of poetry, to be added to the poets' breviary. "What are the eternal objects of poetry?" Matthew Arnold asked in the preface to his own Poems of 1853–54. "They are actions; human actions; possessing an inherent interest in themselves, and which are to be communicated in an interesting manner by the art of the poet.

"The poet, then, has in the first place to select an excellent action; and what actions are the most excellent? Those, certainly, which most powerfully appeal to the great primary human affections: to those elementary feelings which subsist permanently in the race, and which are independent of time. These feelings are permanent and the same; that which interests them is permanent and the same also. The modernness or antiquity of an action, therefore, has nothing to do with its fitness for poetical representation; this depends upon its inherent qualities. To the elementary part of our nature, to our passions, that which is great and pas-

[1] See page 350.

Something of the same enthusiasm, it was, that Shelley demanded of the poet in a memorable letter to Peacock, where he turned from the curious discussion of his friend's Nympholepsy to the question of poetic inspiration:

"What a wonderful passage there is in *Phædrus*—the beginning, I think, of one of the speeches of Socrates—in praise of poetic madness, and in definition of what poetry is, and how a man becomes a poet. Every man who lives in this age and desires to write poetry, ought, as a preservative against the false and narrow systems of criticism which every poetical empiric vents, to impress himself with this sentence, if he would be numbered among those to whom may apply this proud, though sublime expression of Tasso—'Non c'è in mondo chi merita nome di creatore, che Dio ed il Poeta.'"[1]

Shelley, following Plato's idea, develops it in his *Defence of Poetry;* and Sidney in his *Apologie* maintains the same faith in the "divine right" and the supernal inspiration of the poet, as where he tells us, that the poets "are so beloved of the Gods, that whatsoever they write proceeds of a divine fury."

A later poet than Shelley, Edgar Poe, gave another turn to the idea in his lecture on "The Poetic Principle." With Plato and Shelley, the poet has already, as it were, been in heaven, and drunk of the immortal springs. With Edgar Poe, the poet is in the purgatory of an impassioned desire for "divine beauty," the poet's paradise, which is his, as yet, only by prevision. The

[1] In a note to this letter of Shelley's, Peacock adds the passage in question from the *Phædrus*, which goes to corroborate the previous page from Plato: "There are several kinds (says Socrates) of divine madness. That which proceeds from the Muses, taking possession of a tender and unoccupied soul, awakening, and bacchically inspiring it towards songs and other poetry, adorning myriads of ancient deeds, instructs succeeding generations. But he who, without this madness from the Muses, approaches the poetical gates, having persuaded himself that by art alone he may become sufficiently a poet, will find in the end his own imperfection, and see the poetry of his cold prudence vanish into nothingness before the light of that which has sprung from divine insanity."